REVITALIZATION AMID DIASPORA

*Consultation Three:
Explorations in World Christian
Revitalization Movements*

The Center for the Study of
World Christian Revitalization Movements
Funded by the Henry Luce Foundation

The Asbury Theological Seminary Series in World Christian Revitalization Movements

J. Steven O'Malley, Editor

EMETH PRESS
www.emethpress.com

Revitalization amid Diaspora. Consultation Three: Explorations in World Christian Revitalization Movements

Copyright © 2013 J. Steven O'Malley
Printed in the United States of America on acid-free paper

All rights reserved. No part of this book may be reproduced, or stored in a retrieval system or transmitted in any form or by any means, electronic, mechanical, photocopying, recording, scanning or otherwise, except as permitted by the 1976 United States Copyright Act, or with the prior written permission of Emeth Press. Requests for permission should be
addressed to: Emeth Press, P. O. Box 23961, Lexington, KY 40523-3961.
http://www.emethpress.com.

Library of Congress Cataloging-in-Publication Data

Revitalization amid diaspora : consultation three, Explorations in world Christian revitalization movements / The Center for the Study of World Christian Revitalization Movements, funded by the Henry Luce Foundation ; J. Steven O'Malley, editor.
     pages cm. -- (Asbury Theological Seminary series in world Christian revitalization movements)
 ISBN 978-1-60947-049-4 (alk. paper)
 1. Church renewal. 2. Christianity--21st century. I. O'Malley, J. Steven (John Steven), 1942- II. Center for the Study of World Christian Revitalization Movements. III. Title: Explorations in world Christian revitalization movements.
 BV600.3.R49 2012
 262.001'7--dc23
                              2012044476

Photo on the front cover is a picture of the participants

Contents

Contributors / v
Editor's Introduction—J. Steven O'Malley / vii

Part One: The Cases

1. A Multi-Cultural Ministry with an Orthodox Base / 3
2. The East African Revival and the Revitalization of Christianity / 9
3. A Filipino Congregation in Diaspora as a Church Planting Revitalization Movement / 37
4. Mosaic Cultural Ministry with an East Asian Base / 59
5. The Jesus Network / 79
6. Rahab Ministry / 97

Part Two: Interpretation

1. Renewal Ancient and Modern: Reflections from Table One
   —William J. Abraham / 121
2. Mosaic Cultural Ministry in the Interface of Korean and Southeast Asian Communities: Reflections from Table Two
   —Paul Seungoh Chung / 129
3. Theological and Missional Perspectives in Light of World Christian Revitalization in Asia: Reflections from Table Three
   —Bryan Froehle / 141
4. Summary Chapter: Insights and Implications for Christian Revitalization in the 21st Century
   —Steven O'Malley, Beverly Johnson Miller and Michael Pasquarello / 161

Contributors

Editor:
J. Steven O'Malley, PhD
John C. Seamands Professor of Methodist Holiness History
Asbury Theological Seminary

Case One:
The St. Maurice and St. Verena Coptic Orthodox Church
Fr. Pishoy Salama and Professor Wafik Wahba, PhD, Associate Professor of World Christianity, Tyndale Seminary

Case Two:
The East African Revival and the Revitalization of Christianity
Kevin Ward, Ph.D, Senior Lecturer in African Religious Studies; Theology and Religious Studies, University of Leeds

with Revd Manuel Maranga PhD and Revd Amos Karibante, the Anglican Church of Uganda, and Revd. Isaac Kawuki Mukasa, PhD, the Anglican Diocese of Toronto

Case Three:
Narry P. Santos, PhD
Resident Pastor
Greenhills Christian Fellowship
Toronto, Canada

Eunice L. Irwin, PhD
Associate Professor of Mission and Contextual Theology
Asbury Theological Seminary

Case Four:
Reverend John Heonbam Chung
Mission Pastor
Young Nak Korean Presbyterian Church
Toronto, Canada
Paul Chung, PhD

Resident Scholar
Young Nak Korean Presbyterian Church
Toronto, Canada

Meesaeng Lee Choi, PhD
Professor of Church History
Asbury Theological Seminary

Case Five:
Pastor Phil
Pastor Joe
The Jesus Network

Case Six:
Reverend Gladys Mok
Reverend Joanna Yee
Reverend Aloma Yonker
Rahab Ministry in Canada
Toronto Canada

Interpretations
William J. Abraham, PhD
Albert Cook Outlier Professor of Wesley Studies
Southern Methodist University

Paul Seungoh Chung, PhD
Young Nak Korean Presbyterian Church
Toronto, Canada

Brian T. Froehle, PhD
Professor of Practical Theology
School of Theology and Ministry
St Thomas University
Miami, Florida

Beverly Johnson-Miller, PhD
Professor of Discipleship
Asbury Theological Seminary

Michael Pasquarello, PhD
Granger E and Ann A Fisher Professor of Preaching
Asbury Theological Seminary

Introduction

Since 2009, the Center for the Study of World Christian Revitalization Movements, a research group at Asbury Theological Seminary, has been taking the pulse and heartbeat of revitalization movements in world Christianity. Our task has been to see where the Holy Spirit is at work bringing new life in Christ to persons and cultures across the globe. We have been an interdisciplinary team of practitioners and scholars with a common commitment to this task. Our disciplines represent the major areas of theological study, including biblical and theological studies, church history, worship and homiletics, discipleship and Christian education, as well as anthropology and missiology. We have included a wide spectrum of Christian communities, including Wesleyans, Mennonites, Anglicans, Catholics, Orthodox, Pentecostals, Lutherans, and a wide representation from indigenous churches in the Global South and East. In addition to the United States, our national identities have included Canada, Korea, Brazil, Great Britain, Ghana, Kenya, Singapore, China, the Philippines, Australia and Scotland.

During these years we convened three times in annual consultations. At Asbury in 2009 we met to assemble and describe the data of revitalization movements, both historical and contemporary, under the biblical mandate of "Pentecost and the new humanity." At Edinburgh in 2010 we met to interpret and assess that data with the intent of "exploring the dialectic between revitalization and church." Here we considered the normative issues of what constitutes authentic expressions of revitalization, as manifestations of God's ongoing salvation history that has gone forth since the first Pentecost of apostolic times, and how these movements have been challenging, strengthening, and reconfiguring church in its manifold expressions, including the historical church traditions and new ecclesial bodies emerging in the wake of revitalization.

At Toronto in 2011 our concern was to assess, correct and extend the data from consultations one and two in light of six fresh cases of current revitalization movements that reflect the common theme of diaspora, which is an increasingly crucial aspect of revitalization movements in the early twenty-first century. There are now more than 400 million persons living in a state of permanent diaspora throughout the world. These dislocated persons are particularly susceptible to receiving the redemptive message of Jesus Christ and, being scattered as transnationals outside traditional homelands, to finding their identity in the people of God being gathered by the Holy Spirit in the unfolding of salvation history. Most of these persons hail from the Global South and East, where an explosive growth of Christian communities is occurring within the context of revitalization. Communities in the Global North, including the United States, are meanwhile being remapped with the influx of transnational persons. The multiplication of Hispanic and Asian churches has become the major feature of church growth in North American Christianity, with its rapidly declining mainline denominational church bodies.

The cases that were prepared and presented at Tyndale University College and Seminary in Toronto each represented fresh movements of revitalization working at the grassroots level among diverse ethnic communities in that metropolis, which is the most ethnically diverse city in North America. While mainline churches retreat from the urban core, large populations of transnationals, particularly from the Global South and East, have moved into that core area. Ministries of revitalization have manifested themselves through the response of faithful witnesses to the mission of God for these people groups. These ministries have often arisen apart from and even without the involvement of official church bodies. Nevertheless, the resulting revival that has occurred has in many respects become transformative for those living in these developing transnational communities.

In this volume we present these six cases, each of which was written by a team of scholars/practitioners representing an "insider" perspective, or a key participant in a particular mission initiative, joined with the perspective of an "outsider," or an interpreter of that ministry who has empathy and vision for its effectiveness and potential. The cases represent these ethnic communities: Coptic Egyptians, East African Anglicans, indigenous Filipinos living in Toronto, Korean Presbyterians reaching to transplanted southeast Asian Buddhist communities in Toronto and on to their homelands, Anabaptist-based initiatives among Pakistanis and Afghans, and an initiative to reach persons of largely East Asian origin who are enslaved by human trafficking. In each of the cases, there are existing communities of faith that are being revitalized by these initiatives, and there are also new communities of faith being birthed amid this revitalization that display marks of Christian authenticity.

It is our privilege to present these cases here, followed by a group of interpretive essays that carry forward their meaning and significance for the larger movement of revitalization that is going forward throughout the world in the early twenty-first century. These chapters also give attention to new ways revitalization is being manifested in the present day, given the accelerating momentum of revitalization occurring among persons in diaspora.

Finally, it should be noted that this new genre of revitalization is at another level a return to an ancient pattern that God followed from the inception of the biblical narrative of salvation history which is traced to Abraham. Yes, diaspora and revitalization have gone hand and hand from the beginning. The people of God were birthed in diaspora and the grace that revitalized and sustained them in all successive generations was marked by their being gathered into a conscious sense of living memory (anamnesis) and empowerment by the Holy Spirit in light of that divine visitation. Christians trace their genesis as a scattered people of God throughout the earth to their initial expulsion from Jerusalem, whereby they were enabled by the Spirit to actualize the promises bequeathed to them at Pentecost.

This study is a documentation of the latest expression of that forward-moving initiative of our Triune God in history. It is also presented as prologue for the second round of revitalization consultations that will occur in the megacities of the Global South and East, beginning with Nairobi in 2013, and occurring through the funding provided by the Henry Luce Foundation. The Foundation has funded the first revitalization project that was completed in 2011 and also the new project that continues from 2012 through 2016. We are also grateful to Asbury Theological Seminary, of which this research initiative is an integral component in its mission to the world in the heritage of John Wesley, who first articulated our concern for "The General Spread of the Gospel" to all the world.

—J. Steven O'Malley, Editor

Part One

The Cases

CHAPTER ONE

A Multi-Cultural Ministry with an Orthodox Base

Fr. Pishoy Salama
In collaboration with
Wafik Wahba, PhD
Tyndale Seminary

The establishment of St. Maurice and St. Verena[1] Coptic Orthodox Church in Toronto (SMSV), the first multicultural missionary Coptic Orthodox Church in the diaspora,[2] was nothing short of a miracle. Until recently, the Coptic Orthodox Church was known as a Church in which the majority of its parishioners were Egyptian immigrants or second-generation Copts. Within the past few decades, however, a phenomenon had become apparent as Copts began marrying individuals from outside of the Egyptian culture, and some of these members could not find a home for their new families in the existing churches. A small group of parishioners then started praying for the possibility of establishing an English-speaking missionary multicultural congregation in Toronto in order to minister to second- and third-generation Copts, as well as to intercultural couples.

After some preparations, I traveled to Egypt on November 13, 2007 to meet with H.H. Pope Shenouda III in Cairo to request the establishment of such a ministry, which would contribute to the continued revival of the Coptic Church, not only in Toronto, but everywhere in North America. When I traveled to Egypt, the eighty-four year old pontiff was celebrating his thirty-sixth anniversary as the patriarch of the Coptic Orthodox Church. It also happened that he had just been discharged from the hospital, after suffering from some prior health complications. When I arrived at St. Mark's Cathedral in Cairo, I was told by his secretary that the Pope had declined several meetings with government officials, but that my request for a private meeting was going to be presented to him. To my surprise, and that of many others, the Pope agreed to meet with me privately to hear my proposal concerning the establishment of the new parish in Toronto. After some discussion about the logistics of and preparation for such a ministry, I was granted permission to minister in the first multicultural Coptic Orthodox Church in North America. This day represented for me the birth of a new hope that the Coptic Church was taking positive strides to care for and minister to members from all ethnicities and nationalities.[3]

Since November 2007, I have been serving as the priest of SMSV in Toronto. I am responsible for many different tasks which combine to form my vocational identity. My current context of ministry can be summarized as occurring in three main areas: liturgical, pastoral, and administrative.

As an ordained minister, one of my central responsibilities is to celebrate the Church's liturgical sacraments.[4] Members of our congregation have their children baptized as infants and are encouraged to attend spiritual meetings and to be active members in the life of the Church. It is also common that the priest celebrates the Divine Liturgy several times every week and conducts Vespers Prayer services. My pastoral responsibilities include teaching, crisis intervention, counseling youth and families, and providing grief support following the death of family members. I also commonly visit members of the parish in their homes, in hospitals, or at their places of business. Since the Coptic Community considers the priest to be like a member of the family, I am often invited to birthday and graduation celebrations. I also have many administrative responsibilities (such as co-ordinating meetings and events, following up with ministry leaders, and participating in the ongoing planning of the new church building) that occupy a substantial portion of my time.

When the congregation of SMSV was formed, all of its ministries had to be built from scratch. With the help of many volunteers, we have established many ministries which reflect the spiritual needs of the congregation. Some of the ministries which we have initiated include community service, outreach, young adults, new mothers, youth fellowship, small groups, and children's ministry. It was important for me to see lay leaders and multiple ethnic groups represented in the leadership of all of these ministries.

One of my greatest passions in ministry has been the organization of marriage preparation classes. I have led these classes annually for the past seven years, first while serving at St. Mark's and continuing at SMSV. This seven-week course allows couples that are planning to get married that year to come together, once a week for two hours, in order to establish a strong theological and practical foundation for marriage. Some of the topics discussed in this course include biblical foundations, finances, setting goals, conflict resolution, in-laws, intimacy, and explanation of the wedding ceremony. I have also started a regular follow-up meeting for married couples, where they meet to discuss ongoing marital challenges and to make sure that there are no conflicts that may break up their relationship. This meeting is also intended as an opportunity for fellowship among couples in the congregation and to build spiritual ties among members of the one body of Christ.

Following my initial meeting with H.H. Pope Shenouda III in Egypt in November 2007, a small core group of parishioners, who were enthusiastic about the idea, gathered to initiate this ministry. We held a series of prayer meetings and discussions about our goals and intentions in taking this initiative. We then rented a local church building in Toronto, which was used for services on weekdays, and a school gymnasium for use on Sunday mornings. We have made it clear that members of all cultures, age groups, and socio-economic statuses are welcomed and accepted in the church.

It was our first priority to establish a mission statement that would reflect our identity as being rooted in the Coptic Orthodox faith, while also emphasizing and celebrating our diversity. SMSV was established to be:

A Ministry of Love, Integration, and Outreach

- This ministry is for the glory of God the Father, His only begotten Son Jesus Christ, and the Holy Spirit the Comforter.
- This is a Coptic Orthodox Church in its faith, doctrine, traditions, and teachings. It is under the direct leadership of His Holiness Pope Shenouda III and the Holy Synod of the Coptic Orthodox Church.
- A faithful community to the gospel of our Lord Jesus Christ, eager and enthusiastic to grow spiritually and to be a positive influence in its surroundings.
- A worshipping community which offers praise and glory to God.
- A multicultural church ministering to people from every nation, tongue, tribe, and language.
- Missionary in nature; spreading the Good News to the whole world.
- It is a place where no one stands alone.
- Focusing on the love of God through spiritual growth and also on the love of neighbour through community service and humanitarian work. [5]

The multicultural nature of this new ministry was to be its main attraction and mark of distinction. Those who would be willing to join this church would be those who were convinced by its mission and determined to make it succeed. In establishing this multicultural church, the intentions of the founding group were mainly to change people's attitudes, rather than to reform the doctrines or beliefs of the Church. Our goal was to become more relevant to North American customs, culture, and traditions, while remaining true to our faith. Evaluating ourselves steadily and progressively, while remaining conscious of the core of the Orthodox faith, allows us to continue to engage in this cultural versus spiritual/doctrinal dialogue. It is our intention to continue to become a distinctly Canadian Coptic Orthodox Church that simultaneously celebrates our diversity and our uniqueness.

The Coptic Church is not only concerned about the ongoing pastoral ministry of its parishioners, but much thought also goes into the future existence and survival of the Church especially in the diaspora. H.H. Pope Shenouda III has a famous saying that "A Church with no youth is a Church with no future." This statement concerning the significance of youth ministry to the future existence of the Church, along with Pope Shenouda's support of missionary endeavours as means for future survival of the Church, gave us the encouragement to search for positive means and resources to enhance and grow our church through missions. *Future Faith Churches* by Don Posterski and Gary Nelson offers a unique perspective on any Church's chances for growth at the beginning of this millennium.[6] At certain points in my ministry, I thought that any church had the potential to overcome the challenges of the upcoming century, with only minimal consideration of its direction and leadership skills. After reading this book, it became obvious to me that the mission and direction of the twenty-first century Church required much thought, prayer, and planning in order to give it a chance at survival. The authors made it clear that the future church needs to exhibit a balance between love for God and love for one's neighbour.[7] It must be deliberate in its focus on evangelism, social action, church growth, and strong leadership. They suggest that a church that focuses only on the gospel, without emphasis on social action, can be seen as a soul without a body. The model of "Relational Evangelism" requires that congregants feel comfortable inviting friends to the service. The ministry of SMSV has focused thus far on this model of evangelism. We have also initiated outreach programs along the lines of those suggested by Dr. John Bowen in his book *Evangelism for "Normal" People*, which includes a set of practical suggestions for ordinary people to use in reaching out to community and friends in order to attract them to Christ. The suggestions include the Agnostics Anonymous group, tea parties, Valentine's Day celebrations, and visitor Sundays at church, where the programs are custom-made to suit visitors and seekers.[8] In addition, we have started Small Group Leadership training courses, which have produced eleven small groups so far, with several others in development.

I am thankful to report that SMSV has been growing and flourishing beyond anyone's expectations. The congregation needed to move to a bigger school gymnasium only six months after its establishment and to move again after two years. The church has acquired a three-acre parcel of land in Markham, Ontario, and plans are now being finalized to build an eight-hundred-seat church, along with auxiliary facilities such as a banquet hall, Sunday School classrooms, day care centre, and gymnasium. While the new church plant was originally established to minister to second- and third-generation Copts, as well as to intercultural couples, it has become a home for many individuals of multiple nationalities who are interested in Orthodoxy and who are not Egyptian by birth. It is also ministering to other English-speaking, Coptic-born parishioners who were drawn to its principles. The inclusive nature of this new community has become its mark of attraction, and it is becoming well known among Coptic churches in the diaspora. I cannot yet determine the outcome of this endeavour, as this model is still in its early stages and is open to criticism and adaptation. Nonetheless, we have already accomplished a great deal of our mission and continue to seek ways to fulfill the rest.

Notes

1. At the end of the third century, St. Maurice was a soldier in the Theban Legion (modern day Luxor in Upper Egypt) who traveled to Gaul (modern day France) to fight for King Maximian in the Roman army. He was the leader of 6600 soldiers, who were all martyred for their faith. St. Verena was a nurse who accompanied the Theban Legion, and, when they were all martyred, she settled in what is now Switzerland. Both of these saints became very well known in Europe and have also been canonized in the Catholic Church. We chose to name our church after these saints because they were both Copts, Christian Egyptians, who traveled to the west and preached the word of Christ in their teachings, as well as in their works and lives. In the same manner, as Coptic immigrants to North America, we felt the need to witness to our faith and live our calling to the communities in which we live and work.

2. The word "diaspora" here refers to the lands outside of Egypt, the country of origin of the Coptic Orthodox Church.

3. There is no doubt that converts and intercultural marriages had been an integral part in the fabric of many existing Coptic Churches in North America prior to the establishment of St. Maurice and St. Verena. There were also several churches that had programs in place ministering to these members of the community. This ministry, however, was the first one that was intentionally planted to be a missionary and multicultural Coptic Orthodox Church in North America, specifically catering to the needs of believers from all ethnicities and nationalities.

4. In the Orthodox Church, sacraments are better known as mysteries.

5. SMSV mission statement as published on the church website at http://www.smsv.ca/ourmission.shtml accessed on October 12, 2010.

6. Even though, as an Orthodox Christian, my primary sources are those published by Orthodox authors, yet there is much value in other works and scholarships published by Catholic or Protestant theologians, as well as by secular researchers. It is profitable to acknowledge the common grounds that all Christian denominations agree on and also have room for theological debate in areas of disagreement. As a researcher and a priest who is in dialogue with Christians of all denominations on a regular basis, I found it essential to investigate and understand where other denominations stand in terms of their theological viewpoints, which may or may not agree with the Orthodox perspectives.

7. Don Posterski and Gary Nelson, *Future Faith Churches: Reconnecting with the Power of the Gospel for the 21st Century* (Winfield, BC: Wood Lake Books Inc., 1997), 54.

8. John P. Bowen, *Evangelism for "Normal" People: Good News for Those Looking for a Fresh Approach* (Minneapolis: Augsburg Fortress, 2002), 183-185.

Chapter 2

The East African Revival and the Revitalization of Christianity

Kevin Ward, PhD
in collaboration with
**Rev. Professor Manuel Maranga, PhD and
Rev. Amos Karibante**
with a response from
Rev. Dr Isaac Kawuki Mukasa, PhD

Introduction

A 'religious revival' involves a spiritual 'awakening' or 'revitalization' within churches or within an area which contrasts with the smooth flow of daily life. From the Christian perspective, it should be understood as the specific activity of the Holy Spirit deepening people's commitment to God and intensifying their concern about their eternal destiny. Individuals are converted often in large numbers, churches are revitalized and the excitement spreads to surrounding localities. These newly converted or revival Christians become infused with missionary spirit and dedicate themselves to a holy life and not infrequently to cultural and social service. (Jones and Pope 2004, 283)

This appraisal of revival, primarily concerning Wales in the early years of the twentieth century, could equally apply to the East African Revival. With its roots in the 1920s, the East African Revival came to prominence in the 1930s and was a major dynamic force in the life of evangelical Protestant churches throughout the period of decolonization and early independence. In Uganda in particular it remains, to this day, a significant force. But even where it has given place to Pentecostalism as the dynamic force of revitalization, the Revival's legacy remains fundamental to the language and culture of evangelicalism in East Africa as a whole.

The East African Revival is the name recognised internationally for this movement. Within East Africa itself the movement is commonly referred to as *Balokole,* a Luganda word for 'the Saved People', and a word which rightly points to the core identity of revivalists – that they are the people of the cross of Christ, saved by the blood of the Lord Jesus. But, like 'Methodist', the term was initially given by sceptical outsiders, often with slightly mocking implications. In so far as *'Balokole'* is seen as referring to a particular group or sect, the Balokole themselves would reject the term, since they do not see the call to salvation as a call to membership of a particular organisation or sect, nor can anyone rest complacently in membership of a special group. Rather the call is to receive salvation – Kulokoka (be saved) – an active challenge to all men and women, to existing members of the church and to those outside the church. This identity as a people called by God to live a life of wholesale commitment is basic to revivalist self-understanding. They see themselves neither as an organization, nor as a church, with all the bureaucratic and hierarchical trappings which such institutions entail. If it is necessary to have a label, revivalists would prefer to use the term *ab'oluganda* – the brothers and sisters. In English the terms 'the Fellowship' or 'the Brethren' are often used, though the Luganda word is not gender specific. Nevertheless, Balokole has become widely used both by insiders and outsiders to designate the members of the revival. It is widely recognised, far beyond Buganda, as the name for a distinctive type of evangelical Christianity.

The Balokole and the Search for an 'Authentic' African Christianity

In the search for 'authentically African' responses to the Gospel, there have been many examples from the late 19th century and throughout the 20th century of movements for the revitalization of Christianity, often associated with a prophetic figure like the Liberian William Wade Harris in West Africa, Simon Kimbangu in the Congo, and Isaiah Shembe in South Africa. These movements often led to the creation of churches which broke away from the mission-led churches, and created a new distinct brand of Christianity, the African Independent Churches/African Indigenous Churches (AICs). In East Africa the Bamalaki formed in Uganda by Joswa Kate Mugema and the Karing'a Independent Churches of the Kikuyu of Kenya are such movements. The Balokole, in contrast to these nationalist and pan-Africanist forms of Christianity, is often seen as much more closely tied to classical European and American forms of evangelical Christianity. The central focus on the cross of Christ, on sin and repentance, and a refusal to adapt the demands of the gospel to what are perceived as unchristian, pagan practices, whatever their cultural importance, does distinguish the Balokole from the classic AICs, whom indeed they often denounce. It also makes it easy to include the East African Revival movement as an expression of classical North Atlantic revivalism. But this would be to underestimate the fact that the Balokole movement was itself a challenge to those very forms of revivalism as expressed in mission and the church structures built as a result of the missionary movement.

Dr. Joe Church and Gahini in Rwanda

The perception of the Balokole in international evangelical circles was largely mediated through the writings of Joe Church, often regarded as the founder of the Revival. Dr. Church was the missionary doctor at Gahini in the Belgian colony of Ruanda (modern day Rwanda), under whose guidance the revival first became a mass movement. His organizational skills as an evangelist enabled the message of Revival to spread throughout the stations of the Ruanda Mission in Rwanda, Burundi, and the Kigezi district of Uganda, and it was Dr. Church who transformed his hospital-based medical practice to enable him to devote his energies to be a full-time evangelist, accompanying fellow African revivalists (particularly the Ugandan, William Nagenda, on missions to Kenya and Tanganyika, and the Sudan, to other parts of Africa, and to India and Latin America, Britain, Switzerland and the United States, between the 1930s and 1960s. His writings – testimonies, accounts of his evangelistic journeys with the teams, correspondence with the Brethren – all helped to consolidate the sense of this movement as a dynamic outpouring of the Spirit, in the tradition of Wesley, Jonathan Edwards and Charles G. Finney. Later the connection with Billy Graham also helped to reinforce this tradition.

Joe Church was a member of the Ruanda Mission of the Church Missionary Society, established in 1921 as an autonomous mission by two medical doctors, Leonard Sharp and Algie Stanley Smith. The main reason for the insistence on autonomy lay in fears about liberal and modernist theology, which was to provoke a split within CMS in Britain in 1922, and the formation of a rival, biblically more conservative, body, the Bible Churchmen's Missionary Society (BCMS). The doctors sympathized with the conservatives but were persuaded to remain within the larger body of CMS if they could retain a separate identity as the 'Ruanda Mission,' ensuring that only conservative evangelical missionaries were recruited and that the ethos of the nascent church would be definitively conservative biblically and theologically. For the founders and for Joe Church, it was the Keswick movement which defined most precisely what it meant to be conservative and evangelical. The Keswick emphasis on a second blessing beyond conversion, embodied in a strenuous life of spiritual and moral struggle for personal holiness the 'quest for the highest'. This emphasis shaped the way in which the mission developed.

One of the features of the East African revival was that it shattered the expectations of those whose spirituality had been shaped by the Keswick movement. For the African Balokole, the experience of *kulokoka* was not a 'second blessing' but the only authentic conversion to Christ, the only path of salvation. This was a challenge to the integrity of the missionaries where it was felt most keenly: the validity of their own faith experience and their striving for holiness. It put in question a deeply held sense of colonial superiority. These issues deeply divided the Ruanda Mission in the 1930s and 1940s, both in East Africa and in Britain. Dr. Len Sharp, the founder of the mission, never reconciled himself to what he considered the incivility of the Balokole, their arrogance and assertiveness. Stanley Smith, the mission's co-founder, assumed the role of mediator between the pro- and anti-Balokole factions, but this was an extraordinarily difficult task in the face of the uncompromising stances of both groups. The Revival was a subversive force.

It was Joe Church's genius to see that the Revival would not flourish as a mission-led initiative, but that the Spirit was empowering the African converts to exercise roles of leadership and service. The Spirit was leading Christianity in new directions, in response to African needs and aspirations. One could argue that the Keswick movement from its inception in the late 19th century had also recognised this, in its emphasis that living a Spirit-filled life, rather than having acquired the manners and sophistication of 'civilization', was crucial for creating real disciples. But this theological perspective, reasonable in itself, had led to disaster, when young, brash and culturally insensitive missionaries on the Niger, in west Africa, during the declining years of Bishop Crowther's episcopate at the end of the 19th century, had tried to purge the local church of its corruption and immorality. That the Balokole in the 1930s and 1940s avoided this extreme was not because they were really any more sensitive to local culture, but because their critique came from inside the culture. It was not imposed from outside by missionaries.

Simeoni Nsibambi and His Circle in Buganda

As a new missionary, Joe Church had arrived in Rwanda in 1927 as the doctor of the new mission station of Gahini, just when eastern Rwanda was experiencing its worst famine for decades. Overwhelmed by the work, he had recuperated in Kampala, Uganda. Here he encountered Simeoni Nsibambi, a Muganda landowner with property near the Namirembe Hill headquarters of the Native Anglican Church of which he was a baptized and confirmed member. After an experience of conversion to Christ, Nsibambi had for some years lived a life of simplicity and retirement, barefoot and clothed in a white *kanzu* rather than Western clothes, critical of what he saw as the lethargy and complacency of the Native Anglican Church (NAC). He encouraged others to commit themselves in similar ways. It was not so much a school of disciples as a network of committed people with strong personal ties to Nsibambi through family and clan solidarities, and contacts acquired in schooling (which, beyond primary level, was still largely confined to a small privileged group) and by baptized membership in the NAC. Joe Church returned to Gahini invigorated and now part of this network. In the next few years a steady stream of recruits came to work as school teachers or medical assistants at Gahini, including Blasio Kigozi, Nsibambi's brother, and William Nagenda, Kigozi's brother in law, and others who had come into contact with the Nsibambi circle. It was from this group that the revival in Gahini caught fire in 1932. In mission circles Church is regarded as the midwife of the revival, and the wealth of his archives has ensured that his perspectives on revival tend to dominate those scholars who have approached the revival primarily as church historians and missiologists. In East Africa itself, Nsibambi is regarded as pre-eminently the founding figure.

The Ruanda Mission's Attitude to Revival

The Ruanda Mission remained divided about the legitimacy of the Revival until late in the colonial era. However, by the early 1960s, when the nations of East Africa obtained independence, the mission had come fully to accept the Revival, to own it not only as a legitimate expression of its own aims, but to see it as the bearer of authentic Christianity in the churches which it had helped to create. The expectation was that missionaries would be positive about the Revival and committed to its expression and discipline. However positive missionaries were in advance of their arrival on the mission field, the actual encounter with the Brethren could still be a shattering experience, as they struggled to reassess their own previous Christian experience, and to gain full acceptance into the Fellowship. For Ruanda Mission supporters in Britain itself, the message was that this was the authentic form of a heart-felt and committed Christian discipleship which English forms of Christianity, even if ostensibly Evangelical, lacked. By this time the English direction of the society was in the hands of returnee missionaries who had themselves been deeply touched by the Revival during their time of service. Ironically this commitment occurred just as the turmoils of independence, especially during the Hutu Revolution in Rwanda, were having a devastating effect on the cohesiveness of the revival in Rwanda itself. Many Rwandan revivalists were forced to become refugees because they were unwilling to compromise their religious message, of radical equality between Tutsi and Hutu, in favour of a political stance which stigmatised Tutsi as the oppressors and prioritised the development of the Hutu majority only.

Joe Church's writings, the transformation of the Ruanda Mission as an organ for revival values, and the living witness of Balokole missionaries, particularly Anglicans in the United Kingdom, and Mennonites who had worked in Tanzania and went to the United States, all served to emphasise the role of the Balokole as standing squarely in the evangelical revivalist tradition, but also as mediating a distinctively new form of that revival, which had a message to a secular, industrial and consumerist society, where values had become increasingly atomized and private. The practicality of translating Balokole values into an alien culture was not something which unduly worried the missionary Brethren. The fact that the gospel of salvation was so alien was precisely the reason for its relevance in a godless society.

Revival and Culture

Being culturally relevant was not something that worried African Balokole in relation to their own culture either. The gospel message was understood to be a stranger equally to European/North American and to African cultural sensibilities. If the Balokole challenged missionaries' self-perceptions, they equally challenged that of fellow African Christians. They were particularly hostile to the 'bakulu' (Luganda for 'elders'), by which was signified the leaders of the church, bishop, clergy, lay readers – i.e. all in authority, whether Bazungu (European) or African. The criticism of 'obukulu' (a system based on deference to those in authority) applied to the institutional church – particularly a hierarchical Anglicanism, but it was equally applicable to Presbyterians, Methodists, the Mennonites, and the African Inland Mission church, in that all the mission-founded churches had developed hierarchical structures. It also applied, by extension, to the structures of colonial rule, as well as to the traditional rulers. As such, in the 1940s in particular, colonial authorities feared the Balokole as a potentially subversive group. Balokole, for example, were accused of undermining tax collection by attacking the cultivation of tobacco or grain which could be used for brewing alcohol. Traditional rulers also disliked Balokole because they ignored traditional habits of deference and civility. As Derek Peterson's pioneering work has shown, the Revival movement was profoundly antithetical to the development of local nationalisms in the late colonial period. The Revival movement was also seen as subversive of family values, encouraging women to develop roles outside the home, to neglect their domestic duties, and liable to criticize their husbands for adultery, drunkenness and lack of responsibility. In the last decade or so of colonial rule, during the Mau Mau period in Kenya, the Hutu revolution in Rwanda, and the debates over traditional rulers in Uganda, the Balokole represented a critique of colonial pretensions as well as the neo-traditionalism of local nationalisms and the progressive claims of the African nationalist movement. These critiques of the state continued into the post-colonial period. The disjunction between 'salvation' and 'politics' (dini and siasa as Ben Knighton has put it in a Swahili Kenyan context) was continued into the post-independence world, with the Balokole standing out against lavish and ostentatious life-styles, which characterised the new middle class professionals, and which filled the majority who could not compete with envy. (Knighton 2009, p.8) Yet, all Balokole valued formal ('western') education very highly indeed, and sacrificed to put their children through school and university. The high value which they put on monogamy, marriage in church, and the nuclear family also meant that they were, almost against their will, role models for modernity. Their use of hospitals and western pharmaceutical products rather than consulting traditional diviners also put them at the forefront of modernization (the revival movement had, after all, first grown up around mission hospitals). The Balokole movement encouraged an attitude of disregard for wealth, even while it prized better and more hygienic homes, animal husbandry, and systematic approaches to accounting and banking. It valued spotlessly clean, tidy clothes, while discouraging fashion: soap, but not cosmetics; haircuts but not hairdos; simple shifts and shorts rather than suits and haute couture. The Balokole gained a well aimed reputation for honesty and probity, for simplicity of life and reliability.

If the relationship to modernity is complex, the relationship of the Balokole to the traditional spiritual world is perhaps more simple: they reject all aspects of traditional religion which detract from the lordship of Christ as the only mediator between God and human beings. The old gods are powerless, indeed non-existent. No saved person could even begin to contemplate investing any faith in the old divinites and spirits, the Balubaale and mizimu of Kiganda traditional religion, the Bachezi possession cults of South Western Uganda, or the Nyabingi cult of Kigezi and northern Rwanda, or indeed the deities and spirits of any of the ethnic groups of East Africa. The problem with the official church was that, while paying lip-service to this incompatability, church members kept their feet in both camps, paying regard to the old divinities in secret, and sometimes quite openly. Such discrepancy is a familiar reality in many areas of life. But the Balokole are marked by their complete intolerance of subterfuge. It is incomprehensible. It cannot be entertained for one moment.

This Balakoke pattern has not prevented them from being associated with traditional religious practice. At Gahini, in the early years of the revival, young saved women were accused of reviving an earlier possession fertility cult which had been prominent just before the famine. In Kigezi, the authorities (both traditional and colonial) feared a resurgence of the Nyabingi cult, a movement which had mobilized resistance to the imposition of colonial rule in the early years of the 20th century. The practice of confession of sin has been likened to the ritual recitation of prohibited sexual taboos, in deliberately provocative manner, during initiations into the Cwezi cults. These possible likenesses should not be dismissed out of hand. They may throw interesting historical light on the way in which the Balokole has embedded itself in local culture, responding to local anxieties. Nevertheless, the Balokole reject out of hand that these similarities are actual declensions from wholehearted Christian witness.

Balokole Values

If the Balokole are enchanted, it is by the cross of Christ. This is the centre of their devotion. The only way for sinful men and women to come to salvation is through the cross. Bunyan's *Pilgrim's Progress* was translated into Kinyarwanda (it had already been translated in Luganda) just at the time when the

Revival was taking off. The story of Bunyan's pilgrim resonated in the conversion stories of the Revivalists: the shedding of the burden of sin at the cross was the experience of those who were saved, in Rwanda, Kigezi, Uganda and Kenya. The experience of the cross is a decisive event in the life of the sinner. It is open to the nominal church goer and also to the heathen, to the peasant and the chief, men and women, school children and students, educated and uneducated, uncultivated and sophisticated, Hutu and Tutsi, Buganda and Bakiga.

Opportunity to have this experience took place in large public conventions, in small fellowships, and in one-to-one confrontations between an evangelist and a seeker. It was a covenant between God and the soul, a covenant ratified through the confession of sin in detail and in full, before the community. Peterson has pointed out the importance of the careful enumeration of sin, an extension of the accountability and list-making which was the experience of church meetings and school learning, and which marked out Christians from heathens. Forgiveness comes from God alone, once for all, but is re-presented to the believer again and again in the fellowship, and sealed through the singing of *Tukutendereza*, the hymn which thanks God for the cleansing power of the blood of the lamb. *Tukutendereza* is the ubiquitous signature of the Revival, used as a greeting as well as a seal of confession. In Luganda, it is sung far and wide, beyond the linguistic boundaries of Buganda.

Beyond that initial confession made at the moment of conversion, and sealed in the fellowship, confession becomes testimony, in the sense that every Mulokole will feel a joyful obligation to rehearse the confession to new comers. It is his or her business card, as it were. The precise details may become somewhat simplified over the years, but the testimony continues to point to the contrast between the sinner and the saved person, whose former sins have now been forgiven. For the newly converted (especially in the early days of the Revival) restitution of property or other tangible compensation for those wronged and cheated was essential. Balokole would go to extreme pains to visit people who had been cheated or who were owed outstanding debts. At times the wronged person may feel embarrassed by this recalling of often essentially trivial faults, some even took it to be a deliberate attempt at mockery. On the other hand, if serious fraud or even murder was confessed to the District Commissioner or judge, it might raise dilemmas about corroborating evidence, whether justice is served by bringing a case which has been dormant for years or had never become a crime in the first place, and of the appropriateness of punishment. There might also be ethical questions of the propriety of creating a wrong which had never previously been recognised, and which might merely create animosity and dispute (such as the confession of a previously unknown adultery). However, these prudential considerations were not entertained: the importance was truth telling. 'Walking in the light' also included being open and honest about one's feelings towards other

Brethren, and indeed towards other members of the community. Even if this seemed inappropriate or out of proportion (what use, for example, to tell someone that you expected to be given a drink when you arrived and that you were disappointed at the lack of hospitality when this did not happen), such considerations of tact and propriety were seen as secondary to the duty of transparency in one's relations. It has to be said that over the years the values of tact, modesty and politeness have tended to be emphasised, rather than privileging an honesty which might be brutal and insensitive. Civility has in fact become a Balokole virtue.

Preaching to the unsaved could sometimes be interpreted as brutal honesty. It could be ignored or regarded with friendly indulgence in the market place. More intrusive was preaching on buses, where a captive audience was still, by and large, tolerant, amused rather than affronted. William Nagenda's public preaching was, he once admitted, strongly motivated by a vision of unsaved people going to hell. The Balokole make a strong distinction between the things of the Spirit and the things of the world (*by'ensi*), under the dominion of the devil. The Balokole look to the return of Jesus Christ as the ultimate judgement on this world, but they do not indulge in speculation about when and how this will happen, nor are they attuned particularly to the pre-millenarian, post-millenarian debates within Evangelicalism.

> The revival brethren claim that they have victory over sin. They discourage defeatism in their Christian life. They also find that the experience of the Spirit through salvation has given them a new awareness of unseen spiritual realities. In general terms, Revival brethren have a heightened awareness of the presence of evil, the Devil (Satan), and powers of darkness. They are conscious that life is a spiritual struggle against Satan, sin and the flesh. (Birungi in Rukirande 2005, 55).

Balokole want to be good neighbors, and they interpret this as speaking the truth even if it is unpalatable. They do this in the common interactions of life at home, in the market, at work. Yet, they also believe in speaking truth to power, whether in the church or in the nation.

Amos Kasibante's Reflections

In the late 1970s, Kasibante studied for ordination at Bishop Tucker College, the main theological institution of the Church of Uganda. In 1941 Balokole had been expelled from the theological college and for some years the Brethren did not advise its members to seek ordination. But by the 1960s relations between the Revival and the Church had so improved that a large number of Balokole did study for the ministry, and by the 1970s (during the turmoils of the Amin regime) a large proportion of the ordinands were from a revivalist background. Amos Kasibante was ordained in West Buganda diocese in 1979. He now works as a parish priest in England.

In 1966, when I was 13, I came to faith. I was in Primary Five, at Kisowera school. Kisowera is on the Mukono-Bugerere road, a couple of miles from my home at Kabembe. I was sitting under a mango tree when I heard a voice saying 'Repent'. I took the instruction seriously, and walked over to see the catechist (the lay leader of the local church). The catechist didn't quite know how to handle my questions, but he told me that a Fellowship meeting of Balokole was due to meet at 4 pm They met twice a week at the church, on Tuesdays and Fridays, about ten of them. Most were just ordinary villagers, not particularly well educated or with good jobs, but some had been primary teachers. I went to the meeting. The group heard me sympathetically and said that the first thing I should do was to tell my family. They quoted a text, 'I will give my testimony among my own people.' I did tell my Mum. My dad is a Muganda, but my mum was from Kigezi. Mum was somewhat sceptical of the Balokole, partly because she had had a bad experience in childhood, when her step-mother, though a Mulokole, had not treated her well. Although this experience was an important milestone in my life, I gradually settled down. I didn't go to the Fellowship – which was not really geared to primary school kids. Anyway, I lived too far from the school and church (which were in the same compound) and needed to get home straight after school. I got confirmed in Mukono in 1968. This was part of the routine in those days; it was part of the general policy of confirming primary school children. Later, when I went to live with my Dad in Kampala (he was a policeman), I did become committed. I was by then in a Catholic upper primary school at Mulago and used to attend the church daily for the recitation of the rosary. It was there that I met a good friend, Vincent Zake, who unlike me was a Catholic, but he has now become a Baptist pastor.

I remember getting frustrated with my father for constantly promising to give me fees to go to secondary school, but always having excuses for delaying. I confronted him, saying that I did not want to hear lies. If he could not afford to pay then he should tell me directly. He was angry with me for this straight-talking, and I apologised, but he did come up with some money and that helped me to go to Kako Senior Secondary School near Masaka, a school with a strong Anglican tradition. Here I joined the Scripture Union and became very active. The school had a Sunday service, but I preferred to go to the cathedral. One reason was that, because I was poor, I did not have any decent clothes, and the students tended to dress smartly for the Sunday service in school. At the cathedral people came as they were – smart or poorly dressed, it did not matter. The SU was the main focus for keen Christians at the school. The relationship with the local Balokole fellowship at the cathedral was good. However, there was not necessarily much interaction. It was not easy to get permission to leave the school compound. Yet, the watchman knew me and trusted that I was not going to get up to any mischief. He let me and another student, Betty Kyasimire, go to attend the fellowships on Tuesday and Friday at 5 PM. I was encouraged by the cathedral pastor Reverend Kizza, who was a mulokole, and who used to come once a month to the school to celebrate communion.

The Balokole group was a small, intimate fellowship. It included another priest, Reverend Erisa Wamala and his wife. There was also Stanley Kiiza, a man who had a certain amount of prestige because he'd 'been to England,' and thus he was 'omugunjufu' – he 'had civilization'. Then there was a man from Rwanda, Aloni Rugayizihabuka, a Tutsi exile, who had been a lorry driver but now was a farmer in the area. There was a widow called Nora. She was highly respected. Her husband had died in a car accident after only a few years of marriage, leaving her with two small kids. She had never remarried, something quite unusual in those days. The group was no more than 20, and it split in 1973. Some became *Bazukufu* They joined the strict group of Balokole who were dividing the brethren in Kampala. They claimed that the Fellowship was becoming too lax, forgetting its first love. The particular cause of the split in Kako concerned the fact that the Wamalas had admitted into their home some grandchildren who had been born out of wedlock. The strict Brethren felt that these were 'abaana ab'obwensi' (children of the world) and the Balokole should not countenance such immorality.

Meanwhile at the school, the Scripture Union was coming under the influence of the Deliverance Church, one of the early home-grown Pentecostal movements in Uganda. This was part of a youth movement which saw itself as more up to date than the somewhat old fashioned life of the Balokole. They allowed fancy hairstyles and bell-bottom trousers. The Balokole disapproved of both. Nevertheless, the links between SU and the Balokole in Uganda were and remain very strong. These days, the leadership of the SU sees itself as supporting the Church of Uganda, as representative of Revival values, and are rather more suspicious of the less disciplined styles of the Pentecostal churches. (SU is, nevertheless, a non-denominational evangelical body, not an arm of the COU.)

The fellowship in Kako, as well as in other places in the 1970s, was a warm and supportive community. Members took care of each other. If you had a problem, they gave you advice. They were gentle rather than condemnatory, and there was no blaming. Confession was an important part of the fellowship. It tended to be acknowledgement of failing to do things, of jealousies and temptations. Balokole were presumed to have abandoned serious sinful life once they got converted, and it would have seemed strange for people to confess those blatant sins every week. Moreover, the fellowship was ready to acknowledge that we are constantly being tested by Satan, and that we give in to the weakness of the flesh (omubiri). People confessed if they had failed to come to the meeting. The fellowship expected very regular attendance. The sense of mutual responsibility which was such a strong mark of the group depended on that regular disciplined meeting. Discipline and self control were essential. You were also seen as a role model for the wider community, the salt of the earth. Balokole are like 'nkokonjeru' – white hens – they can be, and should, be marked out immediately in a community. There must also be absolute transparency about money, something which began to disappear in the 1980s as a money economy and opportunities for individual enrichment began to undermine the role of the Fellowship in controlling its members.

Manuel Muranga's Views on the Current Life of Balokole in Kampala and Kabale

Manuel Muranga is from Kigezi. As a saved man, he has belonged to Balokole fellowships in Kampala and Kigezi for 40 or more years. For many years a lecturer in German at Makerere University in Kampala, he has recently become the Principal of the Bishop Barham University College in Kabale, an institution of higher learning of the Church of Uganda. I asked him to comment on the present state of the Balokole movement on the basis of living in two areas which have been profoundly affected by the Revival: Kampala, the capital of Uganda, and the center of Buganda; and in Kigezi in South West Uganda.

Muranga's responses to a series of questions on the structure and mission of the Fellowship (ab-oluganda) among the Balokole is provided as an appendix to this case. This interview, in the form of a verbatim, supplements the narrative of this case by providing important documentation on the past and current features of the ab-oluganda, and it conveys core features of this influential revitalization movement within the East African context.

Concluding Reflections by Kevin Ward

Both Kasibante's and Muranga's material show something of the inner life of the Balokole movement at crucial periods in its history, the 1970s and the beginning of the 21st century. This presentation has concentrated on two epicentres of the East African Revival – Buganda in the centre of Uganda, and the distinctive cultural region around South West Uganda and Rwanda. It has tried to show how the Balokole movement was born and developed in different milieux, and how core values of the revival have been expressed differently in these areas. In Buganda, the Revival was primarily a movement calling an already well established church, which had learned to make compromises with the local culture in ways which the Balokole felt were a declension from the central message of the Gospel. The Revival's task was to call the church to awake – *Zukuka!* as Blasio Kigozi memorably put it in his impassioned speech to the 1936 synod of the church, just before his death. The resulting Revival movement in Buganda was always a minority, faithful to this task of witness. It gave the Balokole a strong corporate identity as a separate movement, a member of the Church of Uganda, but critical of it – a 'loyal opposition'. It has remained true to that task with remarkable constancy over the years, and continues to act as an gadfly, a mosquito challenging the larger church and society to repent and reform lives and communities along Gospel values.

In Kigezi, as in Rwanda, the Revival came at an early stage of evangelization. Although there had been faithful missionary work before the arrival of the Ruanda Mission and before the Revival, the church tends to equate the coming of Christianity with the arrival of the Revivalists as evangelists in the area. The Revival created the church, and the church came to reflect its values. In Rwanda the Anglican church was a small minority in a fairly hostile climate where the Roman Catholic church was supported both by the Belgian colonial authorities and the traditional (largely Tutsi) authorities at the expense of Protestant interlopers. The Revival gave the church heart to meet the challenges posed by this inferior position. Unfortunately many Balokole had to flee Rwanda during the political troubles of the independence era. The mainly Tutsi leadership of the church and revival in colonial times was replaced by a largely Hutu leadership. In independent Rwanda, the Church expanded greatly, the older discrimination having been replaced. However, the Revival could not be the force which it had been before 1959. This did not mean that revival Christianity did not continue to be an important force in Rwanda, but it was a new type of revival, generated largely from the revival which affected the schools in the early 1970s. It looked back to the old Balokole tradition, but its dynamism was of a more charismatic kind than the old fellowships.

In Kigezi itself, the Revival went from strength to strength. Under the leadership of Bishop Festo Kivengere, and the clergy, who were overwhelmingly Balokole, the church became a dynamic outward looking institution. Becoming a member of the Church in Kigezi and getting saved were synonymous, at least in popular perception and the church's teaching. The Revival did not fragment into rival groups, as it did in Buganda, nor was there a preoccupation with maintaining the strict identity of the fellowship over against the world. However, as Muranga reported, Revival fellowships continue to exist. They are a minority of the church as a whole, and consist overwhelmingly of women. The difference with Buganda is that the Revival in Kigezi is not judged so much by the effectiveness and vigor of its fellowships, as by the overall dynamism of the church. This may be a loss in some respects, and it may give rise to a lip-service to revival values in the church which are not reflected in the disciplined lives of its members.

Both the Buganda and the Kigezi models have their strengths and weaknesses. The Buganda model may lead to an introversion and irrelevance to a wider society. The Kigezi model may lead to a reduction in honesty and discipline, in that the Church as a whole loudly proclaims revival values, while the reality of church life may show many 'worldly' influences (not least consumerist values, political rivalries, ecclesiastical jealousies).

This article has concentrated on Buganda and Kigezi at the expense of other areas in Uganda (and indeed elsewhere in East Africa) where the Revival has also had an impart. In Northern Uganda, the development has been very different, and from an early age the Revival broke away from the influence of the missionaries of the Ruanda Mission and the largely Buganda, Ankole and Kigezi leadership of the main Fellowship. In Northern Uganda Revival was often much more antipathetic to the established church, much less amenable to live alongside the church. Nevertheless some of the North's outstanding leaders, Archbishop Janani Luwum, Archbishop Silvanus Wani, and the present archbishop Henry Orombi, have been nurtured in the Revival. Outside Uganda, the present state of the Revival movement is rather more problematic. In Kenya, the Balokole are largely seen as a movement of a former generation, dwindling in vitality and creativity as its members grow old and die, while young people are more attracted to the styles of the newer Pentecotalism which is sweeping across Kenya, as it is in other parts of Africa.

Uganda also has its Pentecostal movement, but the Revival has managed to reinvigorate itself and to continue to recruit members from schools and universities. Ugandan Balokole distinguish themselves from these newer forms of revivalism. At heart is the question of discipline, modesty of demeanor and of material aspiration. Where Pentecostals preach the cross, the Balokole applaud. Where Pentecostal churches aim to create a moral community, Balokole applaud. Where they preach a gospel of prosperity, or have a ministry focused on healing, deliverance, and banishing evil spirits, the Balokole are critical. They feel that these emphases detract from the cross.

The strong distinction between faith and politics has meant that Balokole traditionally were wary of its members becoming politicians. It inevitably seemed to involve too many compromises with the world. This has, in turn, been criticized as a pietism which does not engage with the important task of social engagement. Roger Bowen reflected on this possibility in the aftermath of the Rwanda genocide in 1994. However, the Balokole have also adopted brave and unpopular stances at certain times – such as the Mau Mau crisis of 1953-55 in Kenya, during the Hutu revolution in Rwanda from 1959-1964. Archbishop Janani Luwum was murdered by Amin. Bishop Festo Kivengere was forced into exile. Bishop Henry Okullu and Archbishop David Gitari in Kenya have consistently witnessed to Christian values and have criticized presidents and governments for flouting human rights. This shows that, both as a body and as individuals, revivalists have not failed to engage in social and political debate and have acted bravely in times of crisis. The Balokole do speak truth to power in both church and state.

More recent engagement with social issues in Uganda suggests that the Revival has entered a new phase. Archbishop Orombi has constantly invoked the revival tradition of the Church of Uganda in his opposition to liberal biblical and moral stances in the worldwide Anglican Communion, particularly over the question of homosexuality. He has used it as justification for breaking communion with the Episcopal Church of the USA, and for not accepting the 'bitter money' of rich but ethically flawed churches. Orombi is certainly tapping into one aspect of the Revival legacy, characterised as it is by its refusal to compromise with worldly excuses for acting in evil ways. What this position perhaps misses is the refusal of the Balokole to leave the corrupt church to its own devices, and the willingness to persist in engagement with the world church, precisely of being the loyal opposition in adverse times.

In the realm of state affairs, it has been noted that a considerable proportion of the members of the Museveni government have been children of Revivalists. Museveni himself comes from a Revivalist family, and as a schoolboy at the Ntare government school in Mbarara he was prominent in the affairs of the Scripture Union. His time in office has been marked by a re-engagement with these roots. The presence of Balokole, or at least children of Balokole in the cabinet has something to do with the importance of the Revival in South West Uganda, but also with the importance attached to education by revivalists, reinforced by the self-discipline without which study cannot be successful. Professor Apolo Nsibambi, the Prime Minister of Uganda, spoke in August 2010 at the launching of a book about the East African Revival, He spoke of the enormous stresses which children of Balokole had to endure while growing up, the rigid discipline and pressure both to experience salvation and to lead an exemplary life. He joked that as a teenager, growing up in Taata and Mama Nsibambi's home, it was difficult enough to steal a kiss from a girl, never mind have a steady relationship. Children of Balokole are noted for their success in professional and creative life in a number of spheres, and since the advent of Museveni in 1986, in politics too. Reflecting on the legacy of his strict upbringing Simon Nsibambi said that it had given him important principles – punctuality, hard work, honesty, an ability to admit when mistakes are made and to ask forgiveness of those wronged.

These are indeed enduring values. But one cannot imagine that many of the second generation Balokole would relish establishing the full rigors of their childhood in society at large. To try to impose this is likely to lead to an intolerable authoritarianism. But it is also against the ethos of the Revival, in which religion and morals must come from the heart, from the individual's free decision, and must always be motivated from inside, not imposed from outside, whether by society at large or by law. This is what has made the tenure of office of Nsaba Buturo in the newly created Ministry of Ethics and Responsibility rather problematic. In particular the attempt in the last parliament to legislate against homosexuality, the Bahati Bill backed by Nsaba Buturo, has caused considerable alarm both within Uganda and internationally. This is not the place to discuss the relative influence of American evangelicals, dissident American Episcopalians, and the local Revival movement, on these debates. But, it does bring to focus the larger question of the extent to which the Revival should look to implement in society at large its values and aspirations. It would seem bizarre to reject altogether the attempt to implement Christian ethical values in a society, since that would surely be to withdraw from real engagement with society, and the Revival has never done that. On the other hand, questions of public morality do generally require a level of ethical discussion, allowing for different outcomes, and willingness to compromise, which is difficult to reconcile with the rather more clear and absolute demands which the Balokole have traditionally invoked..... difficult, but not impossible, as a number of compassionate and deeply spiritual Balokole leaders have well demonstrated in the past.

Bibliography

Bowen, Roger, 2004, 'Genocide in Rwanda 1994: AN Anglican Perspective', in Carol Rittner (editor), *Genocide in Rwanda: Complicity of the Churches?*, St. Paul: Paragon, 2004.

Church, J.E., 1936, *Awake Uganda! The Story of Blasio Kigozi and his vision of revival* [Second edition, Namirembe: Diocesan Council of Uganda, 1957].*1*

―――, 1938, *Every Man a Bible Student*, London: Children's Special Service Mission. [Second edition, Exeter: Paternoster Press, 1976]

―――, 1966, *Forgive Them: the Story of an African Martyr*, London: Hodder & Stoughton.

―――, 1981, *Quest for the Highest: an autobiographical account of the East African Revival*, Exeter: Paternoster Press.

Coomes, Anne, 1990, *Festo Kivengere: a biography*, Eastbourne: Monarch, 1990.

Godfrey, Nick, 2008, 'Understanding Genocide: the experience of Anglicans in Rwanda c. 1921-2008', PhD dissertation, University of Cambridge.

Guillebaud, Meg, 2002, *Rwanda: The Land God Forgot? Revival, Genocide and Hope*, London: Monarch Books.

―――, 2005, *After the Locusts: How Costly Forgiveness is Restoring Rwanda's Stolen Years*, Oxford: Monarch Books.

Hastings, Adrian, 1994, *The Church in Africa, 1450-1950*, Oxford: Oxford University Press.

Hopkins, Elizabeth, 1970, 'The Nyabingi Cult of Southwestern Uganda' in Robert Rotberg and Ali Mazrui (editors), *Protest and Power in Back Africa*, Oxford: Oxford University Press, pp 319ff.

Jones, Tudur, and Pope, Robert, 2004, *Faith and Crisis of a Nation: Wales 1890-1914*, Cardiff: Cardiff Academic Press.

Kibira, Josiah, *Church, Clan and the World*, I1974, Lund: Gleerup.

Knighton, Ben (editor), *Religion and Politics in Kenya: Essays in Honor of a Meddlesome Priest*, New York: Palgrave Macmillan, 2009.

McMaster, Richard, 2006, *A Gentle Wind of God: The Influence of the East Africa Revival*, Scottdale: Herald Press.

Osborn, H.H., 1991, *Fire in the Hills*, Crowborough: Highland, 1995, *Revival: A Precious Heritage*, Winchester: Apologia Publications.

―――.Peterson, Derek, 2001, 'Wordy Women: Gender trouibe and the Oral Polics of the East African revival in Northern Gikuyuland,' *Journal of African History* 42, pp. 469-489.

―――, 2012, *The Pilgrims' Politics: Conversion, Patriotism and the Social History of Dissent in East Africa*, New York: Cambridge University Press.

Robins, Caroline, 1975, 'Tukutendereza: A Study of Social Change and Sectarian Withdrawal in the Balokole Revival', PhD dissertation, Columbia.

Rukirande, William, Hall, Joan, Traill, E, et al, 2005, *The East African Revival Through Seventy Years 1935-1975): Testimonies and Reflections*, Kabale: Diocese of Kigezi.

Rumiya, Jean, 1992, *Le Rwanda sous le Regime du Mandat Belge (1916-1931)*, Paris: Editions L'Harmattan.

St. John, Patricia, 1976, *Breath of Life: The Story of the Ruanda Mission,* London: Norfolk.
Sharp, Leonard, *Great Truths from God's Word,* London: SPCK, 1944 [second edition, 2007]
Smoker, Dorothy, 1994, *Ambushed By Love: God's Triumph in Kenya's Terror,* Washington PA: Christian Literature Crusade.
Stanley Smith, A, 1946, *Road to Revival,* London: Ruanda Mission.
Sundkler, Bengt, 1980, *Bara Bukoba: Church and Community in Tanzania,* London: Hurst.
Taylor, J.V., 1958, *The Growth of the Church in Buganda,* London: SCM.
Tuma, Tom and Mutibwa, Phares (editors) 1978, *A Century of Christianity in Uganda,* Nairobi: Uzima.
Ward, Kevin, 1991, '"Tukutendereza Yesu": The Balokole Revival Movement in Uganda', ion Z. Nthamburi, *From Mission to Church: A Handbook of Christianity in East Africa,* Nairobi: Uzima Press, pp. 113-144.
____, 1989, ' "Obedient Rebels": the Mukono Crisis of 1941', in *Journal of Religion in Africa,* Leiden: Brill, Volume XIX Fasc.3, October 1989, pp 194-227.
____, 2006, *A History of Global Anglicanism,* Cambridge; Cambridge University Press.
____, 2008, 'The East African Revival of the Twentieth Century; the Search for an evangelical African Christianity', in Cooper, Kate and Gregory, Jeremy, *Revival and Resurgence in Christian History,* Woodbridge: Boydell Press.
____, 2010, 'Christianity, revival and the Rwandan Genocide', in Akindale, A, *A New Day: Essays on World Christianity in Honor of Lamin Sanneh',* New York: Peter Lang.
Ward, Kevin, and Wildwood, Emma, 2010, *The East African Revival: History and Legacies,* Kampala: Fountain.
Warren, Max, 1954, *Revival an Enquiry,* London: SCM
Wild-Wood, Emma, 2008, 'Boundary Crossing and Boundary Marking: Radical Revival in Congo and Uganda from 1948', in Cooper, Kate and Gregory, Jeremy, *Revival and Resurgence in Christian History,* Woodbridge: Boydell Press.

Appendix A

Interview with Dr. Manuel Muranga on the Current Life of the Balokole in Kampala and Kabale, Uganda

The Fellowship (ab'oluganda)

How do you think that the Fellowship has changed since you first became a part of this movement?

1. Is the conduct of the weekly fellowship different from earlier years? Essentially not!
2. Do people still put a great stress on confessing particular sins? Yes, e.g. confessing "spiritual coldness", which one hears quite often.
3. Is there more emphasis on thanksgiving and general testimony of what the Lord has done rather than confession as such? Probably yes! This could be partly a result of influence from the Pentecostal movement, with its greater emphasis on "the good things God has done in one's life".
4. Are the brethren still as concerned about the personal life of its members, in terms of visiting, advising, counselling? Yes, they still are! And they go visiting as well.
5. Is there still a lively international dimension to the Balokole – do people regularly attend Conventions etc in Kenya, Tanzania, Rwanda etc? Yes, very much so!
6. Is the role of the Convention, and other large meetings, still an important one? Yes. And there are annual Balokole conventions, usually in January, in different locations. The annual 3-4 day convention in Kabale is very well attended – around 1000 (one thousand) people attended this year.
7. Are there any specific hymns, music, prayers, spirituality, which the Balokole movement has developed in recent years?

Hymns, yes. There seems to bemore emphasis on Bible exposition, but that is only my impression.

You have experienced the Fellowship in Kampala and in Kigezi. Can you characterise the similarities and differences between how the Fellowship operates in these two areas? Essentially they are the same – only some really superficial differences, such as the brethren at the Namirembe fellowship having a more balanced male-female population whereas the Rugarama one is mainly women, plus just a few men including Cathedral clergy. But I have been told of a weekly early morning fellowship that is attended by more men. We also had a good number of men in the daily Lenten fellowship / Bible study / prayer meetings from 6 to 7 a.m. Most of the Bible expositors during those meetings were men, including BBUC lecturers/clergy. One difference is that at the Cathedral here at Rugarama, there are two felolowship meetings per week, on Tuesdays and Thursdays. In Namirembe there is but one, every Friday.

Youth

Does the Balokole fellowship attract young people? To some extent, yes, though there are many alternative places of fellowship, such as Scripture Union and FOCUS ones, or newer fellowships like KAAYM (Kigezi and Ankole Anglican Youth Missioners) and its many regional offshoots. Members of these are generally faithful to the Balokole spirituality of the COU, though they will be open to a more "oecumenical", like I happen to be, as a result of the Scripture / Christian Union (FOCUS, IFES) movement in the universities.

If so, why do young people feel attracted to the Brethren rather than other charismatic or Pentecostal churches? Those youths that keep with the Brethren rather than with the other movements do so because of the "solidity" and time-proven steadfastness of the Brethren movement, plus the fair number of "icons" (the late Rev. Canon peter Kigozi, Bishop Festo Kivengere, The Most Rev. Eric Sabiiti; the still living Zabuloni Kabaza, The Most Rev. Henry Luke Orombi, gifted living evangelists and Bible teachers such as Eng. Paul Wasswa, Peter Asiimwe, Bishop Zac Niringiye, Rev. Medad Birungi bya Yesu, and many others. And, of course, even influential international Balokole or born-agains from solid, ancient churches, such as John Stott, Billy Graham, C.S. Lewis etc have played a role in giving young people more faith and confidence in their attachment to the Brethren movement and the Anglican Church that has been its home since its birth.

Is it compatible to be a member of the Fellowship and also a member of a Pentecostal church? Yes, it is compatible, especially if one has been through the Christian Union spiritual experience, which, as I said earlier, is quite "oecumenical" in its orientation, the experience of rebirth (John 3:3; 2 Corinthians 5:17) plus the practical consequences of this being the common denominators in this oecumenism. This is a different oecumenism from that of the World Council of Churches, which tends to universalism.

Are the Balokole exclusively Anglican (Church of Uganda) in Uganda? Far from it! Although the Balokole movement started in the then Native Anglican Church, later the Church of Uganda, in the last three decades the world "Balokole Churches" has evolved in Uganda's religious vocabulary to mean the new Pentecostal and charismatic churches which also talk about being born again, or okulokoka. So nowadays people are often heard saying they are Balokole of the Anglican Church/Church of Uganda, or "Abalokole ab'e Namirembe" (Namirembe Balokole).

Do the Brethren still have strict dress codes and are they antagonistic to youth culture in music and dance? Yes, certainly. Outward appearance is regarded as a reflection of what is inside (Matthew 15:16-20; 1 Peter 3:1-7). So a dress code, music and dance that are clearly of "worldly" character, indecent, reflecting lack of anchor in the Gospel of Jesus Christ, will not be encouraged. Here at BBUC, and indeed in the entire Uganda Christian University, we have a dress code that is in fact an outworking of these convictions.

The Church of Uganda

How do the Balokole regard the Church of Uganda as an institution? They realise this is their home, but they recognise that it is a place where you have nominal, merely religious, traditionally church-going "Christians" alongside truly born-again and sincere Christians.

Do they make distinctions between bishops whom they regard as saved and those who are not saved, or who are not members of the fellowship? Yes, the Balokole do make these distinctions. Saved and unsaved bishops and other clergy are looked at with scepticism. Indeed, fortunately, the Balokole have the upper hand in most churches, especially the urban ones. In such places, many an unsaved "Reverend" will try to identify himself with the Balokole; some such Reverends have in the process got saved and admitted they weren't saved before. Glory to God!

Is there still a clear distinction between the saved and the nominal Christians within the CofU. Yes, this distinction is still very much there!

What are relations between the fellowship and the Roman Catholic Church? The charismatic movement in the Roman Catholic Church has helped to melt down the tensions and break some barriers. The bishops and other clergy will, for reasons of church politics, try to relate formally with the RC clergy in the same area; the ordinary fellowship meeting Balokole, especially the church-historically unexposed ones, will normally tend to keep their distance from the RC church members. But the worldwide, cross-denominationally influential charismatic movement (in the Anglican Church called the Anglican Renewal movement) is making of many younger CofU Balokole spiritual friends of, especially the charismatic RC Christians. You can here the greeting "Praise the Lord" exchanged between a born-again RC and a born-again CofU member. This has been the case in the oecumenically orientated Christian Union / FOCUS movement; it is now getting into the old Balokole movement as the "Balokole of the first hour" slowly die off.

Pentecostalism

How do the Brethren regard the Pentecostal churches? The prosperity gospel of the Pentecostals tends to alienate the Brethren. The Pentecostals' emphasis on healing and miracles and financial success and generally on material blessings including posh cars for their leaders – the Brethren regard all these with scepticism.

In general society, Pentecostals are often nicknamed 'Balokole' and Pentecostal churches are sometimes called 'Balokole churches'. Are there tensions between the brethren about whether to share fellowship with members of Pentecostal churches, and is there a generational distinction? Yes, the older Brethren are the greater sceptics with regard to the Pentecostal Balokole. The younger ones are more open-minded. Interestingly, many younger Pentecostals will not believe you if you tell them you are a Mulokole but you belong to the CofU, leave alone telling them that the CofU/NAC is in fact the place where "Okulokoka" began. They have, in a sense, usurped the place of the CofU in the history of the Balokole Movement as known to non-historians.

Women

How do the Balokole regard women priests (bawule)? There is no problem here. Many of the Brethren are women clergy (Rev. Canon Grace Ndyabahika, Rev. Canon Monica Sebidega, Rev. Canon Prudence Kaddu,

Do the Balokole approve of women in professions and in politics? In professions, yes, no problem in a Mulokole woman becoming, for example, a doctor or an engineer or an academic; in politics, even the Balokole men entering politics would be advised to pray seriously about it before entering it. Mr. Peter Nyombi, who has recently been appointed Attorney General of Uganda, and has been an MP for Nakasongola, has for years been a regular attendant of the Namirembe Brethren's fellowship every Friday 5-6:30 p.m. We hope he will continue to do so even as Attorney General.

Do Balokole have any objection to the deference accorded to men, for example in Kiganda culture? (The Bakiga may be more egalitarian?) No there is no objection to this, as far as I know. Even the Basoga practice, for example, women's kneeling before men when greeting. Yes, the Bakiga are outwardly more egalitarian, yet even here the men expect to be respected as the Nyineeka, or head of the home. E.g. the wife must keep a special calabash of bushera (sorghum brew) for the Nyineeka.

Social issues and the Antihomosexuality Bill

How does the Fellowship regard marriage? As an institution set up and sanctified by God. Do they still give advice about who people should marry? They still can, and occasionally do; but most young people nowadays fall in love privately, then they may inform the fellowship about their relationship later. Is a church wedding important? Yes, very important. A couple that does not wed in church will be regarded as not part of the Brethren.

Are the Brethren solidly behind David Bahati's attitude toward homosexuals and the dangers of homosexuality in Ugandan society? If I say they are 100% behind him, I shall at the very least be right with regard to the doctrine the Brethren follow.

How do the Brethren regard the policies of the former Minister of Ethics and Integrity (Nsaba Buturo)? They are fully supportive of them! The Bible is clear about homosexuality being a detestable perversion (Leviticus 18:22, Romans 1:26-27)

Do you think that the Fellowship would want the new government to appoint to the post of Minister of Culture and Integrity? Yes, the Brethren would appreciate a Mulokole in that position. Now a RC father (Rev. Fr. Simon Lokodo) has been appointed to that position. His acceptability will depend on his theology and performance.

Do the Brethren feel that the government should try to promote Balokole values in society? Yes, they do. How do they feel about the children of Balokole who are in prominent positions but as no longer or were never active members of the Fellowship, unlike their parents? They regret that situation and pray for those children.

Are there any distinguishing features of the Balokole movement in regard to attitude to HIV/AIDS, that are different from the attitudes of society in general? Not at all, except, of course, in their talk about HIV/AIDS prevention: The Brethren believe in and preach total abstinence from sex before marriage, virginity for both female and male up to the wedding night, church wedding, and, after marriage, total faithfulness between the partners. However, if someone repents, they are accepted among the Brethren.

Overall Contribution of the Balokole movement

What do you think is the enduring blessing of the Balokole movement in terms of its contribution to personal life, the life of the church, the life of the country? This is a huge question! Personal life finds lasting joy and fulfilment only if one is living as a true believer in Jesus (cf John 15:1-17, Colossians 1:27; Galatians 5:22, 23). A person who bears fruit as a Christian will automatically benefit church and nation.

Do you think the movement is still capable of development and able to adapt to new conditions? Yes, I think so, but only if the foundation is kept. A damaging, unbiblical liberal theology would be contrary to the original revelation and must be kept outside.

Is it still a major force in the religious life of Uganda as it was in the 1940s, 50s and 1960s? Yes, it is! Everybody knows what a Mulokole is, and can tell a true one from a fake one.

Appendix B

A Response to the Case from a North American Diaspora Context: The Perspective of Dr. Isaac Mukasa, a Representative of the Anglican Diocese of Toronto and an Heir of The East African Revival

Allow me to begin my response by sharing the story of David Bakulu-Mpagi, a law-abiding Canadian citizen of Ugandan descent, who arrived in Canada almost three decades ago at the age of twenty-two. David is a third generation *mulokole*. His grandparents were the first to become *balokole* decades ago. His parents followed suit. He joined the fellowship at the age of thirteen and continues to lead his life according to the strict ethical standards of the fellowship. I begin with this story because it illustrates the continuing legacy of the East African Revival in the Diaspora, in terms of its values and potential limitations.

About one year following his arrival in this country, David was taking a short-cut through a deserted alley for his night-shift at a factory in Mississauga. As he turned a corner to go down the alley, he saw what looked like a wallet on the sidewalk. It oddly lying there and looking totally out of place. Instinctively he picked up the wallet but then immediately realized that he was now confronted with a moral dilemma: what to do with it. On the one hand, if there was money in it, that could be an answer to his prayers because he was desperately in need at that point. On the other hand, the ethical standards by which he lived as a young mulokole would not allow him to simply take the money, because this wallet belonged to someone who might be looking for it at that very moment. What was the child of God redeemed by the blood of Jesus and walking in the light going to do?

As David tells the story, when he opened the wallet he found himself looking at a clean, freshly withdrawn bundle of twenty-dollars bills, amounting to five hundred dollars. Further investigation suggested to him that the wallet belonged to someone who lived just around the corner from where he found it. The right thing to do (his conscience now dictated) was to take the wallet back to its owner, which he did. The owner's joy and relief were beyond description. Amazed that all the money was there; that the young man had not taken even a single bill from the wallet, the gentleman gave David forty dollars as a gesture of gratitude.

In sharing testimony about this incident, David credits his heritage as a mulokole and the moral campus inherited from the fellowship. I use it here to demonstrate how the legacy of the East African Revival continues to have an impact in real situations and upon concrete lives well beyond its origins in East Africa. Many Canadians of East African descent who grew up under the influence of the revival continue to live their private and social lives according to the strict moral standards of the fellowship, with appropriate modifications. There are at least two immediate implications.

From the positive side, the values by which these Canadians live make them trustworthy individuals. People feel comfortable to give responsibilities that require considerable honesty. They also tend to have a great deal of respect for authority and a superior work ethic. It is very rare, for example, to find a disgruntled East African Canadian mulokole, or one giving less than what is expected of them at their places of employment. Many who are labor union members dread labor disputes and tend to maintain a very low profile in those situations. Ordinarily their loyalty would go to management. But in a dispute, they are legally bound to side with labor. The moral dilemma leads them to be non-antagonists and minimalists in whatever role they may be required to play under these circumstances.

These and similar behavioral patterns directly related to the legacy of the East African Revival, tend at least to a certain degree to have a positive impact on the relationships in which these people are engaged. They are by and large model citizens; likeable human beings; easy to get along with. They forgive easily, rarely get into fights and are honest and reliable individuals.

I see a negative dimension, though, as well. It relates to the inflexible approach these Canadians take in applying certain ethical values. They insist on a certain mode of behaviour, regardless of the situation or context. The failure to accept the revival as a movement that emerged at a particular time and in a particular context leads to the assumption that the values acquired from the fellowship are timeless, universal and absolute. Such assumptions often put the Canadian "brethren" at odds with reality. This may be reflected in the way they raise their children; their reluctance to associate with people who are not "saved"; the lack of empathy with people who may hold a different set of values and the tendency to pass judgment on other people's way of life. The inflexible attitudes may also lead to dysfunctional behaviours in families. Sometimes families breakup as children attempt to escape the authoritarian tendencies of their parents. From this perspective, the legacy of the revival in the lives of Canadians of East African descent has not been a positive influence.

The most enduring legacy of the East African Revival, in my opinion, is the practice of giving testimony. It is true that in the past this was largely confined to giving testimony about one's salvation. A brother or sister would repeat that story at every fellowship or prayer group meeting. Among Canadians of Ugandan origin today, giving testimony has become part of checking-in with others at any gathering. Along with greetings one may be expected to give thanks to God for whatever has transpired in their lives lately or since the group met. This practice (now very common among Ugandan Canadians) has its origins in the East African revival movement and has significant pastoral and theological implications. People are encouraged and strengthened by the stories of faith they hear. Not every testimony is inspiring to everyone but many find resonance in other people's experience and become a piece of God's grace and blessing upon them as well. The testimonies also add to people's awareness of God as present in people's daily lives; God as watching over us; God as being good to us in practical ways.

Finally let me simply conclude that as far as I can see there is no clear evidence that the ethical values of the East African revival are being passed on to the second generation Canadians of Ugandan descent in any significant way. The ethics of the East African Revival spring from the structure of a communal culture, with emphasis on authority, obedience and recognition of one's place in the hierarchy of the community. The second generation of these Canadians of Uganda descent is North American. They have grown up with ideas such as freedom of speech, individual rights, accountable authority and pluralism. As this generation goes beyond the confines of their parents' community to participate in the wider society, they are likely to be influenced by the values of society than those of their parents' community. Nevertheless, it is possible that some practices like the sharing of testimonies could endure into the next generations.

CHAPTER 3

A Filipino Congregation in Diaspora as a Church Planting Revitalization Movement

NARRY F. SANTOS, PHD, WITH EUNICE L. IRWIN, PHD

Introduction

Thank you for the opportunity to present this case study on the Greenhills Christian Fellowship (GCF) in Toronto. It is an honor. A presentation at the EMS Annual meetings in 2010 featured the church planting aspects of the GCF movement in Canada.[1] We use some of that material for historical background here, but aim to focus this paper on revitalization themes. Thus, the title of "Re-Reading the GCF-Toronto Story."

GCF-Toronto Members and Congregation

On Sunday mornings, GCF-Toronto is a hub of activity. There are 150 members, with 70% of them living in Scarborough (the eastern part of Toronto) and with 60% of them relatively new landed immigrants in Canada. The GCF-Toronto site is located at the Centennial College Residence and Conference Centre (CCRCC), 940 Progress Avenue, Scarborough. For the past two years, the church has been renting a ballroom for the Sunday morning worship service at 11 am – 12:30 pm, two small conference rooms for children's Sunday School (which has an average of 25 kids), and another ballroom for the bi-weekly youth worship service (which has an average of 35 youth). GCF-Toronto also has 17 growth groups (or small groups) that meet regularly throughout the year.

Who Are these Filipinos and Diaspora Peoples, and Why Are They Here?

Experts across disciplines are paying close attention to international migration patterns and its implications on politics, economics, law, religion, and other fields. In particular, missiologists and church-planters are monitoring and analyzing the recent mass movements of people. In "Finishing the Task: The Unreached Peoples Challenge," (*Perspectives on the World Christian Movement: A Reader*, 2003, 534) Ralph Winter writes:

> As history unfolds and global migration increases, more and more people groups are being dispersed throughout the entire globe... Not many agencies take note of the strategic value of reaching the more accessible fragments of these "global peoples."

While it is true that many agencies are responding slowly to the realities of diaspora (unprecedented movements of people) and their strategic value for reaching the "global peoples", we are thankful for congregations that are "reading the times" and are "riding on the wave" of God's movement. The purpose of this case is to showcase such a group – GCF in Toronto, Canada. Specifically, this case is a model demonstrating the effectiveness of diaspora church-planting in the most diverse and multicultural city in the world.[2] GCF-Toronto is a local church that has developed its evangelism, discipleship, and missions programs.

Why is This Case Study Significant to Revitalization?

The case study of Greenhills Christian Fellowship-Toronto is a contribution to a general understanding of missions for Filipinos in diaspora, and perhaps to other visible minorities and even to Christian organizations (e.g. denominations and para-church ministries). In the context of revitalization, it contributes specifically to understanding the role diaspora congregations play in extending church-planting movement transnationally. It searches for connections between vitality of the church and success in their witness among immigrants and diasporic peoples residing in the urban, multicultural cities of Canada.

Methods, Goals, Definitions, Organization of the Case

The research methods employed by the writers are *Case Study and Participant Observation*. The case study approach utilized in this paper is assumed to be the study of a case "over time through detailed, in-depth data collection involving multiple sources of information rich in context" (Creswell, *Qualitative Inquiry and Research Design*, 1998, 61). Interviews and collection of literature on GCF, including documents from archives are used for gathering data.

Participant observation methodology was also utilized for gathering data for this case. Assuming the complete participation of the observer, this method entails the "highest level of involvement...[which] probably comes when [the authors] study a situation in which they are already ordinary participants" (Spradley, *The Ethnographic Interview*, 1980, 61). It is used because one of the authors is the founding pastor of GCF-Toronto and is able to effectively make systematic observations about the birth and development of GCF-Toronto. This is based on first-hand knowledge, close ties, and familiar relationships with the "mother church" in Manila, Philippines, as well as the GCF-Toronto members involved in the past and present activities of the church.

Two definitions provide the framework of discussion that will form part of the response to the paper. These terms are "revitalization" and "an intercultural diaspora movement." Definitions that follow are provided by the CSWCRM leadership.[3]

Revitalization: denotes a process or movement marked by a sense of divine intervention that not only gives new life but breaks spiritual and temporal principalities and powers of human bondage, including conditions of injustice against humanity and the natural order, found within and without the prevailing forms of organized religion. The outcome of the intervention is typically perceived as effecting a renovation of the image of God within humanity and the release of creation from its bondage to decay (Romans 8:18-23).

An intercultural diaspora movement: a cohesive group of people who have relocated from a homeland location to a new social environment, who seek to move beyond the barriers of their community to embrace persons of other ethnic identity from themselves and bring those persons into their fellowship, including their religious identity, or persons from a particular ethnic or religious identity in a diasporic context who join with persons of one or more other ethnic identities to form a new religious community that may draw from features of the old group identities but who find a higher value or meaning in their common fellowship.

The case is organized in four parts:

1. *Canada-wide and Greater Toronto Area (GTA) Diaspora Landscapes*
   Diaspora landscapes of the GTA[4] are included to better understand the cultural diversity of the city and the geographical context of the subject, which is GCF.

2. *GCF-Philippines: The Story of a Church-Planting Movement*
   GCF-Toronto has historical links to the church started in Manila, Philippines. The Toronto church plant marks a status change in GCF, from a national movement to now a transnational one.

3. *GCF-Toronto: Journey to be Sojourners and Missional People among Diasporas*

The situation of the Filipino church planters, along with their commitment to reach other immigrant groups (diasporas) and locals in Toronto, reveals the congregation's call to be multicultural, missional, and metropolitan. The church restructured around these goals.

4. *Reflections on the GCF Movement in Canada: Questions and Conclusions*
   Observations and Questions about the GCF-Toronto movement conclude the paper.

Canada-wide and GTA Diaspora Landscapes

Canada is known to be a nation of immigrants. Early Canadian society was composed of people who were originally immigrants from Europe (18th and 19th Century). In the 20th and the 21st Century, Canada has opened its doors to diasporas from Asia, Africa, and Latin America. In just the last two decades, Canada has extended its immigration policy to include rising numbers of foreign workers (on work contracts) working from the vineyards of British Columbia, to the oil sands of Alberta, to the Tim Horton's donut outlets inside the Toronto airport, to the fishing boats off New Brunswick. There are also thousands of foreign students from the secondary school level to the colleges and universities across Canada. Also, Canada welcomes Asylum Seekers and Refugees (e.g. the political, religious, and climate refugees), who can be found living in high-rise apartments of large cities such as Toronto, Montreal and Vancouver. Evidently, Canada is a hospitable country renowned for its multiculturalism.

By December 2009, Canada had: (1) a total of 404,886 foreign workers as temporary migrant workers; (2) granted initial entry to 253,575 foreign students; (3) welcomed 129,219 refugees; and (4) granted 252,179 people permission to make Canada their home as permanent immigrants. Of these, the Top Ten Source Countries for Permanent Immigrants were (in descending order): China, India, Philippines, USA, Pakistan, UK, Iran, South Korea, France, and Colombia.

According to Canada's migration experts, "visible minorities" or "non-Caucasian Canadians" are predicted to dominate the three Canada's mega cities (Toronto, Montreal and Vancouver) by the year 2017. These people would be coming from Asia -- mainly the South Asians and Chinese. Clearly, these immigrants are established members of the Canadian community. They have already built their own ghettos (e.g. Little Saigon, China Town, Bombay Palaces), places of worship, and have established cultural associations.

The Filipino-Canadians[5] are one of the largest immigrant groups of recent years[6]; particularly the GTA. Like other diaspora groups, they have become active participants in shaping the communities of which they have become a part. People of Filipino descent have connected across the country, gathering locally, and branching out to other Filipinos through media and organized meetings, including political, socio-cultural and religious gatherings.

The imagination of a missiologist is boggled by Canada's multi-ethnic society. The multitudes of people from all four corners of the globe, representing all colors, languages, smells, and cultures are not just a quaint minority in Canada, but are truly Canadians. It is to this Canada that God has called "peoples" to be Canadian disciples of Christ, including the Filipino-Canadian disciples, to evangelize and mobilize diaspora peoples for global mission.

GCF-Philippines: The Story of a Church-Planting Church

GCF was started in Manila, Philippines for the purpose of "reaching the emerging, self-reliant Filipinos who have the influence, and the leadership to do a significant work in spreading the Gospel of our Lord Jesus Christ throughout the Philippines and even to other nations"

GCF-Center (now called "GCF-Ortigas")

GCF is a 33-year-old Baptist church in Pasig City, Metro Manila, Philippines. GCF was founded and pastored for 15 years by Rev. David Yount, a Conservative Baptist[7] missionary. Rev. Yount led the church in its growth to more than 600 members through intentional evangelism and discipleship among middle and upper-middle class people in and around Manila. He also guided the church in the purchase of a lot and in the building of a church facility that could accommodate 1,500 people at the worship hall.

After 15.5 years, Rev. Yount handed the spiritual leadership of GCF to Dr. Luis Pantoja, Jr., who shepherded the church for the last 16.5 years.[8] The ministry of Dr. Pantoja was marked with an emphasis on satellite development (the GCF term for church-planting). Aside from its main church in Pasig City (called GCF-Ortigas), GCF has 20 satellites (or church-plants) in the Philippines and Canada (i.e., 15 in the Philippines and five in Ontario).[9]

GCF-South Metro: The First GCF Satellite

I (Narry Santos) started ministry at GCF on June 1, 1994. After serving as Christian Education Pastor in GCF-Ortigas for three years, I was assigned to plant the first GCF satellite south of Manila, which is called GCF-South Metro. On January 17, 1997, GCF-South Metro was launched (or "birthed"). For ten years, I was the Resident Pastor of this first GCF satellite. On our tenth year, we had 900 people worshiping with us, 300+ students attending our Children's Sunday School, and 88 growth groups (or small groups) meeting weekly.[10]

In 2006, GCF-South Metro was able to buy a lot and to put up its own building that could accommodate 1,500 people and a Christian school that attracted 300+ students from preschool to high school. GCF-South Metro also spearheaded the launch of three other satellites further south of Manila. These three satellites are GCF-Batangas City (which was launched in 2001 and now has 250 people), GCF-Santa Rosa (which was launched in 2006 and now has 300 people), and GCF-Parañaque (which was launched in 2008 and how has 200 people).

Preparation for Vision Beyond the Philippines

How did the mission and vision develop to start GCF beyond the Philippines?

Context for a GCF Diaspora Church-Planting Vision

In such a context of growth, the GCF-South Metro leaders have sensed beginning in 2004 that the Philippines is too small a place to fulfill the Great Commission. We started to realize that God wants us to be part in the fulfillment of the global GCF vision.[11] Our leaders have owned the conviction that the Great Commission is nothing less than global.

The years 2003 to 2005 witnessed a string of five families who were preparing to go to Canada as new immigrants. I was getting frustrated with this disappointing development, however, because after I had discipled, trained, and mentored them for years, they would all go to Toronto. I felt that my investment of time and energy was wasted. In fact, the first family that left for Toronto was one of our GCF-South Metro pioneer families, the father of which served as an able Chairman of the Council of Elders.

In hindsight, such an exodus of families was the trigger that solidified our commitment to go outside of the Philippines to help fulfill the Great Commission. These families were to be the catalysts in starting the first international GCF in North America. I began to see them not anymore as "losses" to GCF-South Metro but as core leaders of what God was about to do for GCF outside of the Philippines. Thus, my frustration and disappointment turned to hope and anticipation.

These transformed sentiments are expressed in the coffee-table book entitled "Ten Years, Ten Values," which commemorated GCF-South Metro's 10th anniversary: "As a global paradigm of missions was sweeping GCF South Metro in 2004 and 2005, who would have known that the initial 'losses' of key leaders and members leaving for Canada in the early years would be the very catalyst for bringing the GCF global dream into reality?"[12]

Confirmation for a GCF Diaspora Church-Planting Vision

God's confirmation for a GCF *diaspora* church-planting vision came to us from both the new immigrants people in Toronto and the leadership in the Philippines. On their end, the five families took strategic steps to move toward owning a GCF church-planting vision:

> These initial families . . . began to conduct informal Bible studies. . . which became a recognized official GCF Growth Group. As the frequency of fellowship meetings increased to twice a month, Pastor Narry . . . visited the group in

2005 to challenge the Toronto brethren to explore the possibility of launching the first-ever global satellite church of GCF. As the fellowship increased, the satellite adopted the small group model for church-planting and February 2006, the first evangelistic event was conducted... (It) continued to grow with the addition of several families from the GCF community and from new members drawn from various activities.[13]

Moreover, the new group registered an official religious entity in Toronto and elected its officers.

On its end, the GCF-Ortigas Board of Elders (BOE) approved the request of Pastor Pantoja in his Pastoral Ministry Report at the Board of Elders meeting on April 21, 2006. The request is for a "GCF Toronto Feasibility Study – the Senior Pastor assigned Pastor Lito Villoria to visit Elder Oddy Bondoc and the GCF core group that intends to organize itself into GCF Toronto. As an outcome of such visit, Pastor Lito will report to this body and to the deacons the feasibility of launching the first GCF satellite overseas."[14]

After the Toronto visit, Pastor Villoria recommended at the June 16, 2006 BOE meeting that "GCF proceed with establishing GCF Toronto as our first GCF overseas satellite and as the parent body, we are asked to provide a fulltime Resident Pastor and to subsidize their annual operating budget. The Senior Pastor intends to ask Pastor Narry Santos to spearhead the project on a minimum two-year assignment as GCF pastor-missionary beginning February 2007..."[15] This recommendation was passed as a resolution by the GCF-Ortigas Board of Elders, as follows: "Motion prevailed to proceed with the plans to launch GCF Toronto... and implement according to the proposed time table" (2006-BOE-064).[16]

GCF-Canada: Historical Account of GCF Members as Diaspora

On my end, I sensed God's hand in opening the opportunity for my family and me to be part of God's global vision for GCF. I knew and already saw that God could start something totally new and exciting. I saw it when God used GCF-South Metro to start GCF-Batangas City in 2001. I saw it when God again used GCF-South Metro to start GCF-Santa Rosa. Even in my absence, God again used GCF-South Metro to start GCF-Parañaque in 2008. Having seen God use us in starting satellites before, I knew that God could use us again in starting satellites for Filipinos and other different groups in Toronto and beyond.

On our 10th anniversary on January 21, 2007, GCF-South Metro commissioned my family and me to be their global missionaries, aside from installing the new pastor for GCF-South Metro. In addition, the GCF-Ortigas BOE approved this motion on March 9, 2007: "Motion prevailed that we officially receive a 'Shower of Blessing' in the form of cash donations for the month of April 2007 as our share in the ministry in Toronto" (2007-BOE-031).[17] On April 9, my family and I left Manila for our new global missions assignment.

GCF-Toronto was officially launched as the 13th GCF satellite on May 6, 2007 at the Centennial Community Centre in Toronto. In its four years, GCF-Toronto has moved from a small basement (that could accommodate 60 people) in a North York library, to three adjacent rooms (that could hold 120 people) at a Chinese Cultural Centre in Scarborough, to its current location in a ballroom (that could put in 220 people) at the Centennial College Residence and Conference Centre.

In our first prayer, vision-casting, and planning retreat as a satellite on June 16, 2007, we discussed three issues of prime importance. In our workshop materials on that day, we summarized the three major issues this way: (1) "We Are All Placed in Toronto by God's Providence"; (2) "We Will Not Be a Filipino Church in Toronto"; and (3) "GCF-Toronto Will Be a Church-Planting Church."[18]

Birth of a GCF-Canada Diaspora Church-Planting Vision

As a result of GCF-Toronto leaders' commitment to a diaspora church-planting vision, the GCF-Canada Triple Vision was born. This triple vision is taken from the Acts 1:8 process of progress. The process begins in Jerusalem, then progresses into Judea and Samaria, and peaks at the ends of the earth.

For the first seven-year cycle (2007-2014), we will trust God for this GCF-Canada Strategic Vision: seven GCF satellites in seven years in the four provinces of Canada (i.e., Ontario; British Columbia; Alberta; Manitoba). This is the proposed breakdown of the triple vision per satellite:

GCF-Toronto Triple Vision (2007-2010)[19]

The vision to launch GCF-Toronto in May 2007   (our "Jerusalem")
+
The vision to birth GCF-Peel in March 2008 (our "Judea & Samaria")
+
The vision to birth GCF-Vancouver in May 2010(our "Ends of the Earth")
+
GCF-Peel Triple Vision (2008-2011)

The vision to launch GCF-Peel in March 2008   (our "Jerusalem")
+
The vision to birth GCF-Etobicoke in October 2010(our "Judea & Samaria")
+
The vision to birth GCF-Winnipeg in October 2011 (our "Ends of the Earth")
+
GCF-Vancouver Triple Vision (2010-2013)
+
The vision to launch GCF-Vancouver in May 2010   (our "Jerusalem")

+

The vision to birth GCF-Surrey in October 2012 (our "Judea & Samaria")

+

The vision to birth GCF-Calgary in September 2013 (our "Ends of the Earth").

Once the GCF-Toronto Triple Vision (1st Cycle) is fulfilled, GCF-Toronto will pause, pray, and plan for its 2nd cycle of its triple vision. God willing, the next GCF-Toronto Triple Vision will be by Countries: (1) GCF-Canada as GCF-Toronto's "Jerusalem"; (2) GCF-U.S.A. as GCF-Toronto's "Judea & Samaria"; & (3) GCF-Australia as GCF-Toronto's "ends of the earth."

Seeing the GCF-Canada Triple Vision Gradually Happen

As God confirmed the GCF-Canada Triple Vision in our hearts, he gradually opened doors to make the birthing of these new satellites possible. Three months in our GCF-Toronto launch, we received a request to start GCF-Peel. In response, we started a growth group in Mississauga and then in Brampton. In September 2007, we conducted two preview worship services. From October 2007 onwards, we held weekly services until GCF-Peel was launched on March 27, 2008 (Easter).[20]

In January and February 2008, we challenged a few former GCF members who now live in Vancouver to consider starting GCF-Vancouver. In response, a growth group was born in March, followed by another one later in 2008. These two growth groups became the core team in conducting monthly and later biweekly preview services in 2009, and weekly services in January 2010. On May 2, 2010, this satellite was launched officially, with Pastor Hizon Cua, a former GCF Satellite Pastor from Manila, serving at the full-time GCF-Vancouver Pastor.

We also received a request last January 2009 from Pastor Reymus Cagampan in Winnipeg that GCF-Toronto consider adopting the new church-planting work he initiated in October 2008 to be part of the GCF family of churches. In May 2009, Pastor Cliff Gonzales, a church-planter in Calgary, was referred to us by Pastor Pantoja, as a possible partner with GCF. Pastor Gonzales was inquiring if the new church-plant he would start in July 2009 can be part of the GCF family.

Initially, we were hesitant about these two requests, because GCF always starts satellite development from scratch. In all the 16 satellites that were launched by GCF in the past 16 years, we intentionally initiated the work in different strategic areas. However, in relation to the two requests from Winnipeg and Calgary, we sensed that these requests warrant our prayer and discussion, and that this may be a new and supplementary way to fulfill God's Triple vision for us.

GCF-Canada Leadership Summit and GCF-Canada Covenant

The GCF-Toronto leaders were open to the mode of "adopting" in satellite development in addition to the "birthing" approach of church planting, primarily due to the corporate decision at the first biennial GCF-Canada Leadership Summit held on May 9, 2009. In that leadership summit, 68 delegates from GCF-Toronto, GCF-Peel, and GCF-Vancouver saw the value of the GCF-Canada Vision in the context of our multicultural realities. As a result of the summit, this manifesto was unanimously agreed upon:

(1) That GCF-Canada shall be missional, metropolitan, and multicultural in its strategy and ministries;
(2) That GCF-Canada shall be one with GCF-Philippines in its fundamental beliefs, mission, and vision but legally, administratively and financially autonomous;
(3) That GCF-Canada shall partner with GCF-Philippines, Canadian Baptists of Ontario and Quebec, and Canadian Baptists of Western Canada in the areas of ministry, missions, leadership development, pastoral training, and other areas of ministry support.[21]

The GCF-Canada Leadership Summit Manifesto catalyzed the formation of the GCF-Canada Covenant, which established the framework of unity and partnership with GCF-Canada in July 2009. The ratified GCF-Canada Covenant specifies four points of agreement; namely: (1) mission; (2) vision; (3) statement of faith; and (4) ethos. These four items are designed to shape the unity of all satellites in Canada and are formulated to serve as the framework for birthing new and adopting potential GCF satellites.

Aside from the four areas of unity, the GCF-Canada Covenant subscribes to three governing perspectives in our satellite development, expressed explicitly at the First GCF-Canada Leadership Summit Manifesto of May 9, 2009. The Covenant states, "GCF-Canada shall be missional, metropolitan, and multicultural in its strategies and ministries." This is how we describe these three strategies in satellite development:

(1) **Missional** Church – the satellites will be intentionally multiplying satellites (through the satellite triple vision) and will incarnationally add value to our communities;
(2) **Metropolitan** Community – the satellites will intentionally and strategically minister in the urban centres (i.e., targeting the cities); and
(3) **Multicultural** Country – the satellites will intentionally be on mission to the *diaspora* (i.e., reaching the immigrants in countries that are open to receive different ethnic groups) of "all nations."

Thus, by God's grace & for His glory, GCF-Canada will be multiplying reproducing missional churches in metropolitan communities in the multicultural country of Canada.

GCF-Winnipeg and GCF-Calgary: Shift from Birthing to Adopting Also

With the ratified GCF-Canada Covenant at hand, Elder Rick Manguerra (Chairman of the GCF-Peel Council), Atty. Abesamis, and I went for an exploratory visit to Winnipeg on July 23-27, 2009. We were sent by GCF-Peel to conduct the exploration, because GCF-Peel owns the Triple Vision of going to Winnipeg for its "ends of the earth" satellite. We met Pastor Cagampan and the core leaders of the new church-plant in Winnipeg, presented to them the GCF-Canada Covenant (containing the GCF Mission, Vision, Faith, & Ethos), narrated our GCF-Canada two-year story of satellite development, joined their two small groups sessions and worship service with 60 people.

On their end, Pastor Cagampan and his leaders agreed to bring to their people the option that their new church-plant be adopted as GCF-Winnipeg, to pray about it for one month, and to inform us of their group's decision at the end of August 2009. In a month, they informed us of the decision of the whole groups to be adopted as GCF-Winnipeg.

To move this decision forward, Pastor Pantoja, Elder Joseph Cachola (Chairman of the interim GCF-Canada Board), Elder Manguerra, Atty. Abesamis, and I visited Winnipeg on September 18-20, 2009 to sign the Memorandum of Agreement (MOA) between GCF-Canada and the new group, GCF-Winnipeg. This marks a shift in our GCF-Canada policy: from simply "birthing" daughter churches, we can now "adopt" young churches as well.

We also trained the leaders on how to do satellite development in their target area. In addition, we continue to mentor and guide the GCF-Winnipeg leaders through our visits, sharing of resource materials, and skype meetings. GCF-Winnipeg is scheduled to be launched as a satellite on October 2, 2011.

In addition to visiting GCF-Winnipeg, the team also explored the possibilities on September 17-18, 2009 of having the new church-plant of Pastor Gonzales and his leaders be adopted as GCF-Calgary. We presented to this leadership group the GCF mission, vision, statement of faith, ethos, and the GCF-Canada Covenant. In two weeks, they committed to be part of the GCF-Canada family of churches. Elder Manguerra and I returned to Calgary on October 14-18 to conduct satellite development training, to take part in their small group sessions and participate in the worship service with 70 people, and to sign the MOA between GCF-Canada and the new group, GCF-Calgary.

When we asked Pastor Gonzales and his leaders why they chose to be part of the GCF-Canada family of churches – knowing that we are just over two years old then and that we have meagre resources to assist them – they replied that they want to be identified with a group that has a clear vision to plant churches in Canada and beyond. Through occasional visits, sharing resource materials, and regular Skype meetings, we were able to mentor Pastor Gonzales and his leaders in doing the GCF ministry in their context. As a result, GCF- Calgary was officially launched as a satellite on May 16, 2010.

GCF-Toronto: Journey to be Sojourners and Missional People among Diasporas

Decisions by a fledgling church planting team in Toronto implied adapting and changing to the new environment without loss of the original vision. There is the clear sense of mission from God to GCF, but as sojourners in Canada on a new journey among diasporas, the team needs to learn fresh lessons in fulfilling this mission. What does ministry look like today?

Worship Life

In our worship services, we value the role of God's Word through preaching and the dynamic worship of God through song and prayer. We seek to make the sermon biblically based and practically applicable in people's everyday life. Church members also regularly share their testimonies on how God works and reveals himself to them. In relation to church music, our weekly praise and worship volunteer teams, along with instrumentalists for guitars, drums, and keyboard, and an adult choir inspire us to sing praises to God.

"Music at GCF can be best described as a fusion. We are a contemporary church that remains in love and attached to Christianity's historical expressions and elements of worship."[22] In addition to the pastoral prayer, we spend 10 minutes of prayer in small groups with the congregation before we conclude our celebration with a benediction and closing song. Our main desire is that we come out of the worship experience inspired to love God more.

Growth Group Life

In GCF, a growth group defined as "a voluntary and intentional gathering of five to fifteen people, regularly meeting together with the shared goal of helping each other realize GROWTH in their Christian life and experience."[23] It also serves as a microcosm of the church that aspires to live out together God's 5 purposes of evangelism, fellowship, discipleship, ministry, and worship. In GCF, these 5 purposes are spelled in its mission statement: "For the glory of God, we commit ourselves to EVANGELIZE and ENLIST people into our fellowship, to EDIFY and EQUIP them for spiritual maturity and service, and to EXALT God together in worship."

The "Five E's" in the GCF mission statement refer to our five purposes as a church: (1) "Evangelize" refers to our commitment to be on mission in reaching out to our "community" (i.e., the people outside the church); (2) "Exalt" refers to our commitment to magnify God in worship among the "crowd" (i.e., the people who come on Sunday mornings); (3) "Enlist" refers to our commitment to the members in nurturing fellowship among the "congregation" (i.e., the people who joined the satellite as church members); (4) "Edify" is our commitment to be maturing in discipleship with the "committed" (i.e., the members who desire to follow Jesus as his disciples);

and (5) "Equip" refers to our commitment to equip for ministry those in the "core" (i.e., the members who volunteer in serving God and his people).

The growth groups seek to fulfill these 5 purposes together (i.e., they worship together; they disciple together; they fellowship together; they serve together; they evangelize together). In the Canadian context, we align our growth group sessions according to the 4 seasons of the year. We meet in homes for the fall, winter, and spring seasons, but we take a break in summer to do more outdoor events (e.g., picnic at the park; barbeque party; trip to the Niagara; garage sale; distribution of bottled water in parks and bus stations).

Witness Life

We desire our witness to be missional and relational for the people around us. Since the church rents the facilities of the Centennial College Residence and Conference Centre (CCRCC) on Sundays, we could focus our outreach to the 100 international students (out of the 400 students) who reside at the CCRCC. After much prayer on how to reach and serve these international students, God opened doors for us in September 2010 when we approached Miss Erynne Levesque, the CCRCC Community Life Coordinator. We asked her how we could serve the international students. She said that we could help carry the bags of new and returning students at the CCRCC on September 6, the Move-In Day for the residents.

After that, Erynne allowed us to hold the following holiday events: (1) a Canadian Thanksgiving Dinner for the 100 international students on October 8; (2) a Christmas Lunch for them on December 19; (3) 3 Ontario Family Day Luncheons for 35 international students with 20 church members who hosted these students at the college-run hospitality restaurant on February 13, 20, and 27; (4) an immigration seminar with a lawyer from our church for 42 international students on April 20; and (5) an Easter Dinner for 80 international students on April 22. As a result, I was able to conduct weekly Bible students with 3 international students (i.e., 2 from mainland China & 1 from India) during the spring semester.

On June 13, Erynne gave me a call and informed me that of all their residence activities for the school year, the events with the international students sponsored by the church received much commendation. It was the first year for the residence to gather the highest number of international students for community involvement. She requested a meeting with me on June 15 to personally thank the church and to ask us to be involved in planning the next school year events for the international students and residents, since CCRCC now considers us as part of their community.

In addition to the CCRCC, the church has seen some open bridges of communication and services this summer to the residents of Tuxedo Court, a high-need area in Scarborough or East Toronto (with approximately 5,500 people housed in 5 buildings, one of which is part of the Toronto Community Housing). In Tuxedo Court, 81% are considered visible minorities, majority of which are South Asians, and in the 2006 census, unemployment rate there is 14.8% (compared to the 6.7% average for the rest of Toronto).

As a result of prayer and a visit at Tuxedo Court last June 18, a couple from church has started a weekly Tuesday Bible Study with 3 elderly Filipino women at 50 Tuxedo Court (Toronto Community Housing). After more prayer and discernment, the church was able to host an after-"Canada Day" celebration at the party room of the building on July 10. We brought South Asian delicacies, rendered a traditional dance, special song numbers, and a message of hope in both the Tamil and English languages. There were 43 residents who came (23 of whom were South Asians), and 39 church members volunteered to help in the food and program preparation. As a result, two people decided to follow Jesus.

Prayer Life

We have seen more breakthroughs in our immediate family and the church family this year, because of a renewed ministry in prayer. A group of 7 members, led by a church elder, Joseph Cachola, sensed a clear call from God to initiate Connection 365, a year-long prayer ministry through 4 major strategies: (1) monthly prayer cards (challenging a group of 30 members every month to pray for the church at particular days of the month); (2) Sunday prayer study at 10-10:45 a.m. before the worship service; (3) quarterly prayer breakfasts (preceded by a week-long prayer and fasting); and (4) 10-minute prayer time in small groups during the Sunday worship services. Encouraged by this prayer emphasis, GCF-Vancouver adopted a similar Connection 365 strategy.

Power of God to Transform

What brings a lot of vitality in the church is when people turn to Jesus for salvation and when they decide to follow him in the waters of baptism. Out of the 150 members, 34 of them were baptized through the ministry of GCF-Toronto. Out of the 19 new members in 2011, 9 of them decided to trust Jesus by faith and were baptized (one of whom was born and bred in Toronto but whose parents originally came from Antigua). We give these transformed followers of Jesus opportunities to share their testimonies at their baptism ceremony, the worship service, and pre-New Year Thanksgiving service.

Discipleship and Leadership Training Life

Discipleship and leadership development is important to our church life and ministry. I hold discipleship sessions at our place with all 13 leaders and their spouses in two batches every month. My wife prepares the dinner for these leaders and leads the discipleship for the wives, while I teach the whole group and disciple the men. We basically follow our church leadership development framework of 3 C's (Character, Care, & Competence).

In relation to lay training, I conduct 5 seminars on the church's 5 purposes (or the 5 E's of Enlisting [fellowship], Edifying [discipleship], Equipping [ministry], Evangelizing [mission], and Exalting [worship]). Having these seminars helps our people learn how to fulfill God's purposes for their personal lives and for the church. Completing these 5 seminars also forms part of the requirements for nomination as a church elder, deacon, or deaconess.

In addition, our church got approval from Tyndale Seminary to give our leaders an 8-course diploma program called "Foundations on Missional Ministry & Church Leadership" through the TIM (Tyndale Intercultural Ministries) Centre. This program is now offered for 15 of our church leaders. The 8 courses are divided into two categories (i.e., 4 on missional ministry and 4 on church leadership), with each course requiring 40 hours of class time and course work. Moreover, the CBOQ (Canadian Baptists of Ontario & Quebec), our church's denomination in Canada, has agreed to credential the graduates of this diploma program as a Level 2 Part-Time Pastor or Church Worker. CBOQ has also given GCF-Toronto a "Barnabas Initiative" Grant, as its support to this church-based leadership development program with the TIM Centre.

Motives for Joining the Church

Since 60% of our members are new landed immigrants in Canada, we normally attract families who are looking for a significant sense of belonging. They seek new friends and a feeling of being part of a bigger family. This is what they often find in the church: GCF (God's Caring Family). We are serious in providing venues for loving relationships for them.

In addition to our small groups, these loving relationships occur in big groups. In the first two years of the church life, we had Sunday pot-bless lunch fellowships (i.e., after the morning worship service). It was an informal time to enjoy each other's company over a meal. When we moved to our current facility, we were limited to have such meals together only on special occasions (e.g., church anniversary; Family Day; Easter; Mothers' Day; Philippine Day; Thanksgiving; Christmas) and quarterly business meetings after the worship services. We also have an annual three-day family camp outside of the city and a sports day during the summer.

Our desire is that our relationships would reflect the GCF-Toronto ethos, which is spelled out through the acronym G.R.E.E.N.H.I.L.L.S.:

1. G = Gifts-based Ministry
2. R = Responsible Stewardship
3. E = Effective Structures
4. E = Empowering Leadership
5. N = Needs-oriented Evangelism
6. H = Holistic Growth Groups
7. I = Inspiring Worship
8. L = Loving Relationships
9. L = Life-Enriching Preaching
10. S = Sustainable Spirituality

Partnership Life

Since there are no Conservative Baptists in Canada, we decided to partner with a like-minded family of churches, the CBOQ for GCF-Toronto, GCF-

Peel, and GCF-York, and the Canadian Baptists of Western Canada (CBWC) for GCF-Vancouver, GCF-Calgary, and GCF-Winnipeg. It is affirming to belong to a bigger family of churches whose mission and vision resonate with ours. In addition, CBOQ committed to support the GCF-York church plant for two years while CBWC has starting supporting the church plants of GCF-Vancouver, GCF-Calgary, and GCF-Winnipeg.

Since we cannot keep "importing" GCF-Philippines pastors for GCF-Canada (which we were able to do for GCF-Toronto, GCF-Vancouver, and GCF-Peel), we saw the need in 2009 to home-grow local leaders. Thus, the partnership with Tyndale Seminary through the TIM Centre was born in 2010. This partnership in the diploma program is also recognized by CBOQ. Current discussions are being made for the GCF western satellites to explore possibilities for a similar diploma program for the leaders of these three satellites.

Since we do not have the experience and expertise to do campus ministry among international students, we saw the need to partner with the International Students Ministries Canada (ISMC) to minister to these students. As a result, Margery Topalian, ISMC's Toronto Director, now worships with us at GCF-Toronto, assists and coaches us on how to connect with and care for the international students in a sustaining manner.

Since we are trusting God for the next seven-year cycle of the GCF-Canada Triple Vision by countries, we are looking forward to a partnership with CBAP (our association in the Philippines) and GCF-Philippines in seeking to have GCF in Australia and New Zealand. At the CBAP biennial conference on November 28 – December 1, 2011, a Memorandum of Understanding is projected to be officially signed in praying, preparing, and planning together to start GCF-Australia and GCF-New Zealand.

In Summary

These eight corporate expressions of GCF-Toronto's life and ministry enable us to see the hand of God at work in revealing himself and his mission, and in enabling us to be the church that reflects his nature and work among his people and for the community where he sovereignly placed us.

Reflections on the GCF Movement in Canada: Questions and Conclusions

The re-reading the GCF-Toronto story for revitalization purposes is an important reflective task that needs articulation. Such articulation comes in two forms; namely: (1) seven observable shifts that the church has gone through in its missional journey in Canada; and (2) three relevant questions that can help shape the movement's future.

Seven "SHIFTS" that Occurred on the GCF-Toronto's Journey into Diaspora Mission in Canada

The journey to become an international movement, to reach diasporas and locals within their new urban contexts, has required GCF-Toronto to gain new skills and training. Regular programs of church-based discipling, mentoring of leaders, and pastoral training, continues, but many are done in new ways. Yet all church members now realize their new identity as Christian (Filipinos)/Canadians who are living out the Gospel and sharing it in neighborhoods and sites where they live. This has transformed them from what could have become merely an immigrant church in isolation from other ethnic groups.

They have become a trusted community as they move from one group to another, and between religious communities. Why? They adapted to the context of Toronto, and the changes they made brought "new life" to their churches. These "shifts" are measurable in the GCF-Canada church planting movement:

From	To
Shift #1: Feeling of Loss	Feeling of Opportunity
Shift #2: Identity as Filipinos	Identity as Christian (Filipinos)/Canadians
Shift #3: Joy of Birthing (Disciples/Churches)	Joy in Adopting them as well
Shift #4: Meeting People	Meeting People's Needs
Shift #5: Reaching Out to Neighbors	Loving Neighbors
Shift #6: Being an Attractional Congregation	Being an Incarnational Congregation
Shift #7: Partnership with GCF network	Partnering beyond GCF network too

1. GCF-Toronto is a safe place for immigrants, refugees, asylum seekers and diasporas. Programs quickly envelop them within relationships where they find members who understand and respond to their needs.
2. The congregation invites cultural diversity. Within the multicultural environment, new members create hybridity of their own understandings because of activities that allow culture-learning and sharing. The congregation is not just for Filipinos.
3. GCF-Canada stepped into new relationship with non-GCF church planting organizations. They demonstrate openness to work as a team to strengthen any work, and in a few cases, accept like-minded church plants that wanted to join GCF but which were birthed through their own model.
4. Members embrace newcomers in their neighborhoods or into the circles

of their congregation's fellowship.
5. The ethos of the church prepares people to move toward relationships with outsiders. This is learned through regular programs of the church. Growth groups provide genuine times of fellowship and service, as well as times of Bible study, and this is the training ground for relational outreach.
6. GCF-Toronto has intentionally decided to become hands and feet to those in need in their neighborhoods. Although they still invite members to special events that attract them to the church, members are learning that community service is an important avenue for explaining the meaning of their faith.
7. GCF-Canada has become open to allowing new church plants outside their own denomination to be part of the movement through "adoption." The church leadership is committing its pastoral training, in part, to denominations and persons beyond their own trusted network of Conservative Baptists. GCF-Toronto now partners with a network of ripple Canadian churches, and we anticipate the effects of her *glocal* ministry (meaning, global and local at the same time).

Relevant Questions on Church-Planting Movements

We observe interesting facets in the "new life" of the GCF-Toronto congregation. These touch on the past, yet raise questions for us about the GCF that relate to diaspora church planting and have implications for revitalization discussions today, as well as for structural considerations in the future.

Legacy of GCF Missionary Pioneers

*Do visions and values remain unchanged? If so, how do these visions and valuse remain as part of any movement?

It is evident that GCF-Toronto is a product of a providential history, from the early missions initiatives of the colonial period in the Philippines to the great scattering of the Filipino peoples of the last three decades. In August 2007, Dr. Mary Wilder of Western Seminary said of the Filipinos, "...100 years ago, the Filipinos were a mission field. Now, they are moving out to take their place in missions, reaching around the world in very creative ways!" Indeed, we affirm GCF-Toronto's role as a diaspora church reaching "the world" in our diverse nation. May her model be emulated by diaspora churches in Canada and everywhere around the globe, wherever diaspora people may be.

Yet, there remains the unfinished task of the Great Commission. For now, however, we give glory to God and celebrate the "colonial" missionaries who evangelized the Filipinos and who gave us a heritage. GCF is a legacy of American Conservative Baptist missionary work through the ministry of Rev. (and Mrs.) David Yount.[24]

The same vision continues 33 years later in GCF and in GCF-Canada. The structures and programs may continue (such as 5 E's, etc.) but a new context of multicultural church planting is the areas where methods and ministry strategies have been broadened. It creates enthusiasm for ministry and vibrancy of worship, with steady church growth because leaders and members trust God to make them into a missional congregation, with vision, equipped and able to minister in the globalized cities of Canada where immigrants abound.

Filipino Global Scattering

*How is the scattering of Filipinos both a loss and a blessing to their contexts?

Scattered The Filipino Global Presence (Pantoja, Tira, and Wan, 2004) is a compendium describing the global scattering of the Filipino people.[25] Evidently, their Filipino glocal is an act of God. They are a providentially dispersed nation, destined to be heralds of the Gospel. While many of them became "born again" Christians while working abroad, many also have lived out their faith wherever they reside. This is the case of many Filipino immigrants in GTA who have become members of GCF-Toronto.

Diaspora Filipinos, therefore, are not only subjects of evangelism but can be mobilized to help fulfill the *Missio Dei*! Revisiting the topic of global partnerships for mission one is amazed at the providence of God in raising Filipinos to partner with the whole Church in bringing the whole Gospel to the whole world.

GCF, specifically GCF-Toronto's glocal vision and mission is to become a missional congregation – ministering both globally and locally simultaneously. It is important to nurture their vision and support their mission in order for them to reach other diasporas in Canada. Practical partnerships with like-minded individuals and organizations are now being appealed in this paper for Kingdom advance. Reaching the diasporas in GTA requires healthy partnerships.

Glocal Missions: GCF-Toronto Agenda and Ripple Effects

*What new movements or structures will emerge due to globalization or revitalization?

Diaspora congregations in Canada are on the rise as the flow of migration continues. However, GCF-Toronto seeks to be different, and while her ties to the homeland and her "hub" are evident as indicated by her choice of name "Greenhills Christian Fellowship" and affiliation with 19 other GCF satellites, GCF-Toronto endeavors to be purposely missional, metropolitan, and multicultural in the city where God has placed her.

Seeking to be "international" and not Filipino by definition, GCF-Toronto seeks to bring people of diverse cultural backgrounds together.-It is our hope that the GCF-Toronto model will inspire many other diaspora congregations to join in this movement of reaching beyond cultural borders, and partnering for the *Missio Dei*. May there be a ripple effect of diaspora church-plants across the country, and even around the world, cropping up as quickly as the waves of migration and God's providence take them.

Conclusion

For diaspora missions in Toronto or through GCF-Canada, every person outside the "Kingdom" of God is priority, and these persons are "everywhere." GCF, specifically GCF-Toronto, remembers that it is God who determines where people will live at certain times, so that wherever they are in the universe, they can call upon Him and find Him (Acts 17:26-28).

Notes

1. This EMS 2010 article, which was co-authored by Narry F. Santos and Sadiri Joy Tira, was later included in the EMS Society Series no. 19, *Reflecting God's Glory Together: Diversity in Evangelical Mission*, A. Scott Moreau and Beth Snodderly, eds. (Pasadena, CA: William Carey Library, 2011), pp. 63-90.

2. Refer to http://www.toronto.ca/ for more information.

3. Terms here are quoted from the document, "Definition of Terms," related to the research project of the Center, distributed by J. Steven O'Malley, March 11, 2011.

4. http://www40.statcan.gc.ca/l01/cst01/demo24a-eng.html; also http://www45.can.gc.ca /2009/cgco_2009_001-eng.html.

5. Canada Census 2006 by Place of Birth and Period of Immigration at http://www40.statcan.gc.ca/l01/cst01/demo24a-eng.html.

6. See Canada at a Glance 2009 at http://www45.statcan.gc.ca/2009/cgco_2009_001-eng.html.

7. The Conservative Baptist Association of America (now called CB-America) started in 1947. In 2003, it had over 1,200 churches and over 200,000 members. For more information on Conservative Baptists, see Bruce Shelley, *A History of Conservative Baptists* (USA: Conservative Baptist Press, 1971). In the Philippines, CBAP (Conservation Baptist Association of the Philippines) celebrated its 50th year in 2006 with more than 400 churches. For a more information on CBAP, see Jim Davis, *From Carryall Beginnings to Crossing Borders: A 50-Year Journey of Conservative Baptist Ministries in the Philippines* (Manila: LifeChange Publishing, 2006).

8. Dr. Larry Pabiona was installed as the new Senior Pastor at GCF on May 28, 2011.

9. For more information on GCF, please visit the church website on www.gcf.org.ph.

10. For more information on GCF-South Metro, please visit the church website on www.gcfsouth.org.

11. Filipino awareness of global mission generally began a decade earlier, triggered by a study program known as the Concentrated World Missions Course, designed to train lay people preparing to work abroad. "Since 1994 over fifteen thousand Filipinos have taken the CWMC (Kairos course). It has helped in seeing a 'missions movement' sweep through the Filipino Church resulting in the Filipino Church moving from being 'missionary receiving' to 'missionary sending'. All thirteen unreached people groups in the country now have one or more fellowships of worshipping believers and

the Filipino Church now ranks as one of the top ten missionary sending countries of the world!" http://www.kairoscourse.org/history.html.

12. GCF South Metro, *Ten Years, Ten Values* (Las Piñas, Metro Manila, Philippines: GCF South Metro, 2007), p.168.

13. *Ten Years, Ten Values*, p. 168.

14. The Pastoral Ministry Report of the Senior Pastor is part of the minutes of the GCF BOE Meeting on April 21, 2006.

15. This is part of Dr. Pantoja's Pastoral Ministry Report to the GCF BOE on June 16, 2006.

16. This resolution is the 64th resolution in 2006 by the GCF BOE at its regular meeting on June 16, 2006.

17. This resolution is the 31st resolution in 2007 by the GCF BOE at its regular meeting on March 9, 2007.

18. This is taken from page 6 of the "For Nothing is Impossible with God" Global Vision Workshop Materials.

19. God willing, one cycle of satellite triple vision takes 3-5 years to fulfill (plus one year to pause & pray after the first cycle, and one more year to plan & prepare for the next cycle of satellite triple vision).

20. Just as GCF-Toronto was officially recognized as a religious institution in Ontario in 2006, GCF-Peel was also officially recognized in Ontario in 2009.

21. Aside from the GCF-Canada Manifesto, the May 9, 2009 leadership summit also focused on the GCF Vision in both its global and Canadian perspectives, and started the formulation of the GCF-Canada ethos.

22. For details on GCF's worship philosophy, see http://www.gcf.org.ph/pages/exalting.

23. For details on GCF's growth group philosophy, see hhtp://www.gcf.org.ph/pages/equipping.

24. The Baptists began their work in the Philippines in 1900. The Younts were deployed to the Philippines in 1967.

25. In their seminal work, the contributors agreed that the Filipinos are widely scattered (in over 210 countries) for a divine purpose. The Filipino diaspora is caused mainly by economic and political reasons. However, Filipino missiologists noted that many Christian Filipinos in the diaspora are actively witnessing for Christ and planting churches. Migrant Filipino workers are found in the 10/40 window, particularly in the Buddhist world, Islamic world, Hindu world, and Jewish world (see *Scattered: The Filipino Global Presence*). They also can be found in the Western world, particularly in North America.

CHAPTER 4

Mosaic Cultural Ministry with an East Asian Base

MEESAENG LEE CHOI, PH.D.
WITH
REV. JOHN HEONBUM CHUNG AND PAUL CHUNG, PH.D.
WITH MEESAENG LEE CHOI, PHD

Abstract:
Purpose of Case Study:

This case will introduce the Mosaic Cultural Ministry (of Young Nak Korean Presbyterian Church of Toronto in Toronto, Canada) in its outreach to different diaspora communities in Toronto, particularly those of South-East Asian cultures, by partnering with the existing Christians from these communities. To describe the ministry properly will require accounts of what is occurring at two different levels. First is the ministry of the Korean Canadian Church of Young Nak, which began Mosaic Cultural Ministry by forming partnerships with the immigrant communities, and second is the ministry at each of the Diaspora cultural communities, in particular.

History of Young Nak Presbyterian Church:

Young Nak Presbyterian Church originated in Seoul, South Korea, in 1945 as Bethany Evangelist Church and renamed to Young Nak in 1946. It has grown to be the largest Presbyterian Church in Korea (and in the world). They have planted churches throughout North America in places such as Los Angeles, CA, Reno, NV, and Toronto, Canada. The church in Toronto held its first worship service in November of 1977 with 86 members and has grown to over 4000 members today. Like its mother church in Seoul, Young Nak Presbyterian Church of Toronto has also become a missions' oriented church that is committed locally to the ethnic and underprivileged communities.

Mosaic Cultural Ministry
(Ethnic Minority Ministries)

Reverend John Chung is the pastor that oversees Mosaic Cultural Ministries at Young Nak. This ministry is an outreach to different Diaspora communities in Toronto, particularly those South East Asian cultures, by partnering with Christians from these communities. Presently Young Nak is partnered with the South East Asian immigrants from Thailand, Vietnam, Myanmar, and Laos. It is important to note that these immigrants are primarily Buddhists (the Karen Tribe from Myanmar being the exception) having been born into a Buddhist family and society. These Buddhist communities are tight knit and hold a high view of morality.

Mosaic Cultural Ministry draws its name from mosaic artwork. In a mosaic, each piece contributes individually and equally to the beautiful whole. In the same way, Young Nak seeks to support the ethnic minorities in Toronto to have autonomous churches that help create the mosaic of the Kingdom of God. This stands in contrast to a philosophy which seeks to create a uniform church where all cultures assimilate to the dominant culture.

Mosaic Cultural Ministry reflects the recent trend of mission initiatives that stem from and are supported by the local church instead of mission societies/agencies or denominational headquarters of mission.

Background Information

The South East Asian countries that have partnered with Young Nak Presbyterian Church of Toronto include Thailand, Myanmar, Vietnam, and Laos. Each of these countries is predominantly Buddhist. Korea also has a religious past that includes Buddhism. In fact, it was not until 1884 when there was first Protestant missionary work in Korea. Presently, only 23% of South Koreans claim Buddhism as their religion. The schools of Buddhism practiced in these South East Asian countries differs from the Buddhism in Korea. However, these differences are not emphasized nor do they impact the evangelism efforts of the Mosaic Cultural Ministry.

In general, Buddhism presents a works righteousness mentality whereas Christianity proclaims salvation is a free gift from God through the mediator Jesus Christ and not through the individual's own effort. Along those same lines, Buddhism follows a cause and effect (karma) worldview. Similar to Christianity, Buddhism stresses high morality.

Part I: The Ministry of Young Nak Presbyterian Church of Canada: Mosaic Cultural Ministry

The Young Nak church casts a vision for its Mosaic Cultural Ministry as follows:

1. Help ethnic minority groups [Southeast Asian diaspora communities] in Toronto start churches in their native language, culture, and tradition and provide support until they are independent financially, numerically, and spiritually.
2. Develop indigenous leadership within their church.
3. Help the churches of those ethnic groups to grow enough to reach out to their home countries of Thailand, Vietnam, Myanmar, and Laos and to plant or support the churches there, and to partner with them in the biblical task of making disciples of all nations.

The main strategy of the ministry, therefore, is to encourage and support *independent* growth and development of an *autonomous* church within the particular Diaspora community. This initiative represents revitalization of the host church (Young Nak) as it deploys human and material resources in initiating this effort and stewarding the nurture of vital communities of faith within these diasporic communities. The ministry *to* a particular cultural group, including evangelism and outreach is done mainly by the indigenous Christian worker and minister belonging to that culture and community. Thus, the ministry is not *cross-cultural* per se, but seeks rather to nurture and facilitate particular ministries *within* that particular culture. Special focus is also given to lay workers who minister within their indigenous cultures, and whose work has been spearheaded by the host congregation, the Young Nak Presbyterian Church.

Specifically, Young Nak sponsors and partners with Vietnamese, Myanmar, Thai, and Laos churches.[1] The pastors and lay leaders, as well as the evangelists of these churches, are members of their respective cultural communities in Toronto. The churches meet at the Young Nak building, but are otherwise independent and autonomous.

From the viewpoint of the Young Nak church, the significance of this ministry to these diaspora communities in Toronto pertains to the particular social setting of the greater Toronto area. Toronto is one of the most diverse cities in the world. It is comprised of 160 different people groups, with 200 different spoken languages. Around 50% of the population was born outside of Canada and nearly 80% are children of immigrants. This trend is predicted to grow as Canada increasingly relies on immigrants for its economy and stability as its birthrate has seen steady decline since 1951.

On the one hand, the vital witness to Christ is fading away within the very society in which the Young Nak church finds itself, namely, within the multicultural society of Canada in general, and of Toronto in particular. This is because new Canadians are increasingly from cultures that are predominantly non-Christian.

On the other hand, this reality opens up a significant opportunity for evangelism; Toronto itself becomes a place in which the Gospel may be preached to a multitude of people-groups *from* the ends of the earth.[2] Furthermore, unlike many of the nations from which these immigrants come, there is both a freedom of religion and due to the cosmopolitan setting of Toronto, a relative openness to different cultures, different modes of thinking, and different forms of religion. Likewise, in South East Asia family and social structures are tight; as the immigrants leave this behind for a looser structure in Toronto there is more freedom for them to participate in Christian activities.

As a result, evangelism in this setting is unusually effective and efficient because these people groups live in the same city, every member of the Young Nak can in effect minister to these communities as long-term missionaries, while living in their homes. In other words, evangelism and church support of these otherwise largely unreached and inaccessible people groups become possible through diverse ways, because every member of the church in their respective jobs, talents, and social status then can participate in the ministry within their *daily* lives, and with only a fraction of the cost and time as opposed to sending missionaries to these countries (in "traditional" missions).

The Young Nak church regards all of these factors not simply in terms of a favorable social setting for ministry and evangelism, but as the *providence* of God. It is viewed as a particular preordained plan set forth by God, who is "shaking the earth," and bringing different people-groups, through various reasons, such as immigration, employment, education, and even tourism to Toronto.

It is spiritually significant for Young Nak that an increasing number of these immigrant communities are those who otherwise would be unable to encounter the Gospel due to religious, political, cultural, and social factors in their home countries. Thus, Young Nak seems to understand this as a Divine strategy of God in which they are just simply participating. This particular way of understanding social setting and history in terms of Divine providence for Christian Mission seems to be inspired by a number of evangelical mission theologies, particularly the work of Ralph D. Winter and the Perspectives movement, in particular. This means that, the Mosaic Cultural Ministry is not understood as the end in itself per se, but is an integral part of a global mission. That is, one piece of its vision is that a vibrant, independent church in the immigrant Diaspora community will become a key player in evangelizing and nurturing the church of its native country, which otherwise would remain inaccessible to the Gospel because of religious, political, and cultural barriers.

What has been described in our account to this point would also be descriptive of a number of different organizations involving Diaspora ministry and evangelical efforts in Toronto. What distinguishes Young Nak's ministry and its approach is its particular experience as being a first generation immigrant church itself. Churches have a particularly strong presence in Korean immigrant communities in North America with a disproportionately large number of churches compared to the relative size of the immigrant population.

In 2007, Christians, both Protestant and Catholic, composed just under 30% of the population in South Korea. This is a figure that has been continuously declining in the last two decades, although the vast majority of Korean immigrants in North America attend immigrant churches. This is not to say that these individuals are Christians indeed, it is difficult to estimate the number of conversions among Korean immigrants because a large number of those who attend immigrant churches do so for non-religious reasons. They come to church to meet other Koreans, to educate their children in the Korean language, culture, ethics, and they seek to form social networking and business connections, among other motivations. Churches therefore serve a particularly important social and cultural function for Korean immigrants and their Diaspora community in North America.

Whether such conditions benefit or harm the church, the Gospel, and the revitalization of the people of God over time is still being debated, but what is of interest here is that because of this, for better or for worse, the Christian church wields a tremendous influence on the Korean immigrant communities in diverse ways.[3] For this reason, a *sustained* encounter with the Gospel becomes nearly impossible to avoid for the members of such communities. Strengthening this encounter with the Gospel, which is to further the cause of Christian revitalization, then becomes an important motivation for partnering with churches of other ethnic, immigrant communities in Toronto.

The unspoken strategy in Young Nak's ministry is to support the churches of immigrant communities of different ethnic backgrounds in Toronto in such a way that each of these communities of faith becomes able to present a sustained encounter with the Gospel to the immigrants of its respective community through various means and in ways resembling the model of how Korean immigrant churches are functioning.

This is best demonstrated in the holiday celebrations, following both the liturgical and lunar calendar, that are held at Young Nak for the partner churches. These are often the first point of contact for the new immigrants, Christians and non-Christians alike. The focus of these celebrations is mainly fellowship and includes cultural presentations, bands, and food. As non-Christians continue to attend these events, they have been known to refer to themselves as "half-of-a-Christian." As the ethnic minorities attend these events, they are invited to participate in worship and hear the Gospel. These celebrations provide an opportunity for the new immigrants to create a social network in their new community. This is extremely important since most of them have left their families behind.

Young Nak also provides ministries for the children of the ethnic minorities. They are encouraged to participate in youth sports teams, for instance the Young Nak Hallelujah Youth Soccer Team, as a means for exercise and encouragement. They also offer an alternative Halloween event to protect children from the non-Biblical Halloween culture and provide a safe alternative in a Christian environment instead of the dangerous streets of Toronto. Friendship evangelism is the key strategy employed by Mosaic Cultural Ministries when addressing the predominantly Buddhist immigrant communities.

Young Nak seeks to provide services that are necessary for these immigrants, especially within six months of their arrival in Toronto. The church extends a hand of friendship in very practical ways, from teaching ESL and providing legal services to inviting them to be "observers" at church functions such as weddings and baptisms.

This strategy is evident in the partnership with Young Nak to provide for the nascent churches of Vietnamese, Myanmar, Thai, and Laos communities a *concrete* and *visible* model and goal on how they can experience church growth. Likewise, growth among the partnering churches can provide like models for others. In addition, Young Nak is able to provide practical know-hows and material support so that its partner churches from Southeast Asia can thrive and have healthy impact on the communities in which they minister.

The chief aim of Mosaic Cultural Ministries is to spread the Gospel to the ends of the earth. With its mission to the diverse ethnic people groups in Toronto, the city of diversity, Young Nak has the advantage of preaching our Gospel to the ends of the Earth by evangelizing to the nearest neighborhood, which can bring the Gospel to their own people and nations in turn, without having to actually go abroad far away to do the same ministries. Likewise, Young Nak is intent on returning Canada to God's kingdom.

Secondary to the goals to spread the Gospel to the ends of the earth, Mosaic Cultural Ministries seeks to meet the needs of the immigrants as they try to adjust to a new life in a new location. Young Nak recommends reaching the immigrants within six months of their arriving and accessing their needs. However, they express a need for wisdom so that the immigrants are not confused and believe that the church exists to provide for social and material needs and not spiritual needs. It is also important to note that evangelism and social responsibility are not separated in Young Nak's missional vision.

Another characteristic feature of Young Nak as an immigrant church, in regard to its ministry, is that it is *mono-lingual* and *mono-cultural* (valuable to its ministry to the ethnic minorities in Toronto). It is notable that Young Nak's English-speaking congregation is composed largely of second and third generation Korean-Canadians that are aware of the limitations of an immigrant church and continuously and consciously have worked to become more multicultural. However, what the next-generation church regards as the limitation of the first generation immigrant church ironically has provided key insights and abilities it lacks.

These strengths include its affinity of experience with other first generation immigrants and their communities of different ethnic backgrounds. To put it differently, a "multicultural" church envisioned in the Canadian – and to some extent in the American context –is hardly "multicultural," because it tends to be English-speaking, and its culture is, so far, predominantly characterized as mainstream and Western. This is precisely the reason why, more often than not, it attracts the second generation or the increasingly "Canadianized" or "Americanized" individuals of the larger community.

Among Korean *diaspora immigrants*, it is therefore the Korean-speaking congregations that *thrive*. Simply put, churches in the immigrant community's native language and culture are much more attractive to first-generation immigrants. The strategy of Young Nak's Mosaic Cultural Ministry is to support churches of first-generation immigrants within different Diaspora communities. What is envisioned is a partnership of different ethnic churches, rather than a single church that reaches out to, and is composed of, individuals *from* different ethnic groups. Through this partnership, the Korean Christian community can share its experience of planting, establishing, and raising churches in the setting of Diaspora communities.

Helping to raise these churches of the Diaspora communities is possible because the Korean church has grown from similar conditions. This becomes a gift of grace to its partners because Young Nak has grown from a similar condition. This similarity of experience is even more pronounced for the current partners, namely the South East Asian churches because of the shared Buddhist religious influences within their cultures, even though the schools of Buddhism influential in Korea and Southeast Asia are, of course, different. However, Young Nak does not focus on these differences, but rather uses Buddhism as a possible point of contact with these communities. In other words, the people of Young Nak can relate because either they were once were Buddhist or they possess an understanding of Buddhism. This point of contact also allows Young Nak to better understand the worldview of these communities.

The Distinctive Themes of the Young Nak Missional Initiative

We have observed that the ministry at Young Nak is greatly influenced by a sense that it is involved in the unfolding of God's plan in mission. This, however, goes further than simply discerning a divine plan in the current social setting of Toronto or the immigrant communities in Canada. The key members and partners of the ministry are moved by personal experience that they understand as the extraordinary guidance of God that has brought them to such ministry, and this into God's mission strategy.

Pastor John Chung, a key figure in the Young Nak missional initiative, was called to full-time Christian ministry in mid life--his late forties, through miracles and independent confirmations--and through a number of individual different backgrounds. He was miraculously sustained during his theological education and first years of ministry, and was introduced to a ministry toward Diaspora communities in Toronto. This was a kind of ministry with which he had been previously unfamiliar. During his seminary years, before becoming a pastor, he was familiar with persons engaged in other ministries within a variety of ethnic communities. These persons helped him better understand the Christian movements in their respective communities.

When he began the ministsry at Young Nak, after a train of unlikely circumstances, he prayed for guidance and then met, seemingly by chance, those persons who have become since the partners involved in the ministry within the Toronto--Vietnamese, Myanmar, Laos, and Thai communities.

This networking can be observed in his initiative to seek ministry partners for the Thai community. He sought direction from a random acquaintance without expecting an answer, but was unexpectedly introduced to a couple he knew from his ESL class. This couple, Frank and Sue, initially voiced their opinion that such ministry was unfeasible for their Thai community. The reluctance stemmed from the fact that there was no previous history of a Thai church in Canada. The difficulties would be great. After a number of prayers and feeling as if he had heard the voice of God through his pastor's words, "Because no one will do it; Young Nak needs to do it." After a number of prayers, Pastor Chung felt strongly led to approach them again. He then discovered that they too had experienced an extraordinary encounter that had changed their minds.

Likewise, after Pastor Chung was involved in advising and helping similar ministries in Canada and Australia, just as he was beginning to really sense the global significance of this ministry, he was invited to this revitalization conference.

Pertinent examples of God's guidance and direction may be offered by other partners of this ministry. Frank from the Thai church recounts how he suddenly had a vivid dream in his homeland of teaching the Bible in Canada, and after discussing it with his wife, they immigrated. However, they believed, because of the predominant faith in Buddhism and its ties to Thai nationalism and culture, that a Christian church among the Thai was not feasible.

Furthermore, they had not met another Thai in the two years they had lived in Canada. However, after meeting with Chung, they prayed that if this is God's will, they should meet with a Thai person. That very day they heard a Thai language being spoken in the supermarket. This person was not only a Thai, but a Thai Christian. So, they began to plant a church which became the first registered Thai church in Canada.

Pastor Tim Nguyen, from the Vietnamese church, recounts how the lease for his church was not renewed, and his church desperately required a place to worship. Suddenly, Pastor Nguyen was approached by Pastor Chung regarding the partnership. After a round of prayers, the leadership of Young

Nak agreed to partner with Nguyen's church and invited the Vietnamese congregation over to their church. That very week, unknown to Young Nak, was the week the Vietnamese church no longer had a place to worship.

This is the role that Young Nak (YN) has played to support its partner churches. Young Nak is a large congregation with over 4,000 members, and thus possesses comparatively greater financial resources and large facilities. It is notable that a major emphasis of its ministry now is designed to enable its partner churches to become independent and autonomous churches, with a significant presence in their respective Diaspora communities, thereby providing a sustained encounter with the Gospel and Christian living. Its record of achievement in this regard can be summarily stated:

1. YN established a regular intercessory prayer teams from the Korean congregation for Myanmar, Laos, Vietnamese, and Thai churches.
2. YN provides free worship space and other facilities without rent or fees in the Young Nak building.
3. YN provides extra financial support for the partner churches' ministries and incomes for their ministers.
4. YN members endeavor to become living witnesses through prayers, love, and friendship evangelism. They seek to befriend and have fellowship with members of the South East Asian communities; especially to comfort and encourage those with difficult pasts such as refugees and displaced people.
5. YN is especially concerned to address the needs and difficulties of Myanmar refugees in the Myanmar/Thai borders. Young Nak members visited the refugee camps with gifts, supplies, letters, and Bibles (there had been no Bibles in the camp in the Myanmar vernacular). They met with Christians to provide encouragement. Young Nak members, along with their partner Myanmar church helped to locate lost family and friends of the Myanmar church members.
6. When needed, YN provides free services, such as funerals and marriages. For example, it provided the facility, kitchen services, etc. when the wife of a member of one partner church passed away in a traffic accident and had no means to pay for a funeral. Likewise, because there was no minister to perform a marriage or communion, YN provided the service. The goal, however, has been to support its partner churches to perform such services on their own.
7. For those who have difficulty coming to church due to finances and the lack of transportation, YN donates vans and Toronto Transit Commission (public transportation) tickets for the respective partner churches.

8. YN joined with the partner churches to help its members search for work in Canada, as well as providing other gifts, such as clothes, food, and other necessities.
9. YN accompanied its partner ministry workers to visit and pray for the sick in their homes and in the hospital.
10. YN annually operates adult and youth leadership forums and seminars for the partnership church leadership development.
11. YN provides financial help and tuition for the partner church members to receive seminary theological education.
12. YN opens its facilities for Thanksgiving, Easter, Christmas, and New Year's celebrations, enabling the partner churches to hold outreach and evangelical events and dinners.
13. YN works together with its partner churches in their home countries. The partner churches provide contacts with local churches in their home countries with which Young Nak also partners with these churches in mission. It helps and advises its support for local seminaries, churches, and various ministries (such as ministry to poverty-stricken areas and jails).
14. YN also facilitates cooperative work between partner churches (South East Asian Mission Fellowship). Many of the events and activities involve not only Young Nak and one particular partner church, but other partner churches as well. One representative event is the yearly joint worship and fellowship of all its partner churches, which involve a large dinner and presentations intended to strengthen the work of God in these communities. Information booths are also set up in the gym to raise awareness of the communities and church ministries. YN again provides the facilities, as well as financial, and labor support for the event.

Part 2: The Outcome of the Young Nak Missional Outreach Initiative (Ministry at Each of the Diaspora Cultural Communities): A Preliminary Assessment

In order to determine a ministry's success, it is important to look at the growth of the ministry thus far, as well as the impact they are making on society. It is important to keep in mind Young Nak's vision for the partner churches to become autonomous and independent financially, numerically, and spiritually and to spread the gospel to the ends of the earth. Here we describe the growth of the ministry so far and its current demographic standing:

1. Young Nak's Mosaic Cultural Ministries has become an example to churches throughout North America, Australia, and Africa. They

were invited to be heard at an OMF seminar on Diaspora ministries at Tyndale in Toronto.
2. As the immigrants from these ethnic minorities become Christians they wish to send missionaries (even their own children) to their homelands to share the gospel.
3. The Myanmar church began with 11 members in 2005 and has grown to more than 80 members. The church has started its own Sunday School and youth group. They are also supporting a sister church in the Jane and Finch area. They have Summer Christian Retreats. The Myanmar church has also sent a lay leader to seminary and is being pastored by an ordained minister. The Myanmar church participated in outreach to the refugees coming into Toronto from the Thai/Myanmar border. They organized coat drives, provided kitchen supplies, and helped the refugees to adjust to social life in a new setting. They also planted a church for the refugees.
4. Thai church planting began in 2005 with 2 members and has grown to more than 40 members in 2011. It opened as the first registered Thai church in Canada on April 10, 2011, with 40 members and 8 newly baptized members that year. This was such a huge event that the Thai ambassador and Thai media were present. The Thai church struggles because of the heavy Buddhist influence in Thailand. They continue to meet (sometimes it is informal worship using videos to share the message) and hold evangelistic events. The Thai church now has its own website and Facebook page.
5. The Vietnamese church began with 40 members and grew to 110 members by 2010. However, a church split occurred in 2011. The Vietnamese church has participated in raising funds to send missionaries to Cambodia as well as sending missionaries into the field. It is interesting to note that the Vietnamese population is greater than that of the Korean population in Toronto. Challenged by the ministry of the Korean church versus the Vietnamese church in regards to numbers, they have begun sending their members to Young Nak for Wednesday evening worship services as well as the early morning prayer meetings to be equipped. The Vietnamese church is also seeking new ways to reach out to their respective community which has included changing the name of their church.[4]
6. The Laotian church formed from a split in another church and grew from 7 to 12 members. However, the church that met in Young Nak dispersed in May 2011. A sister congregation in Hamilton is still growing strong due to joining the Laos Mennonite conference in 2011.

The partner churches still are in a phase of early development. They require varying degrees of financial assistance. Their leadership still remains to be formally developed. Presently, only the Vietnamese and Myanmar churches have a full-time pastor trained in the seminary. The Thai and Laos churches still lack a full time ministry worker because of financial constraints. Like other churches, there is a great need for biblical training and spiritual disciple for its members. Also, like other churches, conflict exists in these churches. Sometimes the conflict arises between leadership and membership. There are also times when there are conflicts between Young Nak members and the immigrant communities, and the ministry leadership is especially careful in these situations. These problems, although endemic in most other church ministries, are especially significant for the Mosaic Cultural Ministry. This is because the churches are nascent, and still developing, and thus otherwise common problems can be relatively more devastating when it is pushed to the crisis point.

Some accounts regarding conversion within the Southeast Asian partner churches are in order to aid assessment of the Mosaic Cultural Ministry's work thus far.[5] What follows is derived from a small set of testimonies and anecdotes. Therefore, it is difficult to discern whether this constitutes a general pattern. This becomes even more problematic since the situation and context differ to varying degrees depending on each congregation and peoplegroups. For example, a significant portion of the Myanmar church belongs to the Karen tribe who is traditionally Christian and is persecuted by the Burmese government as a minority group. This is a very different dynamic from the Thai church which is composed almost entirely of converts from Buddhism. However, some points below may provide a useful starting point.

Because Buddhism is a predominant influence in these cultures, its role is often mentioned in these conversion accounts. Though the schools of Buddhism differ in Korea and the countries of South East Asia, these differences are not stressed, but instead provide a possible initial point of commonality with the South East Asian ethnic minorities in Toronto. When those at Young Nak share their faith they emphasize their shared "Asian-ness;" that is, their shared religious background, cultural beliefs, and position as immigrants in their new society. Their approach is best characterized as friendship evangelism and a partnership in mission as opposed to imperialism or colonialism.

Many of the members of the South East Asian churches express some concern or even stories of alienation from their families and friends because of their decision to become Christian, in particular. This is because the national and cultural identity, as well as family loyalty, in these communities is tied up with Buddhism. For these individuals, the fellowship from the church remains indispensable. The problem seems less significant for those whose family and friends now live in Canada. That is, the possibility of persecution, as is expected, is a much greater concern for those whose family remains in their homelands. The Southeast Asian members also often speak of the importance of being a good example to their Buddhist families and acquaintances, the need to live in peace, and the importance of respecting their religion and viewpoints while still standing for the Christian Gospel.

One Myanmar Christian, who was converted from an early age, speaks of how the devotion and mental discipline in Buddhism is something Christians should admire and emulate. A Vietnamese ministry worker speaks of how Buddhist moral lessons and teachings can often be used as a stepping stone or illustration for further Christian teachings, similar to Paul's ministry in Athens (Acts 17:22-31). On the contrary, as an example that speaks to the differences between the various congregations, or even people-groups within a single congregation, a Karen Myanmar Christian asserts that there is nothing for Christians to have in common with Buddhists.

What is also of interest is the account of the Thai converts regarding what they have perceived as the important distinguishing characteristic of Christianity that convinced them to convert. One mentions how Christians need to worship only one God, the Creator of all things, instead of the many gods who merely rule over their own domain. Few others among the Thai and Vietnamese churches speak of the assurance of salvation by grace, through Jesus Christ, which frees them from having to work arduously for spiritual gain or having to appease many gods (This seems to be due more to the Theravada school of Buddhism is practiced among its Laity, rather than Buddhist philosophy per se).

Another key factor in these members becoming Christian seems to be friendship evangelism. That is, those who became Christians did so not through the evangelization efforts of strangers but through sustained and caring relationships. These relationships take many forms including close friends, family, or in the case of the Thai church, employers who invited the non-Christians to church and to small group Bible studies that were occurring in their own language. Many non-Christians who came to the gatherings and events held by partner churches also report that they come to meet other members of their community, to form social networking webs, and for the "good food."

Among the concerns voiced by the members of the Southeast Asian partner churches is the existing persecution, either by society or by family, especially in their home country. Among the ministry workers, they are concerned about the lack of worship spaced and religious facilities for the churches in their homeland and their communities. Still underdeveloped spiritual discipline and maturity and the need for continued prayers are also concerns. A concern repeated in nearly every interview is the lack of trained ministers and leaders in the churches and their respective communities, especially in their homelands. Several leaders expressed interest in having theological seminaries in their homelands as well as more devout spiritual leaders to mentor the next generation.

Concluding Thoughts

Young Nak's Mosaic Cultural Ministries provides a model for being a long term missionary presence in its own community while still having an impact on the spread of the Gospel throughout the world. This paradigm allows the church to minister to a variety of people-groups offering physical, material, and spiritual aid, especially to the immigrant communities. The focus is not on the differences of the community such as language and religion, instead the focus is on loving like Jesus so that they may experience God's Kingdom on earth and find salvation. This ministry provides an important framework to explore in revitalization efforts as the Western world becomes more and more non-Christian and multi-cultural. The Mosaic Cultural Ministry is key in the Toronto Revitalization Movement as previously unreached people groups are now finding the Gospel accessible not only in words but in actions. This sustained presence of Christ is ushering in new believers in Toronto and around the world.

Addendum from the Discussion

Some of the further elaborations that were made in the presentation and the discussion in the Consultation was the following (by Paul Chung):

1. Senior Pastor of YNC, Minho Song's account of the history of the Church - mainly Protestant - in Korea. It seemed that his analysis of why the Korean churches have thrived, such as its beginnings in Korean diaspora communities in Manchuria, early development of native Korean leadership and church identity, and strong lay ministry, is the implicit basis in the mission strategy of the Mosaic Cultural Ministry. That is, the memory of how predominantly non-Christian Korea has been transformed by its Church is the guideline to how the different ethnic churches in Toronto may transform their own people and nations.

2. Pastor Song's characterization of the 1st, 1.5, and 2nd generation immigrants and the implication of this on mission, is an often-spoken basis on the Mosaic Cultural Ministry's mission strategy.

3. There was a misunderstanding among the participants that the overflowing resources of Young Nak church, with its 4000 members, was what began the Mosaic Cultural Ministry. Simply, the understanding was that Young Nak initiated the ministry, because it was actively looking for ways to use their resources for good.

In response, the idea of the ministry - as far as it can be traced among its current members - began from pastor Song, who was in Phillipines, and not in the "power-structure" at Young Nak at the time, and the ministry itself began first not at Young Nak, but from now forgotten, 10-member "Rejoice-Church" by pastor John Chung, and hosted at a Free Methodist church, pastored by the Reverend Victor Stonehouse. Rejoice Church struggled for a year before closing.

All this is to illustrate and emphasize that the impetus to begin the ministry did not come from available resources, and in fact, its history is marked with difficulties and failures. This makes all the more clear what it means to be called by God for particular mission, and emphasize a major theme in the narrative of the Mosaic Ministry, in which God accomplishes His purpose even when human efforts fail.

Notes

1. Mosaic Cultural Ministry also reaches out to wilkemikong (Native Indian) communities in Toronto. Likewise, Young Nak also supports a Filipino church, but this partnership falls under a different ministry that reaches out to the poverty-stricken areas in Toronto. Each of these outreaches reflects Young Nak's commitment to take the gospel to the whole world and return Canada to the Kingdom of God.

2. Mosaic Cultural Ministry does not replace overseas mission work at Young Nak. They have an extensive ministry that is sending missionaries around the world.

3. Young Nak is a prime example of the centrality the Christian church at large has in Korean communities.

4. The official Vietnamese population in Toronto numbers 150,000. There are ten Vietnamese churches included two Roman Catholic churches. This stands in contrast to the two hundred Korean churches for a population of 120,000.

5. It is important to note that in the Asian communities, conversion is not an individual thing. It is a communal culture versus the individualistic culture known to Westerners. When one person in the community possesses the Gospel, it is necessary for him/her to share it.

Analysis of "Mosaic Cultural Ministry (Ethnic Minority Ministries): The Young Nak Korean Presbyterian Church Ministry to Southeast Asian Communities in Toronto and in the Asian Homelands"

Dr. Meesaeng Lee Choi, Ph.D.

From the early Jewish and Christian histories, diaspora, referring to those individuals living outside their country of origin—the scattered peoples of the world—was God's strategic tool to achieve his mission. Diaspora was an extraordinary group of people who overcame the limits of racial, linguistic, and cultural homogeneity and biases of the host nations. Korean Diaspora, which refers to Koreans residing outside of their homeland in Korea, is ever growing, especially in this unprecedented age of mobility and migration. As of 2009, it is estimated that there are about 6.8 million Koreans living in 174 countries.[1] This population reflects a 14 percent increase during the past decade. As Enoch Wan rightly observes, though they are culturally akin and psychologically attached to the country of origin, Korean Diaspora is challenged to actively engage in world mission.[2] As Sinyil Kim, in "Korean Immigrants and their Mission: Exploring the Missional Identity of Korean Immigrant Churches in North America," explores, the strategic value of the Korean Diaspora is world mission.[3]

When we look at the Mosaic Cultural Ministry of Young Nak Presbyterian Church of Toronto[4] from the perspective of diaspora missiology,[5] it is pretty conclusive that Young Nak Church has gone beyond the Korean boundary as a faith community and participated in diaspora mission, by not only being a practical resource of mission work for Korean immigrants, but also stimulating mission work among other ethnic immigrant communities. Diaspora mission is all about participating in God's redemptive mission among diaspora. Diaspora communities often are inward looking. Many desire to retain cultural identity to the extreme of forming cultural ghettos. For the diaspora church, inward looking behavior has been a long existing barrier to reaching out to the host culture and other diasporic groups. Koreans are not any different.

Historically, Koreans are ethnocentric. However, their ethnocentrism is challenged in the diaspora, when they begin to encounter and interact with various ethnic groups and cultures. Young Nak Church is very much aware of multi-ethnicity of the community in which they live. They believe that it is God who placed them in the middle of more than 160 ethnicities communities. Rather than being confined within ethnocentric seclusion, the Young Nak Presbyterian Church of Toronto is not only serving Korean diaspora residing in the greater area of Toronto, Canada,[6] but, also by crossing ethnic boundaries, practicing diaspora mission among other diaspora communities. They are reaching out to the other ethnic minority groups in Toronto area, especially those from Southeast Asian countries (Thailand, Myanmar, Vietnam, and Laos).

The Young Nak's Mosaic Cultural Ministry is no accident. It clearly reflects the church's mission philosophy, which is based on the basis of both *Lausanne Covenant* (1974) and *Manila Manifesto* (1989):

1) We commit to Missions with the firm assurance that the Church is at the very centre of God's cosmic purpose and is His appointed means of spreading the gospel.
2) We seek to take the holistic approach to Missions which involves both the proclamation of the Gospel and the engagement of the culture. Under God, the result will be the rise of churches deeply rooted in Christ and closely related to their culture.
3) We seek to raise up local leadership through cooperative Missions considering the process and result of the evangelism.
4) We place special attention on the unreached people group[7]

Moreover, it is a direct result of the church's clear understanding of Acts 1:8: "But you will receive power when the Holy Spirit comes on you; and you will be my witnesses in Jerusalem, and in all Judea and Samaria, and to the ends of the earth." For Young Nak, Jerusalem implies immediate families and friends; Judea, naturally, means other ethnic Koreans in Toronto; and Samaria refers to other ethnic groups with different cultures and religions. For this reason, Young Nak Church calls mission toward other minority ethnic groups Samaria mission. They state their vision for this mission: "In the minority ethnic groups' culture, language, tradition, and community that God permits us, we will help them to plant and to self-support, to develop their own leadership, and to expand the kingdom of God through participating their mission to their own countries."[8]

Furthermore, Young Nak Church demonstrates divine hospitality. The Bible clearly shows that hospitality begins with God. God, as a God of hospitality, create a space for hospitality, extending the invitation for creation to dwell with him, "in a majestic display of cosmic hospitality. From the hand of divine hospitality, human culture is born and asked to extend divine hospitality."[9] Young Nak Church clearly exercises a twofold incarnational hospitality: border-crossing into other people's worlds and welcoming others into their world.

Korean diaspora Christians understand the story of Abraham's hospitality to strangers (Genesis 18:3-8) with a strong sense of affinity, because they know the meaning of hospitality from their past experiences of being strangers and living liminally and culturally alienated in a strange world. In diaspora, Korean ethnic churches function as "ricing" communities. Treating "ricing" as an active verb of "rice" to denote hospitality as one of the fundamental components of the church life is original and purely Korean. For Korean diaspora Christians, "the practice of feeding and feasting is to extend hospitality and to strengthen the ricing community."[10] While this ricing tradition continues, Young Nak Church has gone beyond. They have reached out not only "attend to their experience of alienation and isolation," but also "to attend to the strangers who come along the way,"[11] regardless of their racial, ethnic or religious identity.

In the face of growing globalization, Young Nak has met one of the greatest missional challenges for Korean diaspora churches. Korean Diaspora churches are challenged not only to engage more in incarnational hospitality by reaching out to those living on the margins, such as immigrants of other ethnic groups and even asylum seekers and refugees, and welcoming them into their churches as hosts who anticipate the hospitality of God's Kingdom, but also, as Soon-Chan Rah suggests, "move from hospitality to a whole new level of connection: the household and family of God."[12] The fullness of the encounter God offers in Scripture is partnership with him. "Merely practicing hospitality is just the beginning." Young Nak Churh Korean diaspora churches, has made room for other ethnic groups and helped them form an independent worshipping congregation in their own language, by sharing space mutually and becoming a multi-congregational church.

One further challenge is that, though Young Nak church has provided more than mere accommodation my recommendation and hope is that they extend beyond and establish mutual partnership, transitioning from an ownership model to a stewardship mentality to foster mutual partnership, even equal ownership. My prayer is that Young Nak Church continues to align with the eschatological vision of the everlasting city of God in which God's people will be gathered "before the throne and before the Lamb," "from every nation, from all tribes and peoples aund langages."

Notes

1. Young Woon Lee, "Brief History of Korean Diaspora and Educational Issues of Korean Diaspora Churches," *Torch Trinity Journal* 13.2 (2010): 173. The number of 174 is more accurate than what is reported in the article, 151 countries.

2. Enoch Wan, "Korean Diaspora: From Hermit Kingdom to Kingdom Ministry," presented during Korean Diapsora Forum, May 1-21, 2010, in Seoul Korea. See http://www.enochwan.com/english/articles/pdf/Korean%20Diaspora_2010.pdf.

3. Sinyil Kim, ""Korean Immigrants and their Mission: Exploring the Missional Identity of Korean Immigrant Churches in North America," (D.Miss, diss. Asbury Theological Seminary, 2008).

4. From now on, it is referred to as Young Nak Church

5. According to the Seoul Declaration on Diaspora Missiology, "Diaspora missiology is a missiological framework for understanding and participating in God's redemptive mission among people living outside their place of origin."

6. There are 223,322 Koreans living in Canada as of 2009.

7. See http://www.torontoyoungnak.com/inc_en.php?inc=en_minis_missions&type=2only.

8. Kim, 103.

9. "With Arms Open Wide," *The Ooze*, http://theooze.com/family/with-arms-wide-open/, accessed June 11, 2011.

10. SuYon Pak, Unzu, Lee, JungHa Kim, and MyungJi Cho, *Singing the Lord's Song in a New Land: Korean American Practices of Faith* (Louisville, Westminster John Knox, 2005), 88.

11. SuYon Pak, Unzu, Lee, JungHa Kim, and MyungJi Cho, *Singing the Lord's Song*, 91.

12. Soon-Chan Rah, *Many Colors: Cultural Intelligence for a Changing Church* (Chicago: Moody Publishers, 2010), 175.

Chapter Five:

The Jesus Network

Pastor Joe, Pastor Phil, with Steve Ybarrola, PhD

(Pseudonymns have been used for participants and locations)

Community History and Demographics

Hensley Heights is a densely populated, highly diverse, multicultural community. Its physical presence as a multi-unit rental residential neighborhood began to take shape in the 1960s and 1970s. Apartment buildings were being built to house individuals and young families from the "baby boomer" generation, as well as to provide housing for the influx of immigrants who had recently arrived in Canada. Throughout the 1980s and 1990s, there was a continued influx of immigrants moving into our neighborhood. The affordable housing shortage was reaching crisis proportions and many families were compelled to double-up (or worse), just to be able to have a place to live; the local public elementary school became very over-crowded having the largest population of any elementary school in Canada.

Traditionally the community has been a transient one. Recently we have seen evidence of people staying longer in the community. It is a safe, family friendly neighborhood with excellent schools, amenities like the mosque and the church, ethnic shopping places and good level of services. Although newcomers are the most visible population of the community, our neighborhood is home to many established communities including Greeks, East Africans and the Philippines. Today, South Asians are the largest single group of residents of the community. Afghans are the fastest growing segment of the community.[1]

Research Method

In order to obtain a clear and multi perspective picture of the ministry of the Jesus network the author interviewed seven members of the team. Five of those interviewed were born and raised in Canada and who had been members of evangelical churches for many years, the other two interviewed were Muslim background believers. The author prepared a set of interview questions, (Appendix A) and conducted audio-recorded interviews with each of the seven interviewees. Two of the questions were specific to those who had been long-term believers and members of the team from the beginning and two were specifically for the Muslim background believers.

Cross Cultural Barriers

The interviewees identified language, Gender separation mores, ignorance of the meaning of behaviors across cultures, different child rearing values and mutual mistrust as barriers that affect their ministry.

Language barriers

Communicating effectively with the people in our multi-ethnic neighborhood is a challenge because of language barriers. Even our members, who know locally spoken languages other than English, are limited to speaking English with those whose languages they do not know.

A lot of older people and women in our community do not know English well. This hampers our ability to connect with them. English is not as effective to communicate spiritual issues to those to whom it is a second language. Misunderstandings can develop between members of multi-lingual task-groups that work in English.

Gender Separation Mores

Gender separation customs of the cultures in our community is a challenge. This is a challenge for the team members from Canadian cultural backgrounds. For example, Canadian team members have to learn the proper level of eye contact and friendliness with those of the opposite sex, and what is the appropriate way to dress in social settings. The gender separation expectations result in more gender specific group activities than in settings following Canadian mores. The most significant effect is that effective ministry must be carried on mainly by women with women and by men with men.

---

[1] http://www.t.org/#. Accessed on May 26, 2011. (full reference not given due to security concerns.

Ignorance of Behavior Meanings

Not knowing what the meaning of our normal behavior is to someone of another culture can be a barrier to leading people to Jesus. A team member related the following, "I remember one time I had a family over. I was trying to be helpful and took the initiative in doing the dishes and the husband took that as the cue that it was his time to leave and we were not able to convince him that we wanted him to stay. His culture told him that we were trying to shuffle him out the door."

Child Rearing Values

Another person said that the different approaches to child rearing presented a challenge to ministry. They said, "We have great relationships with some families but they do not control their children, so it makes it difficult to spend time with them. Sometimes after a family has left, I sit down and cry because their kids have destroyed my house but you need to make them know that you are glad they are with you because you really are." Developing relationships across cultures requires willingness not only to learn people's different customs but also willingness to live outside one's own comfort zone.

Mutual Mistrust

Building trust where mutual mistrust is the norm is a challenge. One of our Iranian members said that people from his country do not trust fellow countrymen. He has to work hard and be patient to win their trust. Another member said that the mutual mistrust among people in our community makes it hard to navigate relationships among many families of one cultural group and across language groups. Building trust is a challenge when you are a friend to all but they do not trust one another.

Cultural Pathways

Although our team reported some cross-cultural barriers to the gospel, they also reported significant cultural pathways into people's hearts. Pathways that interviewees mentioned are; the high value of hospitality, the importance of relationships, the abundance of children and the openness to share difficulties with trusted outsiders.

The High Value of Hospitality

The first two pathways are intrinsically related to one another. Hospitality is a high value in the peoples of our neighborhood because relationships are very important. One team member confessed, "Hospitality and the welcome of strangers even if the stranger brings a strange message, has transformed me as they welcome me." A Pakistani friend told me that by accepting and giving hospitality that includes sharing food, you form "a covenant of salt" with people. In other words, it establishes a friendship. Therefore, the culture has an accepted and clear path by which to establish friendship.

The Importance of Relationships

People maintain their relational networks. Therefore, when we become friends with one person we become friends with the rest of their network. One of our team members told me, "If I am friend with M and she invites me to her party then automatically I am part of her network and they trust me like M does. You do not have to earn their trust one by one."

The following example related by a team member demonstrates how our team is able to use the relational pathway; "We are helping to sponsor the parents of one family and they came to our home at Easter. They have over two hundred family members in the greater Toronto metropolitan area. By helping, we build trust through their networks. They invite us into their networks." As you can see, God works through the networks of people the Jesus Network contacts. Summarizing this one member explained, "Somehow, God favors us with people's trust but those friends are trusting us with all their friends, families and all of their circles."

The Abundance of Children

Our neighborhood is densely populated and children make up a high percentage of the population. The presence of so many children opens doors to build relationships with families. As explained by one interviewee, "The number of children that people have makes it easy to connect with them. I cannot think of a place to raise kids where they can go out and play with strangers so openly. The number of children is life stimulating." Those team members with children can connect easily with other families with children of similar ages to theirs. Those who do not have children can become involved in serving children in one way or another and that becomes a pathway to build relationships with some of the parents.

The Openness to Share Difficulties with Trusted Outsiders

Our team members' outsider status opens a pathway to people's hearts. One member said, "People are fairly emotionally open. They are not as reserved as Canadians. If they are hurting, they will tell you about it and so it is a great opportunity." Newcomers to Canada have come with high economic expectations. The reality however, is often long periods of unemployment and stress within families. At the same time, people want to keep an appearance of success and respectability. Because our team members share how Jesus has helped them in the difficulties of their lives and families and they maintain standards of confidentiality they find that people often share their problems with them. They could not share these problems even with their close friends and relatives. Therefore, being trusted outsiders opens a pathway to share the gospel.

Intercultural Effects

Our team members have contacts with people from more than a dozen countries and from the Muslim, Hindu, Sikh and Christian religions. The people groups have different histories that affect their attitudes to religion and to each other. One interviewee said, "Each group brings a different history. Iranians and Afghans have had religion imposed on them, this turns them off their religion and religion in general. Others who have religion as a core of their identity find that when arriving in Canada they may feel attacked by the surrounding society and so cling more tightly to their religion. We have people on both ends of the spectrum."

Understanding the different histories helps one team member use different approaches in developing relationships with people. Understanding the uniqueness of the specific culture of a person is an advantage, as another interviewee said, "Each group has their own story that we need to learn. You cannot transfer assumptions from one to the other. It is more important to learn about the differences than the commonalities. It takes more discipline to notice the differences. If you understand some of the differences you can speak into their lives in a way that resonates with them so that they want to hear."

Two of our women members told of two different multi-cultural groups that they have utilized. One said, "The women's committee has Afghani, Bangladeshi, Indian, Pakistani and Canadian members. It has been a four-year process of communicating and working together and over time, I've seen them grow in that and its really encouraging."

The other spoke about a group of ladies, some followers of Jesus and some not, from eight different language groups who have come together at Christmas over the past three years to assemble and distribute food hampers. The ladies are all "from different cultures which made us appreciate each other. This was an advantage, because we always had someone who could speak the language of those to whom we were delivering the baskets."

Religious Barriers

One team member pointed out that our particular Toronto neighborhood has "the largest Muslim pocket of population in North America. People are even more religious than in other neighborhoods." He said, "I was talking with one Pakistani man who said, 'Oh you live in _____ neighborhood; that's where the Taliban are.' People in Canada realize that this is the headquarters for Islam. The entire neighborhood is a religious block. It is not just the religion in general with some Muslims here and there. The religious peer pressure is suffocating." There are four mosques in the neighborhood and a new three hundred million dollar Ismaili Islamic center is being built nearby.

Islamic organizations that seek to make moderate Muslims conform to strict religious practices are present.

Fear

The presentation of this content is intended to be neutral. We do not have data on the possible causes of fear that is reported, and it is difficult to say what is the mixture of justifiable fear and perceptions of fear caused by misperceptions of the Islamic faith. If it is the case that religious authorities in this community have used fear to control its followers, that is not confirmed by observers. Although we do not know whether the reports of fear are legitimate, the case is honoring the experience of the interviewees by using anonymity as it is reported. Reputable ethnography would seek to give explanations of why fear is reported. In the absence of such explanations, it may be supposed that multiple causes are at work, including a legitimate fear of violence or a social order in which deviance is worthy of fear.

Islam, the religion of most of those we meet in our neighborhood, reportedly uses fear to control its followers. One interviewee said, "The way out of Islam is heavily guarded. Liberal minded people have told me that if their child tried to leave the faith they would try to kill them. To leave the faith and confess another could result in death or being cut off."

One person observed, "There is a pharisaical spiritual pride in some Muslims which is very external and it is so hard to break through. There are those who are proud of themselves and the others who are afraid of them. A friend told me that she did grocery shopping outside of the neighborhood, because more conservative women would come up and look into her shopping cart to tell her which things she was buying were haram (forbidden), that she should put back. Women who upon arrival wear western clothes later begin wearing the full niqab with their face covered. Although they explain that they wear this for spiritual reasons it is obvious to our women team members that they have been pressured by peers to do so out of fear of criticism."

Communal Nature of Islam

The rituals of Islam are mostly communal. Prayer, giving, the annual fast, and the pilgrimage to Mecca all are done in public. One observer reorted, "because these are so communal its very hard for someone to go against this without severing important ties in their life", said one team member. They continued, "This communal environment and having no exit make it very challenging for the individual or even a small group of individuals to distance themselves from Islam or to have their minds changed."

Islam is effective in instructing their children in their faith in religious classes held five days per week. However, we observe that Islam does not allow Muslims to question their beliefs. Women are generally not free to make decisions for themselves. One lady team member said, "Women feel obliged to have children and not practice family planning. If their husband says they must have children then the women must obey their husbands."

Religious pathways

Our team members have found some pathways that Islam provides that they are able to use to open peoples' hearts to Jesus. First, Muslims are curious to learn more about Jesus because Islam highly respects him as a prophet. Second, Islam emphasizes the teaching of the final Day of Judgment by Allah and so they take religious questions seriously. Third, many Muslims are open to prayer in the name of Jesus.

Jesus

It is easy to have discussions about Jesus as reported by one interviewee, "I believe that Jesus is unique among the world's holy figures because he appears prominently in Islam and also in Hinduism and Buddhism. I get in arguments with friends about who loves Jesus more. He is revered and spoken about, and this is a huge opening."

Spirituality

Muslims believe that God hears prayers. When our team members pray for a person in Jesus' name and the person receives an answer to that prayer, this engenders more interest in Jesus for them. A team member related the following story; "A lady whom I have known for two years and has given gift baskets, including a Bible and the Jesus DVD, did not notice these things until two weeks ago. We were selling clothing and offering Bibles and Jesus DVDs in the park. She asked about the DVDs and took one. When she watched it she thought, 'Jesus is very wonderful.' She wanted to watch it more. We prayed for her when we visited her and her life was changed. She has a disabled son whose care kept her at home. After we prayed, an organization for disabled people offered a care place for her son. It's a very good program."

Source of Spiritual Power

Prayer

"At the beginning of the Jesus Network, the spiritual power was coming from a group of Jesus followers who had moved into this neighborhood and were praying, calling out to God, providing seed, relationships and response." This is how one of the first four team members described the source of spiritual power in our ministry. Another of the original team members recalled, "When we started we decided to just pray and wait. The first board meeting was only prayer. We did not know what our work would look like, so we prayed and asked God to open doors. The amount of prayer has been the source of spiritual power."

At the beginning, prayer was the primary work. However, even before the pioneers of the Jesus Movement moved into the neighborhood, other followers of Jesus had been praying that God would do something here. The Fellowship of Faith for Muslims held a monthly prayer meeting in the neighborhood in the apartment of one of their members. In the beginning, the team invited Jesus friends to join them on Friday nights for prayer and yearly on the last Friday of Ramadan, and these friends gathered for all-night prayer sessions in a nearby church.

Evangelism

A second source of spiritual power mentioned above is "providing seed." The Jesus Network practices the church planting principle of abundant evangelism, (Garrison 2004, 172), and the primary means of evangelism has been the mass distribution of the Jesus DVD. In the first year, nine thousand Jesus DVDs in sixteen languages were distributed in our neighborhood in the week after Christmas. In the three following years at Christmas, volunteers distributed fifty thousand DVDs each year in our neighborhood as well as in many other neighborhoods across the GTA and beyond.

Presence

Complimenting the strategy of Jesus DVD distribution through the Jesus Network, members live in the neighborhood where they minister. Our ministry is one of presence. We build relationships and respond to inquiries. One team member had developed a relationship with an Afghan family. "The friend had received two or three Jesus DVDs and never watched them. Then he was at the used clothing store and bought a videocassette of the Jesus film in English and it changed his life." (The man asked questions about the film of his friend, our team member, who was then able to watch it together with the man in his language and explain its meaning) "This abundant seed sewing, works together with our having a consistent presence in people's lives so that when the Spirit has prepared the soil God can use us to water those seeds that have been sown."

The Leading of the Holy Spirit

"The leading of the Holy Spirit is an important source of power," stated one team member. "When someone pops into your mind a couple of times in a day, trust the instinct to contact them. Last week we said, " O we haven't seen so and so in a while. We should call her. When we called her she had just gotten out of a hospital after having had a severe allergic reaction. That was a scary experience and nobody else knew or cared but we called when it all happened. Another time I just happened to visit her when the police were coming to arrest her husband and take him away to jail. You know that you are not good enough to know such things – it is just the Holy Spirit telling you this person needs you now so go."

New Believers

The source of our spiritual power has changed over the four years of our ministry. We have fewer prayer gatherings as a team and not many Christian friends from outside our neighborhood gather with us for prayer. "One good reason is that there is a small group of people who have responded to the seed and the work of Christ in their lives and they are the new reactor core of power," explained an interviewee. This new approach is more powerful than the original prayer. Their desires and wisdom are the new source of power. Those born into the Islamic mind-set should be the main voices. We're in a waiting phase, we don't know how to make their voices primary without interfering too much."

One of our important annual activities in demonstrating Jesus' love for our neighbors began by listening to the idea of a new believer. Three years ago, one of them inspired the team to give gifts of food at Christmas to people in the neighborhood who we knew were in need. In 2008, we delivered one hundred and fifty halal food baskets with scripture portions in appropriate languages. The next year the number of gift-baskets we delivered doubled and in 2010, we delivered about four hundred and fifty gift-baskets.

There is a strong vision from the leadership of the Jesus network that we must harness the passion of those who follow Jesus from Muslim backgrounds. One member expressed the vision as follows; "There is such a strong call on new Muslims who come to Christ to share their faith with new people. For the Muslim world to ever be penetrated with the gospel we need to see that incredible explosive chain reaction. It will never happen from the outside in. It has to happen from the inside."

Surprised by God

A Life-changing Experience

What most often surprised our team members was that God had brought about change in their lives as they served. Each person who gave this response expressed different aspects of their lives in which they had experienced change. Some realized that perhaps as important as bringing the Good News to those who needed it, God also wanted to effect change in them. One member summarizes, "But as I walked along I realized that what God is doing in me is a big part of God's plan. It's not just about the people who don't believe. God is doing a work in us." Another member said, "God changed my life so much. Twenty months ago, I lost my husband. I did not want to live and was in bad shape. When I found out that I had a job with the Jesus Network, it gave me strength. I have had many miracles in my life. I'm always looking for a miracle in my life to change me step by step." Another person to their surprise found themselves used by God to bring people to himself. "I never saw myself as an evangelist and never thought that I would be involved in such an evangelistic effort." This observation illustrates how evangelism finds a place within a movement that is revitalizing those persons and communities of faith who are offering that movement their support.

Answered Prayer

Since team members identified prayer as a source of spiritual power in our ministry, it is not surprising that answered prayer is one thing that surprised them. One woman for whom team members had prayed for two and a half years without seeing interest in Jesus became open spiritually through the dream of her mother in Iran. The following is the story that was told to me. "K was not interested herself but her mother back in Iran was having dreams about Jesus and couldn't stop thinking about them and so she asked K to find some followers of Jesus and light a candle on Easter from me to Jesus. K said to us, 'you are the only [lovers of Jesus] that I know. How can I do this?' We had been friends for two and a half years with no spiritual connectedness and although we had prayed for her, given her things and shared our testimonies, it was not until her mom pushed her to do this that something inside her woke up. I do not know if it was that first Easter, when a group of six of us were sitting around and we were each sharing what our struggles were in life, as well as and praying for one another. The two of us were the only Jesus followers in the room. Everyone else was at some stage of seeking. Something about those prayers got her."

Both prayer for seekers and honest, personal sharing with caring prayer in a group has proven powerful in our ministry.

Muslim testimonies to Jesus

We did not expect that some Muslims would testify to Jesus working in their lives. In the words of one team member, "I was surprised to find that people who still identify themselves as Muslims are willing to speak on behalf of the miraculous power of Jesus in their own lives. I did not know that Muslims would distribute Bibles to other Muslims that they would encourage other Muslims to pray in the name of Jesus for a breakthrough in their lives." This was surprising because we have heard about and met other Muslims who secretly trust in Jesus, but because of family and social pressures, they remain secret believers.

The Beginnings of a Community of Believers

God surprised our team members when they discovered that " there were certain people living in this neighborhood who had already were being drawn to Jesus before they arrived." This led to the beginning of very small groups of local believers, as expressed by one person: "It surprised me to see how quickly some have come to Christ. I thought that would take a lot longer. It is also very exciting to see a community of believers starting to form."

One member of the Jesus Network, a believer with Muslim background, described the importance of one of the nascent groups as follows; "We gather together weekly on Friday at Joe's house. This is changing us. We are getting more skill and love for Jesus. We are doing this for ourselves but we also need training and we need the message of God. We need to amplify the source of power to have His love enter into our heart. We pray for the needs of people around us. People in trouble impact us. Some of them come on Fridays but even if they can't they call in advance and ask for prayer."

Images of God Used by Team Members

There are many different images of God used by the members of our team when we communicate the gospel to our Muslim friends.

The Qur'an states, "And We gave unto Jesus, son of Mary, clear miracles" (Qur'an 2:87). Because Muslims are aware that Jesus performed miracles of healing, our team members emphasize this aspect of Jesus' power when praying with friends concerning their needs. Related to this image, our members also employ God as a listener. One said, "Many have portrayed God as a listener, which is very revolutionary for Muslims to know that God listens to the cry of their heart."

Sometimes we emphasize that Jesus is the one who changes your heart, as expressed by one member, "Jesus works from the inside out. What is important to God is what is in your heart as opposed to the external things, like have a long beard. Jesus is the heart changer." The image of 'sacrificial lamb' is used for Jesus because Muslims celebrate the faith of Abraham and the sacrifice of a ram in the place of his son and their annual festival called, Eid al Adha. One of our Muslim background believers portrays Jesus as one who reveals himself in dreams, because that is her experience.

Expressions of Relationship with God

Our team members express their relationship with God in personal terms such as, friend, Jesus, Father and through spontaneous prayer.

God as Friend

This aspect of relationship with God is especially meaningful for the new believers on our team. One said, "I want to be honest and confess something. "When I was a believing Muslim I had graduated from an Islamic school and they showed me that I should be afraid of God. I did not know if God hated me or loved me. If I did something bad, I thought God hated me. After I believed in Jesus, I see God as merciful, wonderful and kind. Why should I be afraid of God? Now I have a kind of friendship with God. It is a very close relationship."

Jesus

One member sensed a new and closer relationship to Jesus than ever before. There is a new sense of the presence of Jesus in prayer. This has resulted in finding new ways to express their relationship to God with the friends in the community. "Sometimes I shy away from using the word Christian because there are so many connotations of that word to Muslims. So I use words like, I am following Jesus or I am trusting Jesus or Jesus is the hope I have in my life, because those terms actually are closer to expressing the meaning I actually feel in my relationship to God, than to say I am a Christian. I would never deny being a Christian, but that word to them has negative connotations. It's good to have words that are simpler and they become more powerful."

Through Spontaneous Prayer

The act of praying spontaneously with people communicates to some of our Muslim friends the closeness of our relationship with God. A team member told me the following illustrative story, "I had a Muslim friend and after I prayed for him he said that the only thing I trust is prayer. He drew a triangle with a line between my heart and his heart and the apex of the triangle that was above his head represented God. He felt that my praying in his presence was like drawing a triangle between his heart, and my heart and God's heart."

The Needs of People in Our Community

Basic Settlement Needs

Persons who arrive for an extended stay in a new country and culture will have a large number of practical needs which they need to learn how to meet in their new life situation. Our team members have found opportunity to serve their neighbors by helping them understand bills, finding medical help, advocating for them with landlords, fixing computers, as well as providing inexpensive used clothing and dry-good foods at Christmas time. One member put it this way, "Instead of offering programs and asking them to come we are really in touch with people's needs. For example, through the Christmas baskets we realized the opportunity to give gifts and meet needs."

Social Needs

Immigrants to Canada leave their home and loved ones behind. Despite the availability of modern internet and phone connections, isolation and loneliness remain common among newcomers. Because they are living in the neighborhood and develop friendships they offer themselves "just by being available." Jesus Network members listen to people's concerns and often pray for those concerns in Jesus' name. Many times God specifically meets those needs in response to people's faith.

Our team members find that many of their friends have marital problems. One member told the author, "There are a lot of marriage problems. Many of the women we talk to have been married at a young age to men much older than they and so feel very alone, isolated and misunderstood." A woman asked one of our women team members for help in getting a divorce. The team member asked to speak with the woman and her husband together. They talked for three hours, and God showed the couple's problem to her and she prayed for them in Jesus' name. After two days the woman called saying that, she and her husband no longer wanted a divorce but that were going on a second honeymoon! The team member reported, "When I prayed for them I felt Jesus was there and that he could do something for them which he did. Because they opened their heart to Jesus, he could change their life. If they are afraid and do not open their hearts to Jesus he cannot go to their heart and change them."

Child abuse is a social need sometimes encountered in our neighborhood. A team member recounted the following story. "We know of a family which is one of the most religious families in our neighborhood. All of that was gone in one night when the police came and took all of their kids away, and put them in jail for child abuse. All of a sudden, their status in the community was gone. Nobody cared about them and wanted to listen to their problems except for us. Suddenly everything changed because we had been pursuing this woman in an effort to get one cup of tea with her. Now when we are walking in the school yard she calls to us, to wait for her and talk."

Our team members also have contact with at least five families that have disabled children in their family. She reports that they are very open to Christ and that we have very strong relationships with them. In one case mentioned earlier, prayer helped the family get their children into a special program.

The Different Needs of Men and Women

The roles the home cultures place on men and women who have settled in our neighborhood result in unique tensions for each gender as they adjust to the pressures of life in Canada. One team member elaborated, "I would say that men and women in this neighborhood live in different worlds from each other even in the same families, and because of that, their needs are so very, very different. For many of the women in this neighborhood their connection to Christ has been an extremely emotional one. Many women feel isolated and hopeless and for them to be prayed for and presented with a loving Jesus is emotionally overwhelming, causing something in their soul to reach out in the presence of other women. Thus, their need is for a comforter, a healer, a guiding light, a source of hope, and Christ is capable of stepping into that role in a very rapid way. We've seen this happen in the right context."

The men generally have a role that requires them to be in control of their family and their own lives. The same team member continued, "The men have a totally different need and their response to that need is much slower. I feel like the men have a huge weight on their shoulders to provide for their family and to give leadership to their family. They do that in the context of culture shock and not having the same status here, which is an enormous source of stress. Many feel humiliated by their experiences and role in Canada. They feel hard-pressed to provide for their families. It was really their vision of hope that brought them here – a hope that they could have more money and better opportunities and they have to keep an appearance of success even among many failures. That makes them totally alone and unable to express the doubts and fears and needs that they have." Perhaps if the men of The Jesus Network demonstrate vulnerability, transparency, as well as a sense of their own depravity and brokenness spiritually and emotionally more often in their relationships, God will be able to touch men's hearts and open up their deep needs to the healing of prayer in Jesus' name.

Key Factors in the Founding of The Jesus Network

Key factors in establishing The Jesus Network mentioned by the members interviewed included the following: the collaboration of a number of denominations, the incarnational and missional calling of original team members, the personality and vision of Joe, the team leader, and God's preparing of people from Muslim backgrounds to become believers [i.e., prevenient grace].

Denominational Cooperation

There was unusual cooperation among certain denominations in the birth of the Jesus Network, which was called 614 T___ P². The Canadian Conference of Mennonite Brethren Churches was the main supporting partner. Other partners at the beginning were the Salvation Army, Vision Ministries Canada and Leaside Bible Chapel. Representatives from these organizations formed the first governing board. The Fellowship of Evangelical Baptist Churches of Canada later entered the partnership.

The groups involved in the partnership have changed over the four year history of our network, as one member described, "It's very much still a collaborative effort in which many groups would be able to say they have input and investment. These groups are constantly changing but I would say they are growing in number." In addition, The Jesus Network has become more independent financially. We are our own official charity and receive very little of our income from the founding groups.

Incarnational Calling

D and his wife who are team members were the pioneers of the current Jesus Network team. D's family home was near to the neighbourhood and as he walked through it, God gave him and his wife a vision to reach it. After they married they moved into an apartment in the neighborhood in July 2003 and became involved in the community. D and his family model the principle of incarnation described in one interview as follows, "Personal, missional, incarnational and evangelistic calling was evident in a strong way in a number of individuals who formed the initial board. The incarnational emphasis was

---

² The full name is not mentioned in this paper for security reasons. "614", is a network of inner city churches organized around principles of renewal as pictured in Isa 61:4.

necessary for people to change their address to move to the margins of the empire, as it were."

One member reported that four years later, "The incarnational part continues to be foundational and it is also a very influential aspect. The incarnational aspect has become a model for many others and has demonstrated that something that people thought was very difficult is actually very pleasant. Something that people deemed to be abnormal is becoming normal. The church community will not always avoid these neighborhoods in terms of believers choosing their own place to live and we are seeing that change in a massive way since the Jesus Network began. Many of the movements of change although they have many different labels on them have direct relational connections to what is happening here."

God's Preparation of Muslim Background Believers

One member reckoned that God's leading of individuals of Muslim background to faith in Jesus was a factor in the establishment of the Jesus Network. "Another factor was that God had already had ripe people on the ground ready and waiting for us to find them. God had been at work. Think of Mr. S,. the first person we baptized. He wanted to be a follower of Jesus but never found anyone who would tell him how. D, who had converted to Catholicism in Holland, was still looking for the real thing that he had been called to in life. It was amazing how much preparation God had done to set up our ministry." Some of these have become team members regularly attending team prayer times and sharing ministry responsibilities.

Over our first four years of existence, the composition of the Jesus Network team has changed. Believers who felt called to come and serve on the team have left. Some have moved on to serve in other ministries and a few left due to personal conflicts and differences of vision. Those team members from evangelical church backgrounds who continue with the team find that their role is changing. Although they continue their outreach to their neighbors, they have a new role of enabling the new believers to fulfill their call to reach their own people. One member put it this way, "The missional call now is primarily of those who have a call to reach their own culture. The new believers have a missional calling as well. At first, it was, 'here is a group of people and you have an opportunity to reach them.' Now we are hearing , 'you have come to Christ from this background, here are the people from your own language background that you feel called to reach.' That is a sharp and healthy transition. It is not an easy transition but one that we are pushing for."

The Personality and Vision of Our Team Leader

One team member mentioned that the personality and vision of Joe was a factor in establishing the Jesus Network. Although other team members have made significant contributions to the development of our ministry, Joe's energy, networking abilities, and vision to establish a cell church led by local followers of Jesus has been a critical element in what God has done through us. His leadership continues to be vital as our ministry progresses.

Conclusion

I am thankful for the opportunity to interview my fellow team members and to record their insights for this case study for the third consultation on World Christian Revitalization Movements. Through the research process, I have gained a much fuller picture of how God has worked among and through us. I hope that this study gives the readers a clearer idea of what he has done in the Jesus Network Ministry.

Bibliography

Garrison, David. 2004. Church Planting Movements. WIGTake Resources. Sri Sudhindra Offset Process. Bangalore, India

APPENDIX A

Interview Questions

1) Re: Social forces:
   a) What cross-cultural challenges do you experience in your ministry?
   b) How do these differences in the various cultural groups affect your outreach?
   c) What challenges does the religion of your contacts pose to the ministry of church planting?
   d) What aspects of the cultures present in our neighbourhood are helpful in church planting work?
   e) Is it essential that the Jesus Network continue its ministry? Why?

2) Divine Encounter:
   a) What are the sources of spiritual power in the ministry of the Jesus Network?
   b) Describe ways that God has surprised you since you have been involved with the Jesus Network.
   c) In your opinion, how does God work through the Jesus Network?
   d) What images of God do the Jesus Network community most use?
   e) How do Jesus Network people express their relationship to God?
   f) What caused you to become a follower of Jesus?
   g) Why are you a member of the Jesus Network?

3) Human Need
   a) What are the needs of the people that make them open to contact with the gospel?
   b) How is the Jesus Network meeting peoples' needs?
   c) What factors were important in establishing the Jesus Network?
   d) In what ways is there continuity with these factors? In what ways has our work changed?

Chapter Six

Rahab Ministry

GLADYS MOK, WITH ALOMA YONKER AND JOANNA YEE

Rahab Ministries

Introduction

The sex industry is like a big elephant in the room that no one talks about but is generally acknowledged. This is partly due to the immorality associated with it [1].[1] The silence that surrounds the industry creates a perfect breeding ground for the unbridled exhibition of human depravity, culminating in a lack of hope for those involved. Baldwin describes the activities and atmosphere surrounding the sex industry as follows: "the scale of it, the dailiness of it, the seeming inevitability of it: the torture, the rapes, the murders, the beatings, the despair, the hollowing out of the personality, the near extinction of hope commonly suffered by women in prostitution" [2,107].

What then is the definition of sex work? It is the provision of sex or sexual services in exchange for material commodities (e.g. money) and/or non-material benefits (e.g. privileges as an example of non-material benefits) [1,3,4]. From an even broader perspective, it is "a social institution which allows certain powers of command over one person's body to be exercised by another" [1,3]. Although these are commonly accepted definitions, these descriptions minimize or disregard the exploitation involved regardless of whether people engage in these activities voluntarily or under compulsion [5,3]. The extent of the exploitation is evident in the fact that a high percentage of people enter into the sex industry at a pre-teenage age (on average, the age of entry is from age 12 to 17) [6]. Moreover, this definition focuses on the sex workers only disregarding the behavior of the men[2] who either buy the services or control the industry, thus freeing them from any responsibility [3] while concealing the suffering of the sex workers themselves.

This perspective on the sex industry prevents people from seeing the inequality and exploitation that takes place and it effectively protects the interests of those who control the trade at the expense of the sex workers themselves. Often, especially in patriarchal societies, women believe that it is their duty and role in society to comply with the demands of men. This is particularly true in cultures where the economic freedom of women is limited. The proposal that prostitution be seen as simply another profession alongside any other line of work will simply lead to further marginalization for the women involved since it "is based on the conclusion that prostitution is a normative life choice for women born into poverty, into minority status, into countries with radical or unstable governments or economies, into male-dominated misogynist cultures, or into child-abusive families...it concludes that this is the way it is and always has been; there is nothing that can be done to change circumstances" [3,158].

To deal with the issue of prostitution without exacerbating the inequality, exploitation and marginalization involved, it is important to understand the structure of the industry.

Supply: Human Trafficking

Human trafficking is essentially the slave trade by another name since it involves selling human beings for economic gain. The United Nations' Office of Drugs and Crime has declared that no country is immune from human trafficking. [7] Although human trafficking constitutes a social problem of its own[3], it is also a major supplier of workers for the sex industry[4].

"Trafficking is highly gendered. Among those who are trafficked internationally, 70-80% are female and approximately 50% are children. Among all females, approximately 70% is trafficked for prostitution and other forms of sexual exploitation" [7,163]. A conservative estimate puts the number of women and children trafficked annually across international borders at 700,000 to 2 million [3]. Domestic trafficking is much more difficult to track but it is estimated that roughly 500,000 women are trafficked annually within Europe [4].

These numbers have caught the attention of many international human rights organizations.

One reason for the growing momentum in human trafficking is the potential economic gain for those who control the industry. It is estimated that once women and children reach the market, the traffickers make between 5 to 20 times of their original price [3]. For children alone, this translates to a multi-billion dollar market industry [4]. Where the women and children are abducted, the profit margin is 100%. Moreover, human trafficking often entails much less risks for the traffickers and organizers when compared to drug trafficking. Not only are humans easier to hide, but many countries do not have adequate law enforcement structures to deter trafficking activities. The high profit margins and low risks could potentially lead to a scenario where "human trafficking will supersede drug trafficking as the number one international crime within the next ten years" according to some [3,148]. The legalization of prostitution in developed countries would serve as a further catalyst for this trend[5] [7].

Human Smuggling

Schaeuer and Weaton point out that "human smuggling differs from trafficking in that smuggling suggests consent of the parties, whereas trafficking includes deception, fraud, coercion, force, or exploitation of the trafficked human by the trafficker" [3, p149]. It is easy to distinguish the two on paper but it is much harder to do so in reality.

People who experience economic hardship often desire to go abroad in order to establish a better life. Although they may make the decision based on the portrayal of the luxurious lifestyles of Western society in the media [7], and without coercion, smugglers often take advantage of their lack of access to the legal means to immigrate. These unscrupulous operators promise to take people to the country of their choice in return for large sums of money, which the immigrants would not be able to repay once they arrive at their destination. They thus end up indebted to the smugglers who would then force them to work in industries such as the sex trade in order to pay back their debt. This is commonly known as the debt-bondage. Since these people have no legal status in the country they have entered and lack a social network that can support them, they have no choice but to comply. The smugglers would often use force to get people to comply, which often involves severe physical and emotional abuse [7]. From this perspective it becomes much harder to distinguish between human smuggling and trafficking.

Migrant Workers

Migrant workers often find themselves in a similar position to the illegal immigrants who find themselves at the mercy of human smugglers. Migrant maids in particular are vulnerable to exploitation. These women often hail from marginalized social and economic settings and they respond to opportunities to work as housemaids overseas. When they arrive, they are mostly offered positions as housemaids. However, Pyle points out that "often...males in the hiring household expect sexual services" [4,71]. Due to the debt that these women may have towards the employment agency who placed them, language and cultural barriers and expectations, limited education, low literacy, lack of financial and social resources, insecure and uninsured status when detach from the hiring household [9], these migrant maids often believe that they have no other option but to endure the exploitation. When they find out that women in the sex industry earn more, they often move into this industry [4,9]. Some may see them as part of the issue of human smuggling or view this as a human rights issue. Regardless of how they are categorized, these women are definitely exploited.

Demand

While it is important to address the issue of supply, we cannot neglect the fact that without demand the market for sex would not exist. This market is driven mostly by men (98% of buyers) [19,p12] and is fuelled by popular myths in virtually all societies that requires a "real man" to be sexually attractive and active. These same legends also legitimize indiscriminate fornication for men and justify the use of women for anonymous sex. These views and the increasing availability of pornography and sexual images in popular media have contributed to the sexualizing of society and personal identity.

Most of the sex market involves men using women or girls (90-95%) [19,12] and there are typically two types of buyers. The first group treats sex as a commodity that they are entitled to buy, while the second comprise lonely men looking for intimacy. While the men who buy sex are referred to as clients as if the women are soliciting the business, the truth is more often that the women are merely workers forced to provide the services demanded by the paying customer. The popular view of all prostitutes as seducers will simply not do (even while there are some who play and adopt that role). The truth is more often that they are forced against their will (at least initially) by a pimp (mostly male, although there are also females that run these establishments) to provide the services his clients desire and have purchased.

Middlemen

The pimp is usually the middleman in the sex industry. They are often connected with organized crime. Their task is to lure (women who are not supplied by traffickers) and groom (break) the women so that they will do what he and his customers demand. The process includes isolating a woman, controlling her every move and changing her name. The purpose is to remove the woman's previous identity and history so that she will become emotionally dependent on him. He will then convince her of her worthlessness and social invisibility and subject her to physical and emotional abuse in order to dehumanize her so that she becomes a commodity that can be bought and sold [19, 35-38].

Workers

Most of the women and children that end up in the sex trade, regardless of how they entered, come from marginalized social and economic circumstances. Homaifar and Wasik describe "the lives of these women [are] often governed by the reality and hardship of socioeconomic demands" [10, 130]. Many of them are unable to find other means to support their family and themselves [5,10]. Many of these women come from backgrounds characterized by: dysfunctional family dynamics, various forms of neglect and child abuse, premature departure from the family home or other care arrangement, low level of formal education, lack of employment opportunities[6], lack of support network, civil unrest, poverty [1,3,6,11,12,13]. These factors are highly correlated to the social and economic development of the country in which they reside.

Although these conditions are dependent on the leadership and people of a country or a society, they also are influenced by pressure from their trading partners and lending nations. Therefore, marginalization is not only a local issue but also a global issue. Due to the changes in commerce and economic systems, many rural people have to move to cities to make a living. During such a migration process they often incur huge debts. Moreover, these people were used to living in a small and intimate community that involved little if any interaction with strangers and they are foreigners to the way of life in the city with little protection against the lures of luxury. The young people are especially vulnerable and easily fall prey to those who wish to exploit their lack of economic and social sophistication [8].

This problem is exacerbated by the structural adjustments required by the International Monetary Fund when poor countries apply for international financial assistance. These obligations usually entail less state spending and more open market policies..., decreases in welfare, health and nutrition programs and education resources"[3,164;4]. All of these conditions force families, whether in rural areas or cities, to increase their labor output in order to make ends meet. Under these circumstances females are often expected to "sacrifice themselves for the survival of their families" [3, 163;6,14]. It is therefore no surprise that international human rights organizations have recognized four waves of international trafficking in women, mostly from poorer regions such as Asia, Africa, South America, Central and Eastern Europe [3].

Inside the Sex Trade

Each of the issues discussed above constitute a huge social issue on its own. All of them, however come together in the sex trade and it is here where Rahab[7] chooses to minister. In order to understand what ministry to these women entails we need to describe the conditions under which the women operate and how it affects their personhood.

Abuse is a common reality for women in the sex industry and they generally lack a sense of control over their lives. Brown et al has done an ethnographic study in an attempt to bring to light the abuse faced by a person involved in prostitution. From the interview responses, Brown concluded with the following statement:

The respondents conveyed accounts of assault and battery from bad dates and pimps, rape, being attacked by gangs or other personal attacks that involved kicking, slapping and being punched in the face. Many physical injuries were sustained...respondents reported daily abuse from partners, both physical and mental, often over a period spanning several years. [12, 386]

Because of such constant abuse and other stress factors, many of the women dissociate themselves from reality mentally and/or through addiction and substance abuse [4,14,15,16]. They would often switch from using less harmful substances to more harmful ones as time goes by [12,14,17]. However, such substance abuse rarely takes away the pain and stress that they experience. As a result, many of them develop depression, post traumatic stress syndrome, anxiety, eating disorders, insomnia, flashbacks and dissociative disorders [7,12,14]. It is very important for those who reach out to them to be sensitive to the presence and severity of these conditions. These conditions, as well as the substance abuse and gambling, would often prevent sex workers from leaving the industry.

As mentioned, they have other stressors as well. A common stress factor for women is their family. Although the majority of sex workers are trafficked, some women enter the industry voluntarily to support their families. Many of the latter are single mothers who have poor support systems from both immediate and extended family. Because they are unable to obtain a decent job due to lack of education, poor language skills, among other factors, they take the risk to work in this industry in order to provide for their children. They often make this choice because working a part-time job would disqualify them from getting welfare or housing assistance.

These women are also under pressure to keep their children, as well as other family members, from knowing what her income source is[8] [14]. This is due to the social stigma associated with prostitution as well as the womens' struggle with pride, despair and rage [16]. As a result they maintain very little connection with their family and become disconnected from the larger community [12], thereby diminishing any support system that they had.

The fact that the women live hidden lives covered by lies has a detrimental effect on their personalities. They often obtain a different name, look and personality for their work. Even the women who are trafficked would often assume a false persona [5]. Over time the women take on this fake persona becoming distant from their real self[9], resulting in a destruction of their beliefs, ideas, desires

feelings [13]. One commentator explains this phenomenon as follows: "[a] prostitute does not exist, so that [the service buyer] can...Prostitution done correctly begins with theft and ends with the subsequent abandonment of self. What remains is essential to the job: the mouth, the genitals, anus, breasts...and the label" [13,27]. In the process the women fall deeper and deeper into despair the impact of which could be so severe that they become suicidal.

In addition the women face pressure from the police force. Outshoorn points out that "women in prostitution continue to be disproportionately charged by police" [1, p83; 4,7,14]. It is not uncommon for the police to let the buyer go without any legal consequences while charging the sex worker. This pattern reflects the inequalities that these women face on a day-to-day basis. Not only are the women often charged by the police, but since many of them are illegal immigrants they can in turn expect little protection from the law when they are harassed, molested, robbed or abused. In fact most of them are afraid to press charges or go to the police. They are thus very vulnerable at every level of life (economically, legally, physically, mentally, emotionally and psychologically).

Ministry to Sex Workers

Sex workers need to be reached at a personal as well as societal level. Many of these women are hidden physically and it is extremely difficult to gain access to them. A lot of their activities are done "behind doors" where outsiders are not allowed in. Rahab, thus, engages with the women through regular outreaches to massage parlors in an attempt to build rapport and trust with the girls who work there. Because they live in a world that is dominated by lies and mistrust it requires sincerity and persistence and we know that it is only through the work of the Holy Spirit that these women can be reached.

We approach the women from multiple perspectives, given the complicated circumstances of their lives. Schauer and Wheaton indicate that "they must be seen as migrant workers, as prostitutes, as women in a male-dominated society" [3,166] and, we might add, as single mothers, as people who are familiar with betrayal, deceptions and lies, and as those who are socially marginalized. Each of these perspectives assists us to understand their needs and the challenges that face while still in the industry or while transitioning out of the industry. It is important to provide assistance with the physical and material adjustments necessary to help them leave the industry by assisting them with access to addiction treatment, housing support, life skills and work training programs, immigration advice, et al. Besides helping them with the practical issues related to their situation, they also need access to counseling and/or mental health programs/treatment in order to help them overcome the emotional and psychological effects of the trauma and abuse as well as the double lives many of them lead. Moreover, we need to be aware of their sensitivity to people's acts and/or words since they are constantly stigmatized. [15]. For this reason we need to find supporters/communities/service providers who are sensitive with regard to how they act and respond to the women.

We also need to address their spiritual life. Many of the girls have been in touch with spiritual mediums as a way for them to find hope and release from the oppressive bondage that they are under and they need deliverance. As a result, prayer and solid grounding in scripture are essential in our interaction with them. We need to walk patiently and lovingly alongside them, introducing the Good News to them while providing a place where they can wrestle with what they have gone through in God's presence. Homaifar and Wasik have quoted a prostitute who has been in the trade since 1978: "I ask God every day to give me the means in order to quit what I do" [10, 130]. While Christ is able to bring restoration and healing, we, the body of Christ, need to provide a place of belonging, rest and safety for the women.

By walking with these women, we who journey with them are awakened to God's heart for His creatures. In addition to praying for them we also need to care for them without lies and conditions, in order that they might experience the grace, love and power of Christ through our actions and words and come to view life from a new perspective. This poses a constant challenge/reminder for Rahab and those who are involved in the ministry to be living testimonies to Christ. That includes helping the women see that we trust God to be our provider with respect to all areas of our lives, including with regard to our physical and material needs so that they too might come to trust His provision for them. The women often remain entrapped in the sex industry because they fear economic hardship. We therefore need to model a different approach to life than the rest of the consumer society in which we live. We therefore need to live in a way that shows that we are not dominated by the power of money, but that Jesus Christ is indeed Lord of our lives.[10]

We can also help the women through advocacy that includes exposing structural evil that facilitates violation of women here (Toronto) and abroad. Addressing these issues would help protect women from inhuman treatment and would help liberate them from bondage in patriarchal societies.[5]. Rahab believes that this level of advocacy should start from within the Christian community and therefore we engage in awareness sessions that encourage churches to take part in this mission to bring light and hope into this dark industry based in degradation and exploitation.[11]

Biblical Model

Rahab Ministries started in response to the Holy Spirit's prompting as the founder, a graduate from Tyndale, considered the plight of Asian women in the sex trade. She recalled Jesus' compassion for sinners and outcasts and the fact that he did not shun the prostitutes of his time, but associated with them, extending them forgiveness and restoring them to relationship with God and his people thereby offering them new life. The ministry is a continuation of the work of God who hears the cries of the oppressed, delivers those in bondage and slavery and is constantly calling people to turn to Him.

The name Rahab was chosen for the ministry because the Canaanite prostitute whose story is narrated in Joshua 2 and 6 embodies the hope that the founder has for these women. In the biblical account Rahab is confronted with a choice when the agents of two kingdoms knocked on her door. The spies sent by Joshua represented Yahweh who by his mighty deeds demonstrated his lordship over nature and human history. The king of Jericho epitomized Canaan and the established world order with its religions, power systems and lifestyles. Rahab believed the accounts she had heard about Yahweh and responded by transferring her allegiance to him, making the choice to turn from her Canaanite identity, community, and ways of life to seek inclusion among the people of God. This decision rendered her immediate existence in Jericho perilous but it ensured her and her family of future preservation. For this reason the letter to the Hebrews includes Rahab among the exemplars of faith (11:31) and she is commended as righteous in the book of James (2:25-26). The life of Rahab describes well how God works to bring about redemption and transformation, providing the hope and new life that these women seek and for which they leave their home countries.

The Church

As the people of God, it is incumbent upon the church to provide a place of belonging for those who like Rahab have heard about the great deed that God has accomplished in the death and resurrection of his Son Jesus Christ and who desire to turn her back on the idols of lust, money and luxury in order to worship God despite the hardship it might cause in the present. It is incumbent upon the church to journey with the girl through the wilderness, as Moses did with the Israelites after the Exodus, helping them to live in accordance with God's commands so that they may leave behind the ways of Egypt.

When Rahab cast her lot with the Israelites, she had just lost her livelihood, but she was assured of protection and sustenance because the covenant described the conditions for life among God's people and it made provision for the foreigner. The church as the corporate people of God is similarly called to provide for the other, including the alien and outcast, thereby exhibiting the pattern of life in the kingdom of God.

Hope

Rahab Ministries defies the powers of darkness, who like Pharaoh try to hold on to the people God has liberated from slavery to human masers and bondage to sin, by befriending those whom society (and often the church) consider unclean. As we talk to the women, we find out that God is already at work.

One of the girls who often had nightmares shared a dream that she had while staying at her brother's place with us. She experienced a sense of serenity and peacefulness surrounding her as she was sleeping. Then a bright white light appeared to enter her heart and forced out all the dark heavy things that had lodged there, leaving her feeling peaceful and secure. In the morning her sister-in-law told her that they were praying for her as she was sleeping. This experience is evidence that God is at work in the lives of the women, delivering them from the powers of darkness in a tangible and visible way. It also highlights the importance of prayer and the need to be available to help the women understand what God is doing and how they need to respond.

References

[1] Outshoorn, J. *The Politics of Prostitution: Women's movements, democratic states and the globalization of sex commerce.* Cambridge University Press, Cambridge. 2004.

[2] Baldwin, M.A. *Split at the Root Prostitution and Feminist Discourses of Law Reform.* In: Spector, J. (Ed.) Prostitution and Pornography: Philosophical Debate about the Sex Industry. Stanford University Press, California. 2006.

[3] Schauer, E.J. & Wheaton, E.M. (2006) Sex Trafficking into the United States: A Literature Review. *Criminal Justice Review* 31(2): 146-9.

[4] Pyle, J.L. (2001) Sex, maids, and export processing: Risks and reasons for gendered global production networks. *International Journal of Politics, Culture and Society* 15(1): 55-76.

[5] Butcher, K. (2003) Confusion between prostitution and sex trafficking. *Lancet* 361: 1983.

[6] DeRiviere, L. (2006) A human capital methodology for estimating the lifelong personal costs of young women leaving the sex trade. *Feminist Economics* 12(3): 367-402.

[7] Hodge, D.R. & Lietz, C.A. (2007) The international sexual trafficking of women and children: A review of the literature. *Journal of Women and Social Work* 22(2): 163-74.

[8] Zhao, G.M. (2003) Trafficking of women for marriage in China: Policy and practice. *Criminal Justice* 3(1): 83-102.

[9] Miller, E., Decker, M.R., Silverman, J.G. & Raj, A. (2007) Migration, sexual exploitation, and women's health: A case report from a community health center. *Violence Against Women* 13(5): 486-97.

[10] Homaifar, N. & Wasik, S.S. (2005) Interviews with Senegalese commercial sex trade workers and implications for social programming. *Health Care for Women International* 26: 118-33.

[11] Cree, V.E. (2008) Confronting sex trafficking: Lessons from history. *International Social Work* 51(6): 763-76.

[12] Brown, J., Higgitt, N., Miller, C., Wingert, S., Williams, M. & Morrissette, L. (2006) Challenges faced by women working in the inner city sex trade. *Canadian Journal of Urban Research* 15(1): 36-53.

[13] Carter, V. & Giobbe, E. *Prostitution, Racism and Feminist Discourse.* In: Spector, J. (Ed.) Prostitution and Pornography: Philosophical Debate about the Sex Industry. Stanford University Press, California. 2006.

[14] Jackson, L.A., Bennett, C.G. & Sowinski, B.A. (2007) Stress in the sex trade and beyond: Women working in the sex trade talk about the emotional stressors in their working and home lives. *Critical Public Health* 17(3): 257-71.

[15] Rabinovitch, J. & Strega, S. (2004) The PEERS Story: Effective services sidestep the controversies. *Violence Against Women* 10(2): 140-59.

[16] Wong, R. (2001) Market forces and powerful desires: Reading Evelyn Lau's cultural labour. *Essays on Canadian Writing* 73: 122-40.

[17] Kuyper, L.M., Palepu, A., Kerr, T., Li, K., Miller, C.L., Spittal, P.M., Hogg, R.S., Montaner, J.S.G. & Wood, E. (2005) Factors associated with sex-trade involvement among female injection drug users in a Canadian setting. *Addition Research and Theory* 13(2): 193-99.

[18] Bales, K. *Understanding Global Slavery*. University of California Press, Berkeley. 2005.

{19} European Baptist Federation, (ed) (2009) Anti-trafficking Resource Book 3:Demand.

II. Rahab Ministries – Theological Reflection

What is in a Name?

The women to whom Rahab ministers are referred to as "sex trade workers", describing them in terms of their "occupation" in order to preserve their personal dignity as human beings. The technical term serves the purpose of distancing the person from what she (Rahab ministers to women only) does. The phrase reminds us as Christians that people never lose their humanness, no matter what their behaviour, because our humanity is rooted not in ourselves, but the Word of God that called us into being. There is, however, also a darker side to the moniker. In the ears of a world based in money and pragmatism the expression sanctifies the profession and justifies its legalisation. From the perspective of this world a person and his or her occupation are disconnected and it is possible, even admirable to choose an occupation based on potential return with little or no regard for the effect that engagement in the activity has on the person. In such a milieu we are all reduced to workers at some form of industry which merit is determined wholly by the amount of money we can garner thereby. Here "sex trade worker" has as much value as "financial trade worker" if that is how a person can make the most money possible.

On the other hand, prostitution carries with it all the negative value judgments of history. The term connotes using one's talents, abilities and bodies for false purposes. In the bible YHWH berates Israel, His chosen people for squandering themselves and the gifts He had provided on pursuing false gods and political allies in faithless contravention of the covenant God established with them. Several of the prophets use the metaphor of prostitution to describe Israel or the nation's capital, Jerusalem's shameless infidelity[12]. Each of these oracles are intended to shame Israel and shock them out of their complacency and pride so that they would turn back to God who made them who they were and laid before them the boundaries within which they would experience life (blessing).

While the shame and degradation that accompanies those who sell their bodies for gain, whether voluntary or forced, is concealed by the term "sex trade worker" the word prostitution lays it bare. Functional language merely hides the true state of affairs and fosters acceptability of the "trade" for those who wish to participate in the industry (buyers, suppliers, middlemen and workers alike). Prostitution, however, implies the cost and effect on the person engaged in the work. When YHWH likens Israel to a prostitute he is indicating that the nation's dealings with foreign gods and political leaders threaten their relationship with him, leading to potentially disastrous consequences. From a biblical perspective, it matters what a person does and to whom he or she binds himself or herself.

What does it mean to be Human?

The issue of what it means to be human is integral to the subject of prostitution. In a pragmatic, money-driven, consumerist society, the person is implicitly viewed as an economic unit and it matters little what he or she does or what occupation he or she chooses, as long as the work allows him or her to participate in the economy. From this perspective a person's occupation is value neutral and any choice is potentially as good as another. The only basis for choosing an occupation is maximizing the return on your assets and if the only asset you have is your body then by all means use it to make a living. Buyers are, by the same token, free to purchase whatever they wish as long as they can pay for their purchase and once the price has been transacted the goods are theirs to do with as they wish. From a theological perspective, however, what a person does, not only speaks to their character, but it also impacts their person. From a biblical perspective, there is no distance between a person and his or her actions.

The enlightenment movement and existentialist philosophy teach that humanity is self-determined, "speaking" him or herself into existence, by deciding and acting upon unbounded possibilities. It is easy to see how this view can give rise to a purely economic view of human beings among other perspectives. The Bible, however teaches that human beings are constituted by the Word of God. God speaks humanity into being (Gen 1), creates the conditions for human life to flourish and calls human beings to affirm the life He has ordained by living into it. The Word of God therefore anchors our humanity and precedes any human speech or action. The only true response is obedience to the Word spoken by God. That which deviates or contradicts that Word cannot be affirmed as good. The Word of God also determines the boundaries within which life is to be lived. By implication therefore that which falls outside of these limits brings about death. In other words "not all possibilities open to human beings are conducive to human life."[13] From a theological perspective it is therefore impossible to affirm that all human choices and professions are equally valid or good for human beings.

Theology of the Human Being

As can be seen from our introduction, how society defines humanity influences what is considered permissible in terms of attitude and behavior. There are several broad approaches to describing what it means to be human, all of which starts from the perspective of humankind. Mythical anthropology takes a non-historical perspective on humankind, depicting human beings as caught in a cause and effect relationship with natural powers, resulting in a fatalistic worldview where the human lacks freedom and accountability. Philosophical anthropology describes the human person in terms of self-knowledge breaking apart the unity between the world of thought and action.

The approaches to the human being described above are limited because they are derived purely from the perspective of the human being without any external reference. The closed system from which any anthropocentric inquiry into the nature of humankind is concluded can only describe what it finds but it cannot pronounce on what constitutes true humanity. In order to avoid the errors produced by a closed system enquiry we therefore turn to the Word of God wherein we find both the initial and the ultimate Word on what it means to be human.

To be human is to be no less than a creature, but from a theological viewpoint, human beings can never be reduced to the merely creaturely, nor are they determined by their creaturely nature. God speaks to us and we are enabled to transcend our own nature in response to Him. To be human therefore means to be in covenant relationship with God. To be made in the "image of God" means to exist as co-humanity in encounter with each other and God the Holy Spirit in the same manner that God encounters and relates to Himself within the Trinity. The pattern of co-humanity as male and female under God is crucial because it reveals sexuality as intrinsic to the order of being, which means that sexual relations are not determined by universal ethics, but by what it means to be human.

The *Imago Dei* pertains to the entire human being and cannot be identified with a specific aspect of the human such as his or her soul or spirit, since humans are embodied souls and can only encounter each other as such. While the *Imago* is present as co-humanity, it is also present in each human, not as individual but in encounter each with the other. Harming the other (physically, spiritually, emotionally, psychically and in any other way) therefore involves affront against the *Imago* present in the encounter, which therefore means offense against both God and humankind. Theology therefore grounds human to human responsibility, not in ethics as a matter of practical concern, but at the level of the order of being (ontology). Turning away from, ignoring, injuring, abusing or oppressing the other therefore constitute contradiction of our own humanity.

From these thoughts we can therefore conclude that the merely creaturely does not have the power to bestow or diminish the humanity of a human being, since the humanity of every human being is guaranteed by the Word of God, which is external to the human person. Since the human being is, however, no less than a creature, whatever is done to impoverish or imperil the creaturely existence of a person remains an offense against the person. In other words, while a person may be severely disfigured, marred and abused physically, emotionally, psychically, relationally and mentally on account of their own actions and the violence others have done to them, they are never reduced to being less than human. Yet this does not mean that we are free to treat the creaturely aspects of our humanity, especially our bodies, however we please, since we cannot be human without them. From the above we also learn that perfecting the creaturely does not lead to humanity, nor can afflicting the creature destroy the human. While moralism, religious perfectionism, health consciousness and workaholism aims at creaturely wholeness, the atonement sets people free to respond to the Word of God, therein bringing about holiness (restored covenant relationship with God) while holding out the possibility of creaturely wholeness. The crucifixion and resurrection of Jesus Christ, the human and sinless Son of God, reveals that sin (denial of the Word of God) and not creatureliness is the cause of the distortion of the human being.

Sin

We have seen that the Word of God is the source of authentic humanity as co-humanity in covenant relationship with God. Sin is the denial of that relationship as the human being disobeys the Divine Word, resulting in a distortion in the order of being and not merely at the level of ethics or behavior. Where the human being turns away from God, unity is disrupted and persons become separated from each other, existing as individuals without the protective context of a community where each is for the other. The individual therefore focuses his or her energy on protecting and sustaining the self at the cost of the society.[14] The autonomous expression of individuality that accompanies denial of the covenant relationship with God includes a sexual component as each person views him or herself as male or female in an egocentric way. When human beings are alienated from God "sexuality becomes an instrument in service of the self and the other becomes an object of manipulation for one's own interest. This leads to anonymous sexuality as the self is concealed rather than revealed in sexual relation."[15] This can take place even within marriage and will often lead to one partner seeking sexual relations outside the relationship. Immoral sexual behavior is therefore an indication of disorder at the level of personhood itself and it is sinful not because of the physical act involved, but because it is a distortion of the fundamental order of being.[16]

From the above it is clear that sin is not merely the violation of a legal principle and therefore ethical or moral failure but it is disobedience to the divine Word. The remedy is therefore not behavior modification that can lead to religious or moral perfectionism, but rather turning back to the true source of being. That involves turning back to God in faith and obedience to the Word that ever calls to the person who has forsaken God and contradicted his or her own humanity. Such faith calls for concrete action in response to the Word of God in the particularity of each situation.[17]

The ministry, life, death, resurrection and ascension of Jesus Christ reveals that the true human being is he or she who is obedient covenant partner to the God who speaks. Anderson states; "There is no authentic human disobedience. Disobedience to the divine command is therefore denial of one's own humanity."[18] Because the *Imago Dei* is, however, an endowment of God, human beings do not have the power to destroy it, even as they may deny or contradict it. The human being who has turned his or her back on God, is still addressed by God. "The sovereign grace of God therefore sustains the humanity of each person, even if he or she is an unbeliever"[19] and may we add, no matter how much he or she has been abused or have contradiction their own humanity. The same applies to the perpetrator of violence against another human being. They too remain human despite the cruelty of their actions.[20]

Salvation

Forgiveness of sins constitutes the basis on which humanity can be restored because it is only as God is willing to restore relationship with us that we can turn back to the source of our humanity and so be restored ourselves. In the life, death, resurrection and ascension of Jesus of Nazareth, God reconciles humankind to Himself so that we may be restored to our true humanity of which Jesus is the prototype. During His ministry on earth he first extended forgiveness to those he ministered to so that they may repent and turn back to God and only subsequently did he pronounce them healed. While forgiveness is proclaimed in the present, wholeness is not yet in sight, but remains a hope anchored in the reality of the resurrected Christ.

Body of Christ

Because God does not abandon the human creature when he or she falls into disorder, but He approaches him or her for the sake of reconciliation to the true goal of human personhood, it is thereby the responsibility of the church as the people of God to declare the Word of forgiveness thereby facilitating faith and repentance prior to ultimate restoration.[21] Such faith and repentance is conditioned at its root by belonging to a community living in obedience to the Word of God in the presence of God the Holy Spirit.

The Body of Christ is therefore the liturgical community, who, while still broken themselves, constitute the place of belonging where authentic personhood can be nurtured through the repeated acts of community life. When Jesus ate with tax collectors and sinners he sanctified them by sharing His life with them, therein enacting the reality of the kingdom of God where people are restored to full value in the sight of God. He did not merely teach it but made His own life an event which included rather than excluded. According to Anderson Jesus "communicated the ontological value of His own person as the Holy One of God to those with whom He ate and drank." The church as the community of Christ carries with it the same possibility even before people make a confession of faith. By standing with sinners the body of believers incorporate them into their own communion with God, thereby opening up the possibility faith, repentance and restoration of the person.

Implications

The theology of the human person grounds ministry and in particular ministry to sex workers because it is possible to affirm the humanness of the women involved in the face of dehumanizing abuse and evil. Because their humanity is affirmed in the resurrection of Christ we understand that sin, while a contradiction of their humanity does not have the power to deprive them of it. For this reason Christians are meant to affirm the humanity of the sex workers in the face of the darkness that threatens to overtake them, knowing that in the crucifixion and resurrection of Christ, darkness and sin lost their power over them, despite appearances to the contrary.

Because the body is an integral part of the human person we can never condone harm done to the body as if we could sustain life as disembodied souls. As we have seen, the physical abuse that the sex workers sustain has a profoundly negative effect on the rest of her life. Because humanity is constituted as co-humanity before God where each is responsible for the other we need to understand that those who "buy and supply sex" are as responsible for creating disorder among humanity as are the women who work in the sex trade.

Since we are constituted as co-humanity there is always a need for belonging, which explains why the women involved in the trade often become attached to her abusers and find it difficult to leave them. Because the pimps deprive the women of their identity (not the same as their humanity), they feel that they will not fit anywhere else and the women therefore assume the ideology of the sex industry in order to belong. This is why it is important that the body of Christ, consisting of those called and sustained by the Holy Spirit, come alongside and provide an alternative place of belonging for these women as Rahab is doing and has done. It is as the women hear the Word of forgiveness proclaimed by the people of God in the midst of a community that accept and love them that they can begin to turn back to the true Word of God where they can find healing and restoration. It is also important to remember that while we are not merely creatures, we need to take care of our creaturely needs and if these women are to leave the industry they will need much practical support, including assistance to live.[22]

In this context it is very important to remember that none of this can take place without the Holy Spirit and that human community without the presence of God, has no salvific or healing significance. While Jesus healed people during His time on earth, he did not heal all and as the people of God we also need to accept that not everyone will be made whole in the here and now. Therefore ministry always requires a long-term commitment and an eschatological orientation that remains steadfast in the hope of our ultimate restoration and wholeness.

Reference

Anderson, Ray S. *On Being Human: Essays in Theological Anthropology*. Eugene, Oregon: Wipf & Stock, 1991.

NOTES

1. The numbers in brackets in this chapter reference studies in human trafficking that are listed on pp. 106-107.
2. 98% of buyers are men [19, p12].
3. The human trafficking industry involves different levels of players: (1) organizers, (2) middlemen like recruiters, transporters, sellers, etc. (3) business operators like brothel owners, nightclub owners (4) people who facilitate the activities of human traffickers such as corrupt government officials and police. Human trafficking also creates other social problems such as illegal use of legal documents, forgery, gang activities, etc. [3]
4. The rest of this section focuses on one form of human trafficking and how it links to prostitution. [8]. See also the *Migrant Workers* section.
5. Netherlands and Germany are two countries that legalized prostitution. After legalization, there was a dramatic increase in trafficking of women and children into these countries. This occurred because legalization promotes sex tourism, which creates a market for "an increasing variety of women and younger children" for sex services [7, p169-70]
6. This is tightly related to gender, race and age equality, especially viewing this from a local perspective. As long as a society is developed and structured in a way that limits the expression and practice of gender, race and age equality, women and children would continue to be made vulnerable by such society.
7. Rahab ministers to Asian women that work in the sex industry within the Greater Toronto Area.
8. The women might continue to hide even when they leave the sex industry. As Jackson et al suggested, "being found out also affects the women's ability or desire to see other types of employment, and may be one of the greatest obstacles to moving to other occupations or jobs...[prostitution is] a label that cannot be shed, and one that is a constant reminder of one's inferior status in the world" [14, p266]. Moreover, being found out would make them vulnerable to harassment even though they might be working in a regular work environment. They might also be harassed by ex-customers and become stigmatized when their co-workers and/or employer found out. Therefore, prostitution is truly "a label that cannot be shed" (either by the person herself, or. by others) no matter how hard she tries to hide it.
9. This process can also be understood from the perspective of slavery. The abuse and violence that the girls go through eventually destroy their ability to discern the evil done to them. When they begin to assume this false persona, which is a direct product of prostitution, it signifies the acceptance of their role and identity as a sex object. This is a sign of complete enslavement [18].
10. See Jacques Ellul: *The Power of Money* for further elaboration.
11. For a list of Rahab's activities please see Appendix A
12. Ezekiel's extended prophesy against Jerusalem as recorded in Ezekiel 16 is a good example.
13. Ray S. Anderson, (1991) *On Being Human: Essays in Theological Anthropology*. (WIPF & STOCK: Eugene, Oregon),166.
14. Anderson, *Being Human*, 108.
15. Ibid., 125.
16. Ibid., 126.
17. Anderson, *Being Human*, 151.

18. Ibid., 83. Refusal to hear too constitutes disobedience, since God's speech creates the capacity for hearing. Denying the ability hear is therefore tantamount to turning our back on God.

19. Ibid.,78

20. Here we can see that faith transcends ethics as universal ethical principles call for the extermination of the violator. Yet God upholds the humanity of all and the community of faith has to act in obedience to the personal Word of God rather than conformance to impersonal moral or ethical codes. To view murderers, abusers and other violaters as human requires that we transcend our natural inclination to despise them and seek retribution in obedience to the Word of God that calls us to transcend our innate responses and to leave judgment and vengeance to Him. This does not mean, however, that they should be allowed to continue their destruction, but rather that we continue to view them as human and to remember that they too still bear the *Imago*. Please read Anderson chapter 10 "Being human in fear and trembling" to elucidate the awesome human responsibility to act in accordance not with universal ethical principles but by faith in accordance with the Word of God in the concrete circumstances of our own lives so that we might liberate people from disorder and bring humanity back to obedience to the divine command (Anderson, *Being Human*, 154 - 157)

21. Anderson, *Being Human*, 129.

22. In the 16th century Cardinal Contarini built houses where women who had worked as prostitutes could live and be provided for. This is an example of the practical arrangements that are required in order to help the women make a transition out of the industry. Much other help will also be required because the spiritual, emotional and psychological damage that the women suffered will also need to be addressed.

III. Rahab Ministry Activities

1) Weekly outreach to massage parlors in Greater Toronto area

    a) 95% on our outreach list are Asians (particularly Chinese), 5% are Eastern Europeans

2) Prayer meeting partnering with a downtown church for Rahab ministry; once a month

    a) This same church has developed a plan to take in women who would like to join/visit the faith community

    b) A few mature Christian women have committed themselves to follow up and care for any of the girls who would like to join church life. These women were originally part of the Rahab prayer meetings

3) Getting together with another church to make sandwiches for a partner ministry within Youth Unlimited that serves homeless people. The sandwich group runs once a week and some of the women that Rahab ministers to volunteer their services with this group. As a result Rahab:

    a) Gets another opportunity to interact with the women

    b) Helps the women discover their skills

    c) Can issue volunteer hours for women who need the hours for their various government applications/programs

    d) Gets an opportunity to pray for the women and share their burden

4) Rahab partners with another downtown church to care for the women's' children

    a) Many of the women have children, some of whom are very young.

    b) Rahab has helped to connect two of the youths to a local church and they attend church youth activities/meetings regularly

5) Rahab partners with a downtown church to provide ESL classes for women in the downtown Toronto area

6) Rahab partners with brothers/sisters who have a heart to serve these women by offering private English and computer lessons. These programs provide:

a) an opportunity to get to know the women better

   b) usable job and communication skills which would help the women to transition out of this industry

   c) opportunities to pray for the women

7) Speaking at Church Fellowships and to small groups to introduce Rahab Ministries and raise awareness of the issues pertaining to sex workers

8) Participating in prayer walks with church small groups

9) Rahab has organized special sessions that address specific needs of the women such as:

   a) Prostitution Law change session: invited two Toronto Police Officers to explain the changes and updates

   b) Immigration information session: invited an immigration consultant to answer questions that the girls have regarding matters related to immigration

   c) Health information session (in planning stage): invite nurses and/or doctor to answer questions that the girls have concerning their health

   d) Legal information session (in planning stage): invite lawyers (family law lawyer, criminal law lawyer) to answer legal questions that the girls have; provide information concerning their rights

10) Other services provided on an on-call basis:

    a) Translation for immigration offices, police offices, etc.

    b) Arranging short term safe homes for the women

    c) Visiting women in immigration hold situations

    d) prison visitations

    e) providing transportation for the women

    f) addressing various other immediate needs

11) networking and building relationship with other organizations and agencies that serve the same group of women (both local and overseas)

12) Providing an educational program for girls who are in prison due to prostitution (in planning stage)

Part Two

Interpretation

Chapter One:

Renewal Modern and Ancient: Reflections from Table One

WILLIAM J. ABRAHAM

It is hard to think of a more incongruous juxtaposition: a rerun of the Revivalist tradition in East Africa and the invigorating presence of the Coptic Church in contemporary Canada.[1] It is tempting to link them merely in terms of geography: they both are connected to the great continent of Africa. However, there the comparison ends, for (it will be said) there is no deep thematic or material continuity. Look below the surface, however, and a fascinating connection emerges both historically and theologically. The two case studies are related by underground activities of the Spirit that are all too readily lost in the search for contemporary sociologically or psychologically oriented conceptions of renewal. Moreover, there are salutary lessons for our whole approach to renewal, an approach than can readily lose its bearings in scholarly labors and bring the whole enterprise of renewal to a screeching halt.

The East African Revival figures from time to time in tales of renewal in the history of recent Christianity. It is not entirely unknown, at least to those who have cultivated an interest in the renewal of the church today. My own impression is that it makes manifest the spirit of revival that one comes across in students from other parts of Africa who show up in seminary classes. I recall the excitement of a student from Zimbabwe in a course I taught on revival in the history of evangelism who, in the work of Charles Finney,

---

1. See Kevin Ward, "The East Africa Revival and the Revitalization of Christianity;" and Fr. Pishoy Salama, "St. Maurice and St. Veronica Coptic Orthodox Church."

had at long last found a theologian who resonated with her own experience of the church back home. It became obvious in the course of the semester that the extraordinary liveliness of her home church was a continuation and development of eighteenth and nineteenth century revivalism that had been transmitted by the missionaries who brought the Gospel to her ancestors in the faith. The ethos and practices of revivalism in North America struck a chord of recognition that made more sense to her than the standard accounts of what she was supposed to feel and think as mediated by contemporaries who claimed to speak on behalf of her people and their history.

Kevin Ward has provided us with a splendid review of the revival identified as the Balokole by its leaders; his review combines the analytical tools of the contemporary historian with the witness of insider participants. One crucial feature of the revival was that its focus was the revitalization of conventional Protestant denominations (Anglican, Presbyterian, Methodist, Lutheran, and Mennonite). The whole point of the revival was not to invent a new version of Christianity from scratch, as often happens in restorationist movements, but to breathe new life into existing ecclesial existence. The aim was to revive real Christianity in world where church members had become complacent, cold, nominal, merely formal, compromised, and the like. Once up and running, the fire could then spread back up the institutional channels available and have an impact on evangelical circles in Britain and the United States.

We might see this as a reapporpriation of the classical revivalism of the Western Protestant tradition. It begins with an intense sense of alienation and dissatisfaction with existing church life that leads to the reawakening of interest in intense forms of spiritual encounter. It ends with the recovery of nerve in mission, the development of new missionary practice, the cultivation of holiness, and more often than not the promotion of cultural and social service. These are very substantial gains in any serious reckoning of renewal in the contemporary church in the West. They do not come on the cheap; those involved invariably have to endure the ridicule of those they seek to help in spiritual renewal.

The practices that are central to the East African Revival are not difficult to enumerate. They include small group meetings and large conventions (the former providing intimacy and pastoral care; the latter giving a sense of universality and non-parochial significance); passionate commitment to scripture, to the centrality of the cross and the Lordship of Christ in Christian teaching, and to conscious experience of repentance and new birth; continuing use of testimony and special songs; the aggressive presentation of the Gospel in public preaching; incisive criticism of institutionalism and church bureaucracy; denunciation of compromise; restitution and truth telling in private and public; the cultivation of personal habits conducive to success in education; the deployment of women in ministry; and the practice of discipline and accountability within the small group ministries. Anyone familiar with the history of early Methodism will recognize immediately the continuities that show up here.

Yet it would be a serious mistake to read what is happening as static and monolithic. The core values and practices are subject to improvisation and development across space and time. At times this can lead to internal division and splits. Moreover, one can readily discern the standing problems of how to transmit the core values and practices across the generations; and there is the perennial problem of how to implement the moral convictions of the revival into a public sphere which is rapidly changing and becoming increasingly pluralistic. Equally, there are the challenges that emerge with the arrival of Pentecostalism and with encounter with forms of revival within Roman Catholicism. The general trend is one of cautious but critical accommodation.

The developments that happened in St. Maurice and St. Veronica Orthodox Church in Toronto occupy entirely difference theological and etiological space than that represented by the East Africa Revival. The crucial catalyst for change was not alienation and spiritual apathy much less institutional criticism. It began with the inability of the host church to meet in a realistic fashion the spiritual needs of those who married into the Coptic community and of those who were second and third generation Copts living in the West. The crucial problem was the problem of multi-ethnic and multicultural ministry. Far from this challenge been seen as antithetical to the life of the institutional Church, the first step was to head to Egypt and get sanction for a whole new missionary outlook and practice from Pope Shenouda III, the eighty-four year old patriarch who was suffering from ill-health. What was centrally at issue was not reforming the doctrines of liturgical practices of the church but changing people's attitudes.

The work itself began from within the life and work of the clergy and by practical necessity required lay initiative and involvement. As the vision progressed it became clear that borrowing from Protestant handbooks of evangelism and ministry were essential to success; yet such borrowing in no way compromised the core commitments and practices of the Coptic tradition; they were supplementary and enriching rather than subversive and destructive. The ultimate payoff is nothing less than the future existence and survival of the Coptic Church in the diaspora.

We can immediately identify a point of contact with the East Africa Revival. Both are concerned about the very survival of the Christian tradition as that tradition is put at risk by either collapse from within or pressure from without. Big issues are at stake here, namely, the very identity and survival of Christianity in the contemporary world. We can begin to extend the points of continuity: there is a passion to preserve the faith once delivered to the saints as represented by core doctrines and beliefs; there is a very strong emphasis on prayer; there is a mix of planning and improvisation; there is a dialectic of conserving the true faith and the urge to be relevant and understood by the host community; there is the inevitable deployment of small groups.

Yet the contrasts should not be minimized. We are living in two completely different worlds when we visit the material in hand. On the one hand, we inhabit a phase of establishment Protestantism which has harbored intense suspicion of Catholic forms of Christianity. On the other hand, we inhabit the world of ancient Coptic Christ which would appear to have next to nothing in common with the volatile spirituality of modern Western revivalism transplanted into twentieth-century East Africa. Any effort to connect the two seems doomed to failure from the outset. Consider in addition the following features of the East African Revival. While its adherents and leaders have stayed within the traditional denominational structures, there is a native suspicion of institutions, organizations, and hierarchies as they develop in the life of the church. The persistent identity is that of loyal opposition rather than docile submission to ecclesiastical hierarchy. There is a subversive element that shows up in the reworking of the Christian tradition and in challenging the political status quo. There is an instinctive privileging of scripture that operates with a hermeneutic of suspicion towards liturgical forms, creeds, and human traditions as they show up in Eastern Orthodoxy and Roman Catholicism. The issue can be expressed with simplicity: the East Africa Revival represents a reapporpriation of classical European and American versions of evangelical Christianity; the changes in the Coptic Church in Toronto represent a venerable Ancient form of Christianity in Egypt.

The internal debate about the nature of revival and renewal require that we move beyond the impasse this sharp contrast evokes. We need more at this point than banal efforts to ferret out points of contact and superficial similarities. We need to go deeper and work through both the contemporary challenges and the unseen historical connections that exist.

First, it is obvious that the emergence of globalization forces all Christians to come to terms with the encounter with radically different expressions of Christian faith and practice. This is not an invitation to some kind of lazy relativism; we have to make firm decisions on the identity and continuity of the Christian tradition. The internal differences between evangelical Protestantism and, say, Coptic Christianity, on how to discern authentic Christianity and the true Church are long-standing and real. However, the stark exclusivism that has marked their histories no longer holds. We can readily discern the work of Christ in each other's life and practices. This means in time the emergence of a new vision of ecumenism that focuses on what we share in the life of the Holy Spirit as good gifts rather than simply work on the convergence of what we have in common.

Second, it is obvious that as the conversation on renewal develops we can see that a crucial impetus to renewal is the challenge of survival and, related to this, the challenge of the new missionary situation in which we now find ourselves both inside and outside the West. Reaching out not just in service to our neighborhoods but in effective forms of evangelism to win and establish new converts in the faith require that church leaders find ways to renew the life existing congregations from top to bottom. We cannot have a recovery of missionary nerve and practice without a theological and spiritual recovery of nerve. This can very clearly be seen in the failure of the leadership of The United Methodist Church to come to terms with the demands of missionary work in the West. The issue is not one of lack of sincerity or lack of effort in restructuring the life of United Methodism. Nor is the issue one of commitment to missionary endeavor. The challenge is to deal systematically over time with the doctrinal and spiritual deficit that has developed in the twentieth century and began in earnest in the late nineteenth century. The judgment that we can meet the missionary challenge of our time essentially by slogans, bureaucratic decree, restructuring, and the imposition of these from above, all the while neglecting the Gospel, the great faith of the Church, prayer, and effective spiritual formation, has run aground, as happened so dramatically at the General Conference of 2012. Yet we should not despair; it is a mistake to think we can meet the challenges of mission immediately or in one generation. We need to revisit the challenge of mission and look again at the comprehensive changes that are needed in the life of the church. Even then, we can trust that providence will harvest what rightly remains of our failed efforts in the current generation.

Third, while we should welcome any and every aid in thinking accurately about the renewal of the Church, and while we should expect there to be enrichment and even significant reform of our initial descriptions and intuitions about renewal as we proceed, there is a real danger that the whole idea of renewal itself ceases to be conceptually and hence practically useful. Not every change for the better is best described as a form or instance of renewal. I think that the Coptic participants are correct to eschew the language of renewal in the accounts of the changes they are implementing in Toronto. We might, of course, say that the Coptic Church is being renewed in its missionary endeavors. However, I think that the language of renewal as it shows up in revivalism and its offspring in evangelical Christianity is more than this. It speaks to much more than the renovation of this or that practice and looks to the recovery of the very heart of the Christian faith itself. There are risks to this disposition which show up in intolerance, in myopia about the place of institutions and offices in the life of the Church, in the tendency to division and schism, in doctrines of radical fall in the history of the church, and in delusional forms of ecclesial utopianism. However, the deep insight is that renewal will involve theological judgments about the meaning of Christianity and not merely this or that innovative change in practice and most certainly not merely secular accounts of revitalization. Unless our work in renewal reaches this level of engagement we shall not have made much progress.

Fourth, it is precisely at this point that we need to take a closer look at the potential for cross fertilization between revivals as seen in East Africa and the identity and resources of the Coptic tradition.

Begin with this observation. The revival represented by Methodism in the eighteenth century was deeply influenced by John Wesley's rediscovery and appropriation of ancient Christianity. This was not a simple or easy journey for Wesley. On the one hand, he found himself in a movement of the Holy Spirit that was genuinely contemporary. Moreover, as a result of his own historical studies, he rejected the conventional High Church reading of the Ancient Church that insisted, for example, on the historic episcopacy. On the other hand, he provided a re-reading of the early life of the first three centuries of the Church that drew on contemporary experience and innovation.

Thus he was insistent that what was happening was a recovery of ancient, primitive Christianity. Thus one crucial fountain head of revival that in time played out in East Africa did not reject ancient Christianity but celebrated the work of God that was visible there. Of course, this kind of historical connection can easily get lost over time. However, what our observation makes clear is that there is no need to play off modern revival against ancient Christianity. On the contrary modern revivalism can learn from the story and developments of ancient Christianity.

Consider a complementary observation. Early Methodism and hence early revivalism can be seen as a form of monasticism for the common Christian. Monasticism was, in fact, one of the earliest forms of renewal in the ancient Church. It was an effort to secure authentic spirituality in the teeth of developing forms of nominal Christianity ushered in by the establishment of Christianity as the official religion of the Roman Empire. It was at one and the same time a lively embrace of the faith as personal and transformative and a real threat to the status quo. It could readily have derailed into the rejection of crucial Christian values, like marriage; it could have become a rival enterprise, syphoning off crucial financial and personal resources; it could have lost the intellectual treasures of the Church in scripture and tradition by turning inward and rejecting the life of the mind in favor of personal piety. Hence it was subject to exactly the kind of pathology that shows up in revivalism. Yet it did not do so; but instead became a crucial reservoir of spiritual nourishment. Modern evangelicals have of late come to see how much it has to learn from the spiritual resources of monasticism and in its own way is experimenting with new forms of monasticism. This is a healthy development. It reveals the potential for fresh cross-fertilization across what initially look like rigid boundaries.

Consider a third observation. What revivalism and monastic Christianity in the Coptic tradition have in common is an intense interest in ascetic theology. The language deployed, of course, is quite different. Revivalism speaks of piety; monasticism of spirituality. The former readily gravitate to talk of new birth, justification, repentance, and the like. The latter often gives the impression of not having a clue about justification and comes across in its model prayers as excessively penitential. However, the potential for a deeper understanding of the Christian life is enormous. If a Coptic congregation can learn from evangelical resources on evangelism and outreach, revivalists and evangelicals can plunder the Coptic tradition for similar treasures doctrinally and spiritually.

Permit yet one more observation. As I mentioned above, the monastic tradition could all to quickly have gone off the rails; its best practices and insights could easily have been set against the institutional life of the Church. The results of such a development would have been tragic. However, the reason this did not happen was relatively simple. The wider church happily had far-sighted and wise leaders, like Athanasius in the fourth century, who readily saw the need to harvest the fruit of monasticism and integrate it into the life of the Church as a whole. This is clearly what has happened in part in

East Africa. Regrettably it has not happened as often as it should have in the West. What is at issue here is the need for contemporary bishops and their colleagues down the line in the establishment to harvest the fruit of renewal and ensure that that fruit is not lost to the Church as a whole. Alternatively, as the experience in parts of East Africa reveals, we must simply wait patiently until those who have been transformed by revival and renewal become in time leaders of the church in the West.

The obvious objection to this raft of constructive proposals is to say that neither evangelicalism nor Coptic Christianity can really embrace the kind of borrowing and cross-fertilization I am recommending. What we really have are two totally irreconcilable versions of Christianity that should be far more critical in their disposition towards each other. We can readily imagine aggressive adherents of both sides coming to agreement on this stance. They could, and no doubt will, defend their respective dispositions in terms of a defense of preserving the authentic gospel, the true Church, the faith once delivered to the saints, the non-negotiable core of orthodoxy, and the like. I welcome this kind of contestation, for, as I noted above, revivalists are committed to nothing less than the recovery of authentic faith within their denominational homelands. The concern is for the real thing and the interest is neither causal nor superficial. They are not afraid to call into questions developments where the Gospel gets lost in the name of creative innovation or under the banner of liberal or progressive reform. So we can expect worries about betrayal and apostasy from critics of the positive suggestions I have enumerated. The crucial question is how we deal with these developments. Do we simply dig deeper into our ecclesial ghettos and hold the stranger at bay? Or do we patiently listen and learn?

Three comments are needed to back up the second response. First, neither evangelical Christianity nor Coptic Christianity should be read as monolithic, rigid entities. They are inwardly contested; and they change across space and time. Globalization and immigration only serve to force them to learn from each other and assimilate each other's treasures of faith and practice. Second, the kind of exclusivism expressed in the objection under review is a deep denial of the work of the Spirit in our midst. This can only be sustained in the teeth of the signs of the Spirit's work across our divisions. At best it is a matter of spiritual ignorance; at worst it is a form of blasphemy against the action of the Holy Spirit. Third, and most importantly, what is really at issue here are rival ecclesiologies that can benefit from vigorous, self-searching criticism of each other's proposals. It is not enough, theologically speaking, to sit pat on our privileged identities and ignore the alternatives offered by other serious Christians who share our passion for renewal. Renewal itself requires we go all the way to the bottom and think through what is needed for the comprehensive renewal of the Church today. We need all hands on deck at that point, whatever their ecclesial disagreements may be; and we need to make a virtue out of those disagreements in thinking through how best to understand the Church.

Renewal in the end is an ecclesiological and theological matter of the first importance. We cannot have renewed churches unless we have a relatively thick description of what the Church truly is before God. For my part, by far the best ecclesiology is one that sees the Church as a gift of the Spirit to the world; we need a pneumatologically oriented ecclesiology. What exactly that means is an issue for another occasion. At the very least such an ecclesiology will be keen to appropriate all that the Holy Spirit seeks so generously to make available to all Christians across space and time. Hence it can readily be rooted initially either in the work of revival as seen in East Africa or in the work of the Holy Spirit in the Church which spread from Jerusalem to Egypt and which continues in the life of the Coptic Church today. The wise observer will make sure that in the end we receive and cultivate all the gifts the Holy Spirit has so generally poured out upon God's people across space and time.

Chapter Two

Mosaic Cultural Ministry in the Interface of Koeran and Southeast Asian Communities: Reflections from Table Two

Paul Seungoh Chung, PhD

In our questions rest the seeds of our answers. That is, what we ask, and how we ask it, defines, shapes or even limits what we eventually learn. However, the questions we ask arise from where we are. Take the term, "Christian revitalization." How the West understands this process is based on its historical memory of the Church *re*forming and *re*vitalizing itself for two thousand years amid the changing religious, social, and intellectual climes.[1] Despite the waning and waxing of its influence, Christianity had an ubiquitous and constant presence in the West, and this, I believe, is inseparable to the self-understanding of Western Christianity. However, what of the *new* churches of the world, with considerably shorter history? What of those who are the first Christians in their respective culture or nation? What of those who do not see themselves living in a *post*-Christian society, where the Church needs *revitalization*, but in a *non*-Christian world, which needs *evangelization*? In what sense are their ministries "*re*-vitalization?" How would these Christians describe what they are doing? The Mosaic Cultural Ministry and Greenhills Christian Fellowship, along with several other case-studies presented in the Consultation at Toronto, begin precisely from these questions, and thereby compel us to re-think what "revitalization" means for Christianity.

What is being Revitalized?

The conceptual framework through which the case-studies of revitalization movements in Christianity was examined, both in the previous volumes and in the consultation at Toronto, is derived from the work of Anthony F. C. Wallace. Wallace defined revitalization as "deliberate, conscious, organized efforts by members of a society to create a more satisfying culture," when the existing culture fails in its role to meet the physical and psychological needs of the society and its members.[2] Thus, a culture may transition from a steady state, in which it fulfils its role, to a period of stress where it fails to do so and the needs of its individual are no longer met. This leads to a period of cultural distortion where its beliefs and practices become increasingly less coherent, convincing, or workable. At this point, a culture may undergo "revitalization," and Wallace argued that there is a common set of patterns or stages to such revitalization movements, including a number of revival movements in Christianity.[3]

Wallace's theory has been revised and expanded since. Some questioned his assumption that there is a relatively unchanging "steady-state" to cultures, and critiqued his overemphasis on individualistic psychology and cognitive dimension to revitalization process, while others asked how his theory ought to be applied in the contemporary setting of an "urbanized, globalized world," with numerous diaspora communities living in major cities.[4] From the Christian perspective, his account lacked the dimension of Divine initiative and intervention by the Triune God. This critical discussion, from Wallace onward, thus formed the basis for the questions regarding the experience of Divine action, human needs, and social forces and changes, particularly in the setting of cosmopolitan Toronto, which largely framed and constituted the presentation and understanding of each case-study in the Consultation *as* a revitalization movement.[5]

To a great extent, this framework did successfully identify the different factors and experiences that shaped both the Mosaic Cultural Ministry at Young Nak, and the Greenhills Christian Fellowship.[6] For example, the city of Toronto, with its numerous diaspora communities from diverse cultures and ethnic groups, presented a very different sociocultural setting and thus a different kind of mission field. It has compelled both ministries to understand its mission in a global context, seeing beyond its local ministry to having a vision and detailed strategy of impacting the people of all nations and cultures of the world. Both ministries have been propelled by experiences of Divine provision and intervention, and strongly see a plan of God in how Toronto has become a home to the immigrants and foreign students from places that were predominantly non-Christian, or even hostile to Christianity, presenting unprecedented opportunities to the Church for engagement and proclamation of the Gospel. Also, as churches planted by, and successfully flourishing in diaspora communities, both have drawn from their past experience to formulate their own approach to church planting and building to pioneer new churches in similar situations. The actual physical and psychological needs of individuals within the diaspora communities that both ministries have encountered have led them to hold a more holistic conception of evangelization, where social work, charity, and genuine personal friendship is an inseparable part of presenting the gospel of Jesus Christ. Simply put, the existing questions and framework enabled the participants to analyze how these novel approaches to planting new churches were borne out of an awareness of Divine providence, and in response to their particular sociocultural setting.

However, one of the notable features of the narratives of Mosaic Cultural Ministry and the Greenhills Christian Fellowship is the lack of dissatisfaction by individuals or by groups regarding how their "culture," or rather their church, is failing to meet their needs, and thus needing "revitalization." There was no indication that any problem in their beliefs or practices has served as the impetus for their new formulation and vision of ministry and mission. Young Nak church, which hosts the Mosaic Cultural Ministry, and the Greenhills Fellowship church in Philippines, from which its offspring in Toronto was commissioned, are both thriving, and continuously growing congregations. There is in this sense, no clear *object* of *"re-vitalization."* This absence was apparent also in many of the other cases in the Toronto Consultation, as noted by a number of participants.[7] Furthermore, the actual terms and wording that those who participated in the Consultation *used,* to describe what was happening were not only *uniquely Christian,* but lacked for the most part the kind of language that would be consistent with the metaphor of revitalization – that of bringing a dying organism back to life. Rather, they spoke of "making disciples," "new mission field," the "harvest," "heart of God," and the "sovereign plan and provision of God."

What then is being *revitalized* in these movements? Of course, there seems something vital and significant about these ministries. However, are we to include every such ministry under the umbrella of the term, "revitalization?" Could we do so without risking the loss of all useful meaning of the term? One answer is that such movements energize the churches involved. The churches in question were already flourishing. One may easily say the reverse and argue that because the churches are *already* "vital," that these movements began. Another answer may be that such movements revitalize the increasingly diminishing Christianity in the West. Certainly, members of Mosaic Cultural Ministry and Greenhills Christian Fellowship specifically identified the secular West, including Canada, not as a Christian or even a *post*-Christian society, but a place that need *missionaries,* much as their homelands, Korea and Phillipines once did. However, their words are the language of *evangelization,* not revitalization. Furthermore, such "revitalization" or perhaps "re-evangelization," has not yet happened; if anything, it may even be that the unanswered intellectual and social critiques and controversies that have challenged Christianity in the West, will simply make their force known to the more "vital" churches in the rest of the world, as their respective societies "modernize." At this point, I, as one of the "insiders" of the case of Mosaic

Cultural Ministry, am afforded the frankness to ask this question: is Mosaic Cultural Ministry, for example, really a revitalization movement?

What do we recognize as Revitalizing?

Again, in our question there rests the seed of answers. *Why* consider the ministries examined in the Consultation, such as Mosaic Cultural Ministry, as "revitalization movements" in the first place? Why were they – or rather, we – *selected*? After all, none of the ministries *labelled* itself as a "revitalization movement." None of these movements have had significant evangelical, social, or cultural impact that has brought about a "revitalization" of Christianity in the larger world; again, the *potential* is there, but most of these ministries are still relatively small in terms of the scale and the number of people involved. It cannot be that each fulfilled some sort of a check-list of criteria that define "revitalization" in some theory of revitalization, since the discussion whether they do so came *after* the selection, and the question of how we are to understand and describe Christian revitalization is that which was still being asked at the Consultation. Then, why did the conference organizers decide that *these* should be the cases, the stories, they ought to examine to understand Revitalization?

If I were to organize a consultation on the subject of Christian revitalization, what would we be looking for? Perhaps we would use a kind of heuristics, which identifies some general features that these ministries share with the previously examined examples of revitalization movements from other consultations. However, prior to detailed discussion and examination of each ministry, what would be the deciding factor that identifies these as revitalization movements?

First, it entailed a recognition of sorts. That is, we somehow *recognized the presence of God* in each ministry, that the "hand of God was upon it," so to speak. However, this is still too vague, since we say God is present and at work *everywhere, everywhen* and in *everything*. This is not theological hair-splitting; what it is precisely we are recognizing, as the "presence of God" *in this context* may pinpoint what we seem unconsciously to recognize as revitalization in Christianity. Again, thinking back, I, *as a Christian*, concerned about revitalization of the Church myself, recognized in each ministry the transforming power of the *Gospel* of Jesus Christ at work, which reveals therefore the undeniable hand of God. Yet again, is that not simply the definition of what the Church ideally does?

In the six case-studies, it may be observed that not only could we recognize the presence of God and the transforming power of the Gospel, but this was found particularly in *unexpected* or even *abandoned* places – that is, I saw God working in areas where *I* previously neither *perceived nor even imagined that* He would be working. There was, therefore, a sense of surprise at what each ministry is doing. The Rahab ministry and the Jesus Network reached out to groups that were, for social, cultural, or economic reasons, generally overlooked or even excluded from both the mainstream society and Christian ministry. Their main theme of Incarnational ministry is literally a call for the *living presence* of God, by *becoming* the people in which the Gospel is embodied, *in* the midst of these groups where the Gospel and its reality has been *absent*. East African Revival movement was a call to be a living witness of the Gospel and holy living in a society and more importantly, the Church, which has *lost* this witness. St. Maurice and St. Verena Coptic Orthodox Church recounts how a Christian tradition, which one might have presumed to be constrained largely to Egypt and its culture, transformed itself to be both faithful to its particular tradition, yet be relevant, vibrant, and growing witness to the Gospel in a very different culture of Canada. Finally, Greenhills Christian Fellowship plants churches *intentionally* where there are few or no active churches, and it becomes involved in the communities there to live out and present the Gospel, while Mosaic Cultural Ministry proclaims the providence of God in the multicultural setting of Toronto, and envisions a place in which the Gospel becomes *inescapably present* in diaspora communities from cultures where it was previously and conspicuously absent. Even the city of Toronto exemplifies our increasingly secular, post-Christian, pluralistic society, *yet* these ministries began and are thriving within it.

The imagery these ministries present is not so much a dying creature being revived, but that of a vast painting, or a construction being completed. That is, the presence of God "enters" places we once believed were devoid of His presence, as if each of these revitalization movements is a stroke of a Divine paintbrush that dances across different blank portions of a canvas. Such a "blank" place may literally be a geographic area, where the Gospel was rarely if ever proclaimed. Or, it may be a particular people-group, or a marginalized, forgotten segment of society. Even more abstractly, it involves different spheres of our society and culture, in how we do business, run economies, bring forth arts and literature, pursue scientific or philosophical truth, and so on. Whenever the presence of God – indeed, the Spirit of God – comes to indwell and transform these groups, or a particular sphere of our life, where once we did not perceive His presence, we seem to recognize as a moment of "revitalization." Of course, too many times it is the churches themselves, which have become devoid of the presence of God, needing just such revitalization, but, in the cases examined in the Toronto Consultation, especially the Mosaic Cultural Ministry and Greenhills Christan Fellowship, Christian revitalization seems to reach "outward," beyond the Church.

Furthermore, there seems to be an inherent narrative to such a movement to this transforming work of God – a *uniquely Christian* narrative. Past consultations and discussions, I believe, have recognized this narrative, calling it the *Missio Dei*, the Mission of God, although I would also call it colloquially the "march of the Kingdom of God."

Revitalization, the *Missio Dei* and the Promised *Eschaton*

Let me take a brief detour to a passing remark by Michael Rynkiewich in the previous volume regarding how Thomas Kuhn has demonstrated that "science began to accrue some of the characteristics of religion."[8] Many have observed the parallel between the reigning scientific paradigms described by Kuhn and the the theological paradigm in religion.[9] However, one of the more interesting questions that Kuhn's work raised is what justifies the periodic revolutionary shifts in a comprehensive, overarching theoretical framework – namely, the reigning paradigm – throughout the history of science? Since the standard of justification and definition of "evidence" for each new paradigm is incommensurable with its predecessor, it seemed to suggest that there was no rational reason why scientists would choose the new paradigm over the old.

In one interesting response, Alasdair MacIntyre argued that the rationality of choosing one paradigm over another is understood only through the historical narrative of that particular science. However, according to his later works, such a narrative is a very particular kind of narrative; it is a narrative of the journey toward the particular *telos* – or goals – of the practice. In the case of science, this would be the complete knowledge of the fundamental laws of nature that explain all the workings of the universe. The historical narrative of the practice, including its sometimes revolutionary changes, describes how the difficulties, problems, and obstacles in its progress to the ultimate *telos* have been overcome so far, bringing its journey closer to its *telos*. It is this *telos*-centered narrative that explains why scientists would abandon or adopt different paradigms.[10] However, the general conception of what this *telos*, or the *end*-state would be like, such as the complete scientific knowledge of the universe, is defined by a kind of primary exemplar – let me call this the *alpha* paradigm – a particular accomplishment in the past, which initiated the practice in its current form.[11]

It is not my purpose, by any means, merely to present yet another parallel between religion and science. What I am suggesting is that there is a certain kind of action, of which scientific inquiry is but one variant, in which just such a telos-centered historical narrative is essential to understanding it – that is, any kind of practice that has a particular purpose, which is to journey toward a definitive, though yet-unreached and distant, historical end-point. Christian revitalization is just such a practice.

The Anatomy of Large-Scale *Telos*-Driven Practice

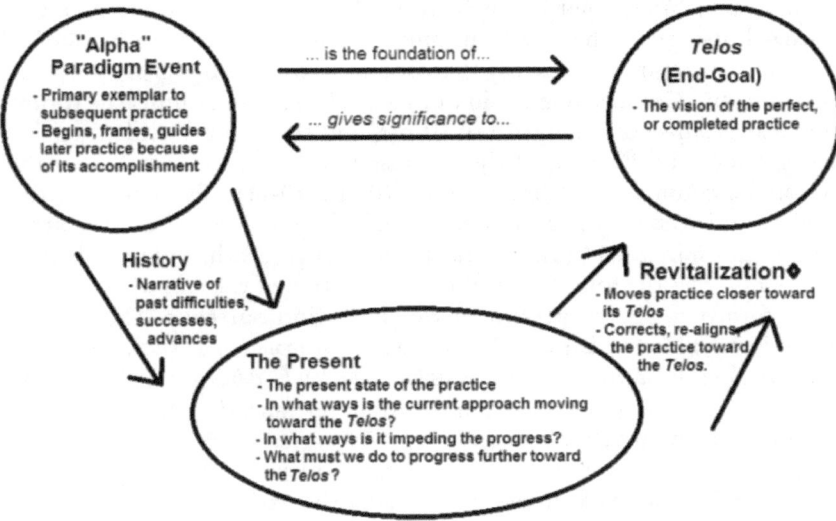

The narrative inherent to the revitalization movements examined in the Consultation. This is the narrative of the *Missio Dei*, that of God's redemption and salvation history, which begins from the very moment of the Fall. It continues through the entire history of humanity and particularly of Israel, and culminates in the life, crucifixion, and the resurrection of Christ, the fullness of which then unfolds through the Church, by the power of the Holy Spirit, until its final, eschatological fulfilment in the promised return of Christ. Christian "revitalization" is defined by an understanding of the Church and its place in this salvation history – between the saving work of Christ, and His promised return. As such, the participants of revitalization, either implicitly or explicitly, understand themselves to be a *part* of this grand biblical narrative of the *Missio Dei*. Furthermore, this narrative has a *directionality* – that is, their ministry is participating in a particular way to the course of salvation history that is *leading* to an eschatological *telos*. Thus, both the Mosaic Cultural Ministry and the Greenhills Christian Fellowship understand themselves as fulfilling the Great Commission, to "make disciples to the ends of the Earth." They aim toward an eschatological end in which every nation, tribe, and tongue will confess that Jesus is Lord. Their ministry is quite literally a particular strategy to bring the present closer to this *end*.

This narrative understanding of Christian revitalization movements requires then three points of reference in history to orient itself. First is the past, which includes the biblical narrative of the Gospel of Jesus Christ, which is what I would call the "alpha paradigm" of Christian living. This is followed by the first apostolic Church, and the subsequent history and the traditions of the Church, including its past struggles, accomplishments, and revival movements. For both Mosaic Cultural Ministry and Greenhills Christian Fellowship, this included their history of how their respective homelands were evangelized. It is from this, we form our understanding of the Kingdom of God – that is, what it means to say that God has saved, God was present, God has worked, and God has reigned in our past. The second point is the future, the biblical promise of the return of Christ, and the point in which we find the eschatological fulfilment of the promise that "every knee shall bow and every tongue confess that Christ is Lord (Phil 2:10-11)." Furthermore, this biblical narrative about the past is inseparable from the promised end – that is, the revelation in Jesus Christ in His life, teachings, death, and resurrection, and the Church, is the foundation of the completion of the *Missio Dei*.

The third point is the present in which we find ourselves. The primary question is, *from what we know God has revealed to us about His Kingdom in the past, what is to be done in the present, to propel us toward what God has promised shall come in the future*? Ii is here proposed that a Christian revitalization movement is by definition an answer to *this* question.

The general answer, of course, is quite easily answered. It is to participate in the *Missio Dei*, the work of God in bringing the world to Himself. It is to bring people to confess that Christ is Saviour *and* Lord, to change people, societies, and cultures, *so that* they conform to the reign of Christ. Again, it is the past – the biblical revelation, historical experience of the church – that informs our understanding of what it means to conform to the Kingdom of God. However, it appears that the aspect of *re*vitalization specifically occurs when the Spirit of God *re-equips* the Church to bring that which presently is *not* under the reign of Christ – people, societies, cultures, churches(!), etc. – into His reign. This may happen when the churches have somehow lost the living presence and thus the reign of God, which in terms of biblical narrative, would resemble the Prodigal Son, or the faithless Israel, and so forth. In such cases, a revitalization movement transforms the Church to bring it *back* into the reign of God. However, many times, as with the case-studies in the Toronto Consultation, this *Missio Dei* is directed *outward*, because Christian revitalization is not merely a movement from the vital past – by reformulation of culture – to the present, but a movement from the present *toward* the promised *eschaton*. Such movements, thereby, seek *new domains* in which the Gospel of Christ may be lived out, and the Kingdom of God may be realized.

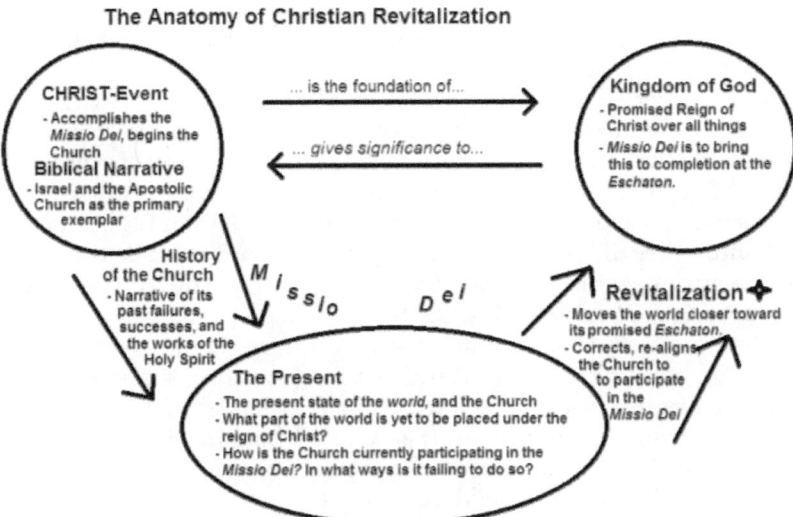

The Anatomy of Christian Revitalization

To do so requires changes to the established pattern of how the Church interacts with the society, or communicates the Gospel, thus giving rise to new forms of ministries. However, the *impetus* for such movements lies not in the particular state of the church or Christian communities in question, but in the overarching narrative of the *Missio Dei*. What "revitalization" movements in Christianity, "revitalize" is *not* necessarily the vitality of the particular church or faith community to *perpetuate itself*, but the vitality of the Church to *move the world toward its promised eschatological end*. This opens many possible answers to what it means to participate in this Kingdom narrative. To bring the reign of God to "new domains" may mean evangelical work to new *geographical* areas, but it may mean different, hitherto overlooked segments or different cultures or worldviews, or even how our social, economic, or intellectual world operates.[12] Thus, a myriad of possible, "mini-revitalizations" may therefore occur in the history of the Church. On the other hand, different aspects of the *Missio Dei* may come to be understood, rightly, as a *single* ministry, as was suggested by the increasing awareness that evangelization and social work go hand in hand. This may reflect ministry representing note *separate* activities, but a *singular* act of bringing the world closer to what that ministry envisions to be the coming Kingdom of God, under the reign of Christ.

This also explains one of the seemingly peculiar conclusions by the participants examining the Greenhills Christian Fellowship and the Mosaic Cultural Ministry. Both have seemingly contradictory visions of the church, the former intentionally seeking to build *multi*cultural churches, while the latter intentionally planting *mono*cultural churches of their target groups. However, unanimously, both groups recognized the importance of the other's approaches. Yet, this would be odd indeed if the purpose of revitalization movement is merely a new vision of what church ought to be. However, if the purpose of revitalization is not a new vision of the Church per se, but any activity that further fulfils the *Missio Dei* and propels the Church forward to its *eschaton*. Then these different visions could readily be seen as complementary.

However, what I have written so far may seem as if these revitalization movements are initiated *by* people, based on their particular beliefs and understandings of the Church's journey to the *eschaton*. Yet, this is what makes the narrative of the Mosaic Cultural Minsitry and Greenhills Christian Fellowship so interesting. According to the stories of both John H.B. Chung and Narry Santos, they did not begin with any clear vision or goal to their ministry. There was no spiritual dissatisfaction on their part toward their church, nor its approach to mission. Indeed, Santos recalls his reluctance and fear when his senior pastor asked him to leave the flourishing ministry in Philippines to plant a church in North America. Chung, who was called into ministry in his late forties in a series of extraordinary events, recalls how fearful he was in even becoming a pastor. Furthermore, he initially did not even know why God seemed to want him to start a ministry of any kind, let alone what Mosaic Cultural Ministry would become. The narratives of Santos and Chung speak not of how they began their ministries out of the dissatisfaction with the existing approaches; rather, they were compelled out of a place of satisfaction and comfort, and into uncharted domains. They did not initiate the events that shaped their respective revitalization movements. The events were *thrust* upon them.

In this sense, the narrative of the *Missio Dei* that propels the Christian revitalization movements is literally the mission *of* God, carried out by God, sometimes *despite* the Church.

Christian revitalization movements are necessarily pieces of a puzzle, the whole of which is the Divine narrative. These movements therefore are necessarily incomplete, not merely in the sense that the Church will need to be revitalized again and again, but in the sense that each movement in itself only completes one particular piece of the narrative toward the eschatological completion of the Kingdom of God. Each movement, furthermore, requires a time to orient itself, to ask *where* it is in the unfolding Divine narrative, and *then* what is to be done. This act of re-orientation is constantly required throughout the history of the Church because if what I have said is correct, the Church is essentially on a *journey*, and it needs *navigation*.

It is perhaps this need for navigation which has brought about this Consultation. Sometimes, theologians and scholars may feel distant from where the action is, seemingly commentating and debating like spectators. However, in this case, they do so *as* Christians, *as* participants of the *Missio Dei*. What they may potentially accomplish – and in my opinion, it is their responsibility to do so – is to serve as navigators, mapping the past journey of the Church, and ever-looking forward to its final promised destination. Thus, they may hopefully better illumine for the rest of us the direction in which God seems to be leading His Church.

Notes

1. The role of the historical memory of the Church in its revitalization is observed by a number of scholars, including a chapter by J. Steven O'Malley, "What is it about Christianity that is ever generating Revitalization and Reform Movements?" in J. Steven O'Malley, ed., *Interpretive Trends in Christian Revitalization for the Early Twenty First Century* (Lexington, Ky: Emeth Press, 2011)

2. Anthony F.C. Wallce, "Revitalization Movements: Some Theoretical Considerations for their Comparative Study," *American Anthropologist* 58: 268-275. The quote is from p. 279. Wallace and his theory of revitalization is mentioned a number of times in the previous volume, *Interpretive Trends in Christian Revitalization for the Early Twenty First Century*.

3. This, of course, is the main body of his work, and his theory of revitalization, though dated – the article was written in 1957 – is still considered a classic in the field of anthropology and sociology. However, for our purpose, I am more interested in the definition of, and the overarching framework within we understand the term "revitalization."

4. A summary of the critical assessment of Wallce's theory in the context of the studies of of World Christian Revitalization is found in Michael A. Rynkiewich, "Models and Myths of Revitalization: Wallace's Theory a Half-Century On," in *Interpretive Trends in Christian Revitalization* and for further discussion on the understanding and definition of Christian revitalization as such, in the same volume, see Eunice L. Irwin, "How Do You Spell Revitalization?" Definitions, Defining Characteristics, Language", 229-244.

5. The different factors, forces, and patterns that shape Christian revitalization, are categorized and described succinctly in the first chapter of the previous volume by Beverly Johnson-Miller, "Dancing with God: The Forms and Forces of Revitalization," in *Interpretive Trends*, 9-20.

6. The details of these two ministries are described in John and Paul Seungoh Chung, and Meesaeng Lee Choi, "Mosaic Cultural Ministry," and Eunice L. Irwin, and Narry F. Santos, "Re-Reading Greenhills Christian Fellowship-Toronto Story for Revitalization Purposes," in the present volume.

7. For example, in what sense is the Rahab Ministry or the Jesus Network is "revitalization?" Both ministries do not speak of unmet needs of individuals *in* the culture – or in this case, the Christian Church – but, rather those *outside* it. It is only the East African Revival that seems to have the feature of the need for "revitalization" in their narratives. For detail, see the East African Revival case in the present volume. The question of what is therefore being "revitalized" was a key question in the final plenary session.

8. Rynkiewich, p.39. The work he refers to is Thomas Kuhn, *The Structures of Scientific Revolutions* (Chicago: University of Chicago Press, 1964).

9. For example, Ian Barbour, *Myths, Models and Metaphors* (New York: Harper Collins, 1974), and see also Barbour, *Religion and Science: Historical and Contemporary Issues* (New York: HarperCollins, 1997), chapter 5.

10. For MacIntyre's work in this regard, see Alasdair MacIntyre, "Epistemological Crises, Dramatic Narratives, and the Philosophy of Science," *The Monist*, no. 60 (1977). See also MacIntyre, *Whose Justice? Which Rationality?* (Notre Dame: University of Notre Dame Press, 1988) and *First Principles, Final Ends and Contemporary Philosophical Issues* (Milwaukee: Marquette University Press, 1990)

11. It is rather a difficult question what such "alpha paradigm" is for a given practice. But, I believe a good candidate for Physics would be Newtons's *Philosophiae Natu-*

ralis Principia Mathematica (1687) which not only was a comprehensive physical theory of the time, but presented the compelling case that every motion in the universe both in the heavens and on the earth may be governed by simple, *discoverable* mathematical laws. Risking over-generalization, the *practice* of physics have ever since been conducted by that *faith*, justified and strengthened by each subsequent scientific successes. MacIntyre also writes about the conception of *arche*, or "First Principles," of an intellectual enquiry but I am expanding on his account by focusing on the particular *accomplishment* or *event*, which forms such a concept.

12. I note here that the ecological aspect of revitalization, raised by Dr. Snyder in the previous volume may be understood as a possible revitalization movement in itself, rather than *an* aspect of Christian revitalization. See Howard A. Snyder, "Renewing the Church, Restoring the Land: The Larger Ecology of Revitalization," in *Interpretive Trends*, 185-196.

Chapter Three

Theological and Missional Perspectives in Light of World Christian Revitalization in Asia: Reflections from Table Three

Bryan T. Froehle

World Christian revitalization in the twenty-first century is "global" in a new way. It must see broadly, in such a way that does not ignore particular people groups, whether large or small. Contemporary social reality simply does not allow religion or religious revitalization to be simply within a single context.

This chapter considers the continent with the world's oldest civilizations, largest populations – and remarkably small number of Christians. World Christian revitalization needs to take account of exactly such a reality, one far removed from a "fortress" like ghetto mentality of other times and places, in light of contemporary challenges. Any understanding of revitalization in the contemporary moment must also take account of the new reality of global urbanity. The twenty-first century is remarkable as the first century in human history to be marked by the global dominance of urban lifestyles and all that this more densely networked lifestyle represents. Perhaps this is nowhere more clear than in the sheer scale of rapid urbanization in East Asia. The internal movement of people in China is on a scale never before seen, as hundreds of millions not only move from rural areas to the long-established metropolises of the eastern Pacific Rim, but even more significantly from rural hinterlands directly to mushrooming provincial cities.

Woven into this new reality is the global city. The new hinterland of the global city is not the area within a 50 or even several hundred miles' radius.

Rather, the new hinterland of the global city are other metropoli around the world. Toronto is a perfect example: the most diverse city in North America, with half of its population born overseas, a plurality of whom are Asian. It is arguably more connected to cities half a world away than to its own backyard: such is the nature of the global city.

Toronto offers remarkable opportunities to supply retroductive warrants regarding world Christian revitalization, particularly in the case of Asian reality and those otherwise ignored as non-persons, as sinners, victims, or followers of alien religions.[1] Retroductively generated arguments regarding world Christian revitalization presented here stem from two in-depth case studies presented earlier in this volume. The first is the Rahab Project, which focuses on the largely Chinese migrant women used as workers in massage parlors throughout Toronto. The second is the Jesus Network, which opens the Christian story to members of the largest, most densely populated, and largely Muslim, South and Central Asian migrant community in Toronto. Both cases are about Asian migrants, both are easily and readily overlooked on the economic, social, and religious scene in Toronto, and yet both represent a critical dimension of reality with which world Christian revitalization must contend.

The Rahab project takes its name from the end of the Exodus story (Joshua 2: 1-21 and Joshua 6: 22-25). As the Canaanite prostitute on whom the Israelite's future depends, and who later becomes spouse to a prominent Israelite leader, Rahab is mother of Boaz and ultimately an ancestor of the royal line and of Jesus. As such, she is a powerful protagonist of deep symbolic resonance in both the Hebrew Scriptures (1Chronicles 2:3-15; Ruth 4:20-22) and the New Testament, as a named ancestor of Jesus (Matthew 1:4), and a critical figure in James (2:25-26), and Hebrews (11:31).[2]

The Jesus Network takes its name from the realization that Muslims have considerable respect for the person of Jesus, mentioned and highly esteemed in the Quran as a major prophet and precursor of Muhammad,[3] even while the word Christian evokes strongly negative images. The term network reflects an approach to sharing the story of Jesus through friendship and family ties in the very large and overwhelmingly Muslim neighborhood where the Network and its members are located.[4]

Those responsible for the Rahab Project and the Jesus Network provided descriptive-empirical studies of their work, which in turn received commentary from outsiders and discussion from a group of scholars and practitioners of diverse backgrounds and Christian commitments. The goal in all this was to consider the data in order to better understand what God is saying through the cases and the implications for the various disciplines and commitments represented. The results offer a broad, interdisciplinary synthesis and call to action suggestive of ways in which world Christian revitalization, as set forth in an earlier volume, *Interpretive Trends in Christian Revitalization from the Early 21st Century*, might be both challenged and corroborated. This in turn promises to lay out groundwork for future work on world Christian revitalization.

Context

Asia through Toronto

If there was such a thing as a "generic" person today, such a person would be Asian and non-Christian. If there were such a thing as a "generic" Christian today, such a person would be a person of color in the global south, a woman living alone with her children in poverty on the fringes of a large urban conglomeration.[5]

The urban reality and the larger globalized socio-economic reality of which it is a part, is intrinsically a product of capitalism in late modernity, where a process of reducing products touched by human work – and humans themselves – to commodities has advanced well beyond earlier levels.[6] This is a political economy, however, never simply an economy, and so it is important to understand power relations as they relate to the image of empire, with its implications for command and control grounded in domination systems based on violence. For this reason, the Jesus Network describes its location as at "the margins of the empire."[7] To be on the margins of empire in what is a powerful global city is typical today. In global cities such as Toronto, distance is now no longer physical but virtual. One can be easily removed from power, at the margins, yet physically very near it. In a sense, this is nothing new, powerful human beings have long seen past marginal ones.

This is exactly what happens to prostitutes and unreached immigrants identified with alien religions. People in dominant, privileged groups – in other words, those neither "public sinners" nor "victims" nor "others"[8] in any way – see right past the powerless as a matter of course and, when necessary, actively, willfully so. Massage parlors are everywhere in Toronto, all in the open – but yet not seen. Such places of prostitution, where sex workers are Asian migrant women trafficked specifically for the purpose, number well over 400, and may be as many as 3,000.[9] They are common everywhere, in the suburbs and central city, yet ignored more than seen. They are also ignored by the churches.[10] Not only are prostitutes far – again, in virtual terms – from the "decent" people, they are also visible minorities.[11] There are thus racial, ethnic underpinnings to the invisibility of prostitutes and unreached migrants.[12] There are also class underpinnings: those who are or aspire to middle class respectability and economic power have good reason to fear the possibility of becoming or remaining forever underprivileged and working class. As those in the Rahab project point out, these divisions point directly to structural evils[13] built into the system, evils that produce and maintain marginalization.[14]

Prostitution

The social psychological process of labeling is a reliable and typical means to produce such marginalization among prostitutes. The neutral, distorting language of the sex trade itself reinforces such marginalization.[15] Sex "workers" serve their "clients," as commonly used language would have it, thus maintaining the deceit that prostituted, sex-trafficked women look for business, rather than being commodified sex sold by another to a purchaser. This is hardly an ordinary business. Certainly for the women encountered by the Rahab project, this work is dehumanizing, reducing women to commodities that are bought and sold.[16] As the Rahab Project notes: "As long as a society is developed and structured in a way that limits expression and practice of gender, race, and age equality, women and children would continue to be made vulnerable by such society."[17]

In such a society, women become all too familiar with betrayal, lies, and deceptions.[18] The Christian church itself bears no small measure of responsibility for this. Countless churches preach now, and have long proclaimed, strong "family values," which often include an underside -- a double standard that prizes "sexual purity" among women more than men, who quietly are permitted a place for, and the acceptability of, sexual activity outside marriage.[19] Today, as this standard changes, it is not to hold men to higher standards, but to reduce them overall. In this way, prostitutes remain as "expendable women whose sexual availability not only serve[s] to satisfy the alleged indefatigable sexual urges of men but also ensure[s] that the honor and integrity of other women would not be threatened." Such a theory of essential differences between women and men results in the everyday acceptance of the commodification of women.[20] And it simply does not work. Far from being held in check, commodification has been a powerful, destructive force even while it has seemingly increased. It is certainly "questionable... to what degree [prostitutes] are sinners [rather than] victims of oppression and injustice.[21]

Yet it is the prostituted who are seen as the face of sin far more than the real criminals, "the barons and entrepreneurs of the sex industry."[22] This goes back to the labeling process described above, and is deeply seated within notions of purity that have found their way into the very heart of the Christian tradition. Yet it is hard to see such notions of sexual purity at the front and center of the Gospels – this is not to deny such values, only to question how they have come to be so very close to "godliness" itself.[23]

Unreached Persons

Prostitutes in Toronto massage parlors, and throughout North America, are not only "public women" – "public sinners" – by definition those seen as rejecting the church (and who often also feel rejected by the church).[24] The Asian women who commonly provide sexual services in massage parlors are also for the most part not baptized Christians. In this, they share marginality with all those people who adhere to truth systems other than Christianity. Nowhere is this more strongly felt that in Asia, given the sheer number of adherents that embrace ancient, deeply rooted religious systems other than Christianity.[25] But perhaps no other system is as marginalized or as threatening as that of Islam, in part because Islam shares with Christianity common roots in the Abrahamic tradition and a similar missionary impulse.

Further, while other religious traditions have declined as a result of revolution and social change, or have been limited in appeal within a particular culture, Islam has grown in population and militancy in areas precisely where it most threatens Christianity, whether in lands where Christians have long been a part or places where both Islam and Christianity are dramatically on the rise, as in Africa today.[26]

Second, Asia is the continent where vast majorities are not Christian and unlikely to be Christian anytime soon. Asia largely explains why a similar proportion of the world is Christian today as in 1900: Asia's very large population accounts overwhelmingly for the majority of the world's population that is not Christian. Further, in those countries (primarily in Europe and the Americas), where Christians once accounted for overwhelming majorities of the population, the Christian proportion has declined, sometimes significantly, due to increases in persons of other faiths and no faith. How then do we understand what God is saying to us today about world Christian revitalization and the future of the world Christian movement precisely at a time when the limits – as well as the gifts – of world evangelism are becoming increasingly clear? What does it mean to be Christian in a situation of global religious pluralism? What does it mean to be a minority faith among many, globally speaking? Questions such as these are central to world Christian revitalization and may perhaps best be explored in Asian cases such as these.

Claims

Three major claims may be made about the future of the world Christian movement based on the data regarding the Rahab Project and the Jesus Network, both of which are oriented toward the Asian community in Toronto, the largest multicultural city in North America. The future of the world Christian movement and ongoing processes of revitalization and renewal are likely to be increasingly distinguished for, (1), a strong incarnational element; (2), a prayerful component, and (3), communal dimensions.

Incarnational

The greatest such emerging emphasis, and the one on which the other two rest, is an incarnational dimension that promises to radically transform reigning theological understandings.

In this, it might be helpful to recall the insights of the Franciscan philosopher-theologian Duns Scotus (1256-1308)[27] and the medieval Franciscan movement more broadly, an experience that arguably prefigured later Christian developments, including the Wesleyan tradition, in important ways.[28] As Duns Scotus well understood, the doctrine of the incarnation offered a different but no less orthodox vantage point on the doctrine of God and soteriology. As the Subtle Doctor put it, "[T]he incarnation of Christ was not foreseen as occasioned by sin, but was immediately foreseen from all eternity by God as a good more proximate end."[29] Such an incarnational focus can be seen reflected well in the opening sentence of *Gaudium et Spes*, a crowning document of the Second Vatican Council:[30] "The joys and the hopes, the griefs and the anxieties of the people of this age, especially those who are poor or in any way afflicted, these are the joys and hopes, the griefs and anxieties of the followers of Christ. Indeed, nothing genuinely human fails to raise an echo in their hearts."[31] The level of embodiment and engagement is striking.

As such theological understandings would suggest, and as the experience of the Jesus Network specifically shows, the principle of incarnation is personal and missional. It is also been a critical part of the Jesus Network since its start: "the incarnational part continues to be foundational."[32]

The incarnation points to God's radical solidarity with humanity and all creation, one that embraces embodiedness and reflects God's love. An emphasis on the primary of an incarnational spirituality is thus deeply relational.

In this way, it again harkens back to Franciscanism and early Methodism, as was observed in the group that examined these cases.[33] Such an incarnational approach is ultimately more about feeling and doing, or practice, than about logical, propositional thinking. As a result, new theological insights may emerge that go far beyond existing theological understandings but are nevertheless perfectly orthodox. For example, the witness that Francis famously gave to the sultan can be seen as an expression of incarnational theology that goes far beyond the *extra ecclesiae nulla salus*[34] formula typical of the times.

While many different accounts exist for Francis' meeting with Sultan Malik al-Kamil of Egypt,[35] common to all is an emphasis on the mutual respect at the heart of their encounter. Francis' openness to such an incarnational, profoundly respectful approach seems to have grown out of his original, foundational encounter with a group of lepers years before, an encounter central to his conversion. In that moment with those most excluded and poorest of his society, he came to the "cardinal insight of his life: namely, that all men and women, regardless of class, economic condition or physical appearance, were brothers and sisters, *fratres et sorores*, one to one another, each fashioned and shaped by the same creator God."[36] Francis' loving, incarnational engagement found inspiration in the embodied forms of prayer characteristic of Islam, involving a mix of standing and prostrating, and touching one's head to the earth. Thus for him, the incarnational led directly to the prayerful, a connection very similar to the experience of the Jesus Network.

This incarnational orientation does not mean a denial of one's experience of Christ and Gospel convictions. Rather, precisely because of those Gospel convictions, the Jesus Network is not about expressing judgment, "just love."[37] "It is about being honest and vulnerable."[38] Something very similar happens in the case of the Rahab Project and its incarnational theological stance towards prostitutes.[39] Such incarnational approaches flow from the Incarnate Word of God, Jesus Christ, for whom the marginalized and oppressed were at the center, not the periphery.[40]

This is about one accompanying the other on a journey together, as equals, to "patiently and lovingly walk alongside" each other.[41] It "involves sharing in the joys and trials" of a common life.[42] An incarnational stance includes rather than excludes, following the pedagogy of Jesus: "come and see,"[43] "go and listen."[44] The incarnational model is even more than that, since it flows from Jesus's very identity as God incarnate. Not only is Jesus an embodiment of God: the Gospels present Jesus as incarnate in the poor and marginalized. Just is not merely symbolized by the Other, but somehow incarnate in the Other: "Whatsoever you do to the least of these, you do to me" (Matthew 25:45). Put another way, "the prostitute is Jesus."[45] In this way, Christ himself assumes the stigmatizing label prostitutes are made to internalize through the degradation process, redeeming and radically de-centering human distortions of reality in the process.[46]

Ultimately, the incarnational model is the only way for the marginalized and expendable to become subjects. In this sort of praxis, it becomes clear why the Incarnation itself is salvation and central to God's plan. God's saving power is in the Incarnation just as it is in the Resurrection. John makes precisely this point: "The Word became Flesh, and dwelt among us" (1:14)

Oddly, in the case of prostitution, cultural and ecclesial conditioning might suggest that salvation is from the contagion of impurity of a sexual sort, but that is hardly the case in Scripture.[47] The woman central to the close of the exodus story, the harlot Rahab, was prized for her faithfulness, not condemned. Indeed, as the Franciscan practical theologian Guider points out, harlotry was apparently not an issue for God – "Rahab was a harlot when she made her declaration of faith and when she took action for Israelites. No amount of nuancing can change that."[48]

Nonetheless, as a result of long Christian tradition and social context, mores of sexual purity have been central to Christian life and practice until very, very recent times.[49] The delinking of Christianity from notions of sexual purity as central to the Gospel is not about a rejection of sexual fidelity but rather a move that turns from the disembodied toward the material in a more profound, creation-embracing way.[50] Recovery of the primacy of the incarnational lifts up two critical dimensions: the anthropological and the intersubjective. Both are closely related. The anthropological is central because an incarnational approach insists, for example, that so-called objectified persons are not object but persons, not peripheral but central, not prostituted but whole persons. No one is born to be a prostitute.[51] This leads straightaway to an experience of intersubjectivity where the "minister comes to terms with the essential difference between an experience of ministry that is understood as problem solving and an experience of ministry that is understood as involvement in the mystery of being. This is a creative, life-giving move from function and technique to wonder, humility, and reverence for the other."[52] Such intersubjectivity, as Marcel points out, is about solidarity: not as "I think" but "We are."[53] Such insight is tightly bound up with prayer and a lived mysticism of ordinary life.[54]

Prayerful

"The devout Christian of the future will either be a mystic, one who has experienced something, or will cease to be anything at all."[55] This seems to describe the reality for world Christian revitalization, one encountered clearly in the praxis of the Rahab Project and the Jesus Network. It is about the encounter with the Holy Spirit and radically reduced reliance on technical, preplanned solutions. Such an approach might have been sufficient under modernity, and was certainly reflective of the era, with its one-size-fits-all scientism and strong affinity with mass-scale social and religious engineering.

Today, the moment in which ongoing world Christian revitalization and renewal finds itself is heavily informed by a pentecostal-type impulse, with roots that drink deep of the Wesleyan holiness tradition and other antecedents, as well as a turn toward ancient sources of Christian prayer forms typically found within Catholic and Orthodox expressions of Christianity. In short, a post-modern, globalized Christianity is less about propositions of the head and more about presence in the heart. Large scale evangelism is still very much part of the mix, of course – a Jesus DVD is distributed by the Jesus Network on a massive scale, but the expectations for it are quite modest, as are the results. In any case, such activities fit within a much broader vision that begins and ends in prayer.[56]

It is not only about beginning in prayer and being rooted in prayer, it is about seeing ministerial action as itself the work of the Holy Spirit. The Rahab Project recognizes, for example, that only through the work of the Holy Spirit can the women for whom it exists be healed – precisely in the same way as every human person depends on the work of the Holy Spirit for healing.[57] Such an approach ultimately makes prostitutes, public sinners, victims, and all unreached persons, no longer victims and outsiders, but protagonists and insiders, together in community with the whole human family and all of creation. The sort of "incarnational presence"[58] affirms the religious imagination – the real faith lives – of prostitutes, women, Muslims, and all people beyond the control of institutions, including churches, that relatively devalue such persons and their religious imaginations.[59]

Such notions of presence and prayer suggest critical pneumatological insights every bit as much as the Christological insights around incarnational dimensions.[60] This is all the more so if the Holy Spirit is not constrained but rather "blows as she will"[61] Theologically, the experience of prayer and presence in an ecclesial context leads to a consideration of such issues as the *sensus fidelium* and *sensus fidei*.[62] In the contemporary experience of world Christian revitalization, these theological concepts may have a renewed power. A renewed focus on the *sensus fidei*, the sense the individual believer has of the faith, and *sensus fidelium*, the community's sense of the faith,[63] naturally feeds into "ordinary theology," as developed by Jeff Astley and others on the British scene.[64] Engaging these various forms of embodied and emplaced theologies, seeing material religion as theological expression,[65] leads to a challenge, something that takes us further into a critical opportunity for practical theology today. This draws from a focus on engaging lived spirituality in dialogue with theological theory. The theological theory can be ecclesiological, pneumatological, Christological, sacramental, and so on, usually some fruitful mix engaged correlationally, in the context of the ordinary, messy, everyday lived spirituality of people, globally.[66] This suggests a fruitful, new sort of systems-seeing that might offer a means of getting past the centuries-old break between spirituality and theology, theory and practice, proposition and prayer.

Understanding of the *sensus fidei* and *sensus fidelium*, particularly when leavened by the praxis of incarnate presence central to contemporary world Christian revitalization as suggested by the data from the Rahab Project and the Jesus Network, point toward the *koinonia*, the *communio* of believers.

Communal

The praxis of incarnate presence to the prostitute leads to new insight about the nature of church. The *missio ecclesiae* cannot be inward looking and must be outward-engaging: not a fortress but a servant. The namesake of the project of relationship with prostitutes points toward this. Rahab herself has long been seen as a model of the church, a symbol of the Christian community, as set forth by Jerome,[67] Clement of Rome,[68] and Augustine.[69] The relational praxis of contemporary world Christian revitalization can be understood in light of the Trinity.[70] Such a communal reality is rooted in the practice of solidarity.[71]

These developments suggest that part of the challenge from which Christianity needs revitalization and renewal is the on-going reality of institutional, organizational life. "Who says organization, says oligarchy," as Michels put it,[72] and Christian ecclesial life shows this human dynamic every bit as much as political parties organized to promote democracy and fight oligarchy. When churches split one from another, or new church groups of whatever level or type are formed, it is not long before the same dynamic can be observed. Leaders often find themselves doing exactly that which they viewed as problematic when it was done by other leaders. Given that Christianity is inevitably an ecclesial-institutional expression, world Christian revitalization has always been rooted, in part, in struggle with this dynamic. Even more, without being oligarchic, but simply in its existence within a given time-space cultural-historical reality, ecclesial life itself inevitability causes limitations. Its very incarnational presence leads to contradictions far greater than any scandal of particularity. The institutional church is inevitably implicated: there is no other way.[73]

The problem and challenge of revitalization rests in exactly this ecclesiological – and hamartological – reality. By ultimately, unavoidably prizing purity above inclusion, or judgment before welcome, or promoting family values that emphasize an essentialist, subordinate role for women and a sexual double standard, the church itself contributes to the construction of the problem of prostitution. In this sense, prostitution is not just a "cultural and social problem but an ecclesial problem needing an ecclesial solution,"[74] without any guarantee, of course, that the church itself is capable of conversion.[75] Further, as the Jesus Network knows, the church itself has created a "Christianity" of negative connotations even as Jesus bears position connotations.

Conclusion

In light of these claims, for which the data from the case studies provide ample warrant, several conclusions can be drawn about the nature of world Christian revitalization today, when the curtain has fallen on a "cocooned" or "fortress" Christianity and the contemporary context is analogous to that of a diverse global city where believers and non-believers, those ecclesially more valued and less valued, the marginal and the mainstream, are all present together, to each other.

This analysis presents three major conclusions regarding world Christian revitalization today. It depicts revitalization as retrieval and renewal, shows that revitalization upends common Christian categories, and insists that revitalization is relationship.

Revitalization as Retrieval and Renewal

Revitalization today is both retrieval and renewal of practice and understanding. It mines ancient insights missed or overlooked through a retrieval of embodied practice rather than a merely propositional approach. This means, of course, that it is also about on-going conversion as well: *ecclesia semper reformanda est.*[76] Such an approach prioritizes the *missio Dei* before the *missio ecclesiae*: it is not that the church has a mission; rather, the mission has a church.[77] Seen in this way, revitalization itself leads to a more adequate theological understanding.

Identity is not about a label such as "Christian," though it is not to be denied, but rather as someone who loves and follows Jesus.[78] Revitalization, in other words, is more about a verb than a noun. Further, there is a direct connection between the Great Commission and the Great Commandment. It all begins with God, with the *Missio Dei.*[79] In this sense, Christians are to cooperate with God in building up the church, but the one who does so is ultimately Godself. Revitalization thus comes from God and the appropriate Christian practice is one of openness to the incarnate presence of God in community. This is why contemporary world Christian revitalization nourishes and relishes the call for a deeper, more adequate theology of the Holy Spirit.

Thus, one might describe those who enter into revitalization movements among prostitutes and believers in other traditions, among Others, as "moved by an imitation of Christ that expressed itself in the desire to be one with others… aware that participation in the *missio Dei*—understood as God's universal loving will for all humanity—was not without its risks and consequences. Grounded in this knowledge and experience, they dared to come face to face not only with the mystery of God's love, but with the problem of God's love as well.[80] Renewal of the church inevitably follows with the retrieval of the Incarnational understanding that presence among such Others (as defined in human terms, including ecclesial ones) is an end in itself.[81]

In light of the communal experience of incarnate presence critical to these cases of contemporary world Christian revitalization, promising patterns for the renewal of Christian praxis are clear. They involve attitudes (of seeking, availability, and awareness).[82] principles (of creative fidelity, hope, and love), and practices of secondary reflection (contemplation of experience), participation, (understood at three levels – incarnation, communion, and transcendence) and creative testimony (which brings together justice and truth).[83]

Revitalization Upends Categories

Revitalization upends existing categories, including religious, theological, and ecclesial ones. This includes common Christian categories that have turned from heuristic proposals into reified idols, from something that helps the life of discipleship to something that gets in the way. Revitalization, in other words, is about a kind of creative destruction. It reveals the inadequacy of mere evangelism or any kind of strategy, technique, or proposition. It shows the insufficiency of church, and even how church is implicated in creating the need for revitalization in the first place, or in getting in the way or revitalization. Ultimately, revitalization relativizes everything – except God's grace.

As noted in the extensive consultation and group theological reflections on the Rahab Project and Jesus Network, the incarnational, loving approach profoundly complicates things.[84] Revitalization demands that Christians attend to learning from the limitations and sets of constraints they experience, much of which comes from the accumulated detritus of the tradition itself – very much incarnational and embodied, but not necessarily with the Spirit of Christ.[85]

One category that is roundly upended is any notion of the sufficiency of the church – contemporary revitalization shows, once again, that sufficiency is in the *missio Dei*, the Incarnational/Salvific Christ-event. Church – and experience of church – is necessarily limited precisely because of its incarnational aspect.[86] The point here is not that revitalization necessarily calls for the church to change on particular issues in a given cultural context. Rather, it is a more significant categorical issue, one on which contemporary revitalization might well hinge, according to the data at hand. The point might be about the very identity of the church as "problem solver" in favor of something altogether less, and more, ambitious.

Sometimes incarnational presence for the church, when truly communal, helps it be seen that a theoretical, propositional, generalizing approach to Truth is not appropriate, even if true. Rather than serving, and saving – providing access to and parceling out truth – sometimes the church may simply be called to participation and encounter. This is the great lesson of the Rahab Project and the Jesus Network, both of which never reject any Christian truth, but which are both fundamentally more about presence than pushing. There is a recognition in this that *imitatio Christi* (understood as incarnational presence in community) can all too often be short-circuited by *tentatio humana* (understood as the classic temptation to be like God, as in the Garden of Eden and as expressed in the pious desire to save, even to serve, readily distorted into a move toward control).[87] The imitation of Christ is not a license to control others, and contemporary world Christian revitalization demands a very different praxis.

Such a form of practice may well be entrepreneurial and informal rather than formal and structured. Such an entrepreneurial, independent Christian action may often be precisely what is needed in the present ecclesial and social context. It is certainly apparent that it "works" today in terms of Christian revitalization. Unofficial ministry is, in this context of revitalization, arguably more ministerial than ecclesially sanctioned ministry.[88] This should not be surprising: such was the nature of Jesus' ministry and countless movements of Christian revitalization through the centuries, whether that of Paul, Catherine, or Martin, and all those before, between, and after.[89]

Revitalization is Relationship

Revitalization is relationship, and the action implied by relationship is ultimately God's action. Such a conclusion flows from the dual move of practice retrieval and renewal, on the one hand, and a radical realization of the insufficiency of existing propositional categories on the other.

Revitalization is ultimately about how Christians in the world are called to be "artisans of a new humanity,"[90] and this artisanal metaphor is best understood in an apprentice-master relationship, where Christ is the master and those who would follow are the apprentices.

What Christ teaches – through the Incarnation – is that God is more of a great lover than a great fixer. Awareness of the profound presence of the Holy Spirit in all creation and the transforming love of Christ leads revitalization in a profoundly relational direction, one inspired by the relational theology of the Trinity and stemming from the very nature of the Godhead as it is experienced.

Such an encounter leads to a revitalized understanding of God and God's presence in the world as well. It is certainly orthodox to describe human sinfulness and need for redemption as why Christ came into the world. But it is no less orthodox to say that God became human out of love and desire for relationship, and that salvation is most adequately understood in light of the very nature of the Godhead: Love.[91]

Experiential understanding of the Incarnation – revitalization that is relational – does not reject classic Christian understandings of salvation, but resituates it in a way that flows from contemporary experiences of revitalization, thus shaping future work in world Christian revitalization. It thus removes any possibility of the distortion that would claim that Incarnation – God's loving nature – was caused by human sinfulness. Even more, it responds to the distortions that are "human efforts to influence God and to control evil through heroic and charismatic acts of expiatory suffering and messianic virtue."[92]

In this way, a more adequate account of ecclesiology – the *missio ecclesiae* – emerges, one that puts the eschatological, in the sense of seeing as God sees,[93] before the soteriological and harmatological, without ever changing anything to the fundamental Christian revelation of the gift of salvation and the reality of sin.

In relationship with the Cosmic Christ revealed in the Resurrection as the first fruit of the new creation – the *missio Dei* – a more adequate vision of *imitatio Christi* emerges, embedded in the *missio ecclesiae* rightly understood. In this way, the Great Commandment and the Great Commission truly come together, pointing toward a more profound understanding of world Christian revitalization founded in incarnation, presence, and communion. Growing the Gospel and growing in love – the relational, creative love that is God – are ultimately exactly the same.[94]

World Christian revitalization is about recognition of the on-going restoration of all things in Christ. It is Christ, after all, who brings restoration and healing to prostitutes and migrants, to those who are Christian and those who are not – and to us Christians who fall easy prey to seeing ourselves as the ones who save, as anything other than a simple child of God. The praxis of revitalization reveals the role of the body of Christ with a new humility and a new clarity. The Rahab Project puts it this way in terms of prostitutes, but it could be just as well for the entire work of revitalization today: Christians are to "care... without lies and conditions, in order that they might experience the grace, love and power of Christ through our actions and words.[95]

Notes

1. As Francis Schussler Fiorenza put it in *Foundational Theology: Jesus and the Church* (New York: Crossroad, 1985), xvi, retroductive warrants are neither deductive nor inductive. Rather, they "argue from the variety and diversity of inference that can be drawn from a hypothesis. The argument is not accepted because of logical cogency as in deduction or because of generalizations of data as in induction. Instead, the argument is accepted because the hypothesis generates illuminative inferences. Quoted in Margaret E. Guider, OSF, *Daughters of Rahab: Prostitution and the Church of Liberation in Brazil* (Fortress Press: Minneapolis, 1995), 5.

2 *Rahab Project Report*, 12. See also Guider, *Daughters of Rahab*, 28-31.

3. Quran 5: 46-47.

4. *The Jesus Network Report*, 4.

5. As Philip Jenkins puts it, "If we want to visualize a 'typical' contemporary Christian, we should be thinking of a woman living in a village in Nigeria or in a Brazilian favela." See *The Next Christendom* (New York: Oxford University Press, 2007), 1-2. As Emmanuel Katongole notes, this is particularly true for Catholicism. See "Performing Catholicity: Archbishop John Baptist Odama And The Politics Of Baptism In Northern Uganda," 2, presented at the World Catholicism Week Conference, Center for World Catholicism and Intercultural Theology, De Paul University, Chicago, Illinois,

April 12-13, 2011. Nonetheless, as Guider, *Daughters of Rahab*, 116, notes, the generic vision of a poor person, and a person in general, remains of a male head-of-household in a patriarchal system.

6. "Rahab Commentary," in the *Rahab Project Report*, 12-13.

7. *The Jesus Network Report*, 14.

8. The notion of the other has many roots, include Hegel's master-slave dialectic in his *Phenomenology of Spirit*, work on alterity by Lacan and Levinas, and Gabriel Marcel, among others. See Marcel, *The Existential Background of Human Dignity* (Cambridge: Harvard University Press, 1963).

9. For numbers, see "Behind the Sign: Investigating the Growing Number of Erotic Massage Centres in Toronto, National Post, May 7, 2011. See http://news.nationalpost.com/2011/05/07/behind-the-sign-investigating-the-growing-number-of-erotic-massage-centres-in-toronto/. For more on the Rahab project, see http://www.tyndale.ca/~missiodei/2010/03/finding-rahab/.

10. To paraphrase an observation Guider makes about prostitution, "In many ways, the church [does] not know how much it [does] not know." *Daughters of Rahab*, 115.

11. This is characteristic of much of North America and is certainly the case in South Florida, where the author lives. When one begins to have eyes to truly see, it is truly astonishing how often one sees such places.

12. This analysis also has much in common, and is in part inspired by, reflections on racism in the church, particularly in the Americas, especially in the United States. More than once in history, the church has legitimized racism and practiced exclusion. Such realities reaching back into the past and through the present day, need to be taken very, very seriously.

13. Such structural evils make possible the violation of women on such a massive and continuing scale in Canada, North America, and globally. See *Rahab Project Report*, 11.

14. *Rahab Project Report*, 11.

15. "As the life histories and personal testimonies of prostitutes repeatedly confirmed, such women rarely had fallen into prostitution. More often than not, they had been pushed." See Guider, *Daughters of Rahab*, 114. Thus, prostitution is not such much a "deviation but an expression of the norm; it is an all too common example of the exploitation and degradation experienced by women in general." See Guider, *Daughters of Rahab*, 90.

16. *Rahab Project Report*, 2. As John Paul II noted in *Familiaris Consortio*: "Unfortunately, the Christian message about the dignity of women is contradicted by that persistent mentality which considers the human being not as a person but as a thing, as an object of trade, at the service of selfish interest and mere pleasure: the first victims of this mentality are women. This mentality produces very bitter fruits, such as contempt for men and for women, slavery, oppression of the weak, pornography, prostitution—especially in an organized form—and all those various forms of discrimination that exist in the fields of education, employment, wages, etc." (24) See also Guider, *Daughters of Rahab*, 1. Guider goes further, arguing that "in effect, prostitution was the reality of all women" (92), in terms of strongly patriarchal societies where women are reduced to an object to be controlled by men.

17. *Rahab Project Report*, 6 (footnote 5).

18. *Rahab Project Report*, 10.

19. For more reflection on this double standard, see Guider, *Daughters of Rahab*, 109.

20. Guider, *Daughters of Rahab*, 109.

21. Guider, *Daughters of Rahab*, 99-100.
22. Guider, *Daughters of Rahab*, 93.
23. See Charles Taylor's work on this topic in *A Secular Age* (Cambridge: Harvard University Press, 2008), published in article form in "Sex & Christianity: How has the Moral Landscape Changed?" *Commonweal*, September 28, 2007 at http://commonwealmagazine.org/sex-christianity-0. See also Janet R. Jakobsen and Ann Pellegrini, Marriage Plots" at http://blogs.ssrc.org/tif/208/01/08/marriage-plots/.
24. Note that only women can be "public sinners" in this sense – and that it is the church who ultimately offers this definition. Even more, a synonym for "public sinner" historically has been "public woman," meaning prostitute. Such a notion flowed from an ecclesially sanctioned understanding of women in an essentialist manner, as not having an acceptable public role, but rather an exclusively domestic one.
25. Fewer than 10 percent of Asians are Christian. See Todd M. Johnson and Kenneth R. Ross, editors, *Atlas of Global Christianity 1910-2010* (Edinburgh: Edinburgh University Press, 2009).
26. See Phillip Jenkins in "Global Schism: Is the Anglican Communion Rift the First Stage in a Wider Christian Split?" at http://aseekingspirit.wordpress.com/global-religious-schism-among-christians/. The ancient Christian populations of the Middle East and North Africa has declined dramatically over the past half century, to the extent that some commentators describe Christian "extinction" or near-extinction in a number of places where significant and sizeable Christian communities have been present for millennia. See John Allen, Jr., *The Future Church: How Ten Trends are Revolutionizing the Catholic Church* (New York: Doubleday, 2009), 113.
27. Scotus was a realist, arguing against Aquinas that the existence and essence of a thing cannot be separated. Between this position and his remarkable argument that existence is the most abstract category possible, it is clear why he would have insisted on the concept of *haecceitas*, tied to an understanding of particularity and individuation, all of which point toward a strong underpinning for incarnational theological understanding. See, for example, Woosuk Park, "Haecceitas and the Bare Particular," *The Review of Metaphysics*, 44, 2 (December 1990), 375-397.
28. George Hodges, *Saints and Heroes since the Middle Ages* (BiblioBazaar, 2009), 303; 308-309. For other similarities between the Franciscan movement and Wesleyanism, see Mark Anthony Smith, *John Wesley: A Pattern of Monastic Reform* (University of Kentucky Ph.D. dissertation, 1992). For a retrieval of the medieval Franciscan understanding closely tied to the incarnational dimension described here, see Ilia Delio, OSF, *A Franciscan View of Creation: Learning to Live in a Sacramental World* (St. Bonaventure, New York: The Franciscan Institute, 2003).
29. John Duns Scotus, OFM, *Ordinatio* 3 (sup.) dist. 19 (Assisi com. 137, fol. 161vb); quoted and translated in Allan B. Wolter, OFM, "John Duns Scotus on the Primacy and Personality of Christ," in Damian McElrath, OFM, ed., *Franciscan Christology* (St. Bonaventure, New York: Franciscan Institute Publications, 1980), 153. See Guider, OSF, *Daughters of Rahab*, 139.
30. The Second Vatican Council was a gathering of all Catholic bishops around the world, the twenty-first such ecumenical council in its history. It was convened on October 11, 1962 and closed on December 8, 1965.
31. *Gaudium et Spes* (The Pastoral Constitution on the Church in the Modern World), December 7, 1965. See also http://www.vatican.va/archive/hist_councils/ii_vatican_council/documents/vat-ii_cons_19651207_gaudium-et-spes_en.html. The quote is taken from the first paragraph.
32. *The Jesus Network Report*, 14.
33. The Jesus Network Discussion, E-4 (author's notes).

34. "Outside of the church there is no salvation." This is taken from the saying by Cyprian of Carthage in Letter XXII, "Ad Jubajanum de haereticis baptizandis," and while it grew up in that context, there have been times when this has been taken literally, meaning that no one who is not visibly in communion with the church can be saved. This is what the Fourth Lateran Council (1215) of Francis's time would seem to imply, or what Calvin seems to imply in the *Institutes of the Christian Religion*: "beyond the pale of the church no forgiveness of sins, no salvation, can be hoped for" (Book IV, Chapter 1, Section IV).

35. John V. Tolan, *Saint Francis and the Sultan: The Curious History of a Muslim-Christian Encounter* (Oxford: Oxford University Press, 2009) and Paul Moses, *The Saint and the Sultan: The Crusades, Islam, and Francis of Assisi's Mission of Peace* (New York: Doubleday, 2009). Many other accounts exist, not all of equal scholarly value.

36. Taken from Michael F. Cusato, OFM, "The Democratization of Prayer: What Francis of Assisi Learned in Damietta (1219)," Third Summer Lecture, Franciscan Institute, St. Bonaventure University, July 19, 2011. As Cusato notes, one of the results of Francis' visit to the Sultan was to ask local leaders to encourage that all people pray together as Muslims do: "May you foster such honor to the Lord among the people entrusted to you in such a way that every evening an announcement might be made by a messenger or some other signal so that praise and thanksgiving be given by all the people to the all-powerful Lord God" (9).

37. The Jesus Network Discussion, D-7 (author's notes).

38. The Jesus Network Discussion, D-8-9 (author's notes).

39. The Rahab Project itself "started because its founder recalled Jesus' compassion for sinners and outcasts and the fact that he did not shun the prostitutes of his time but associated with them, extending them forgiveness and restoring them to relationship with god and his people thereby offering them new life. See *Rahab Project Report*, 11.

40. Guider, *Daughters of Rahab*, 130. The ministry of Jesus has marked this incarnational love for prostitutes and public sinners. This can be seen in ministries today such as the Rahab Project, just as it can be seen in the Ministry to Marginalized Women, sponsored for decades by the Catholic Bishops of Brazil, or the Equiperes du Nid (a Catholic religious order) among the prostitutes of Paris. See Guider, *Daughters of Rahab*, 81. A particularly classic example of ministry among prostitutes is that of Renaissance and Counter-Reformation Rome in the work of the first Jesuits, including Ignatius of Loyola. See Lance Gabriel Lazar, *Working in the Vineyard of the Lord: Jesuit Confraternities in Early Modern Italy* (Toronto: University of Toronto Press, 2005), especially 37-70, "Chapter 2, Training the Vine: S. Marta and the Compagnia della Grazia."

41. *Rahab Project Report*, 10.

42. Steve Ybarrola, "The Jesus Network Commentary," in *The Jesus Network Report*, 22.

43. John 1:39.

44. Guider, Daughters of Rahab, 96.

45. Guider, Daughters of Rahab, 72.

46. *Rahab Project Report*, 8.

47. Rahab Project Discussion, C-3 (author's notes).

48. Guider, *Daughters of Rahab*, 35.

49. See Charles Taylor, "Sex & Christianity: How has the moral landscape changed?" *Commonweal*, September 28, 2007 (http://commonwealmagazine.org/sex-christianity-0), taken from Charles Taylor, A Secular Age (Cambridge: Harvard University Press, 2008). See also Janet R. Jakobsen and Ann Pellegrini, *Sex in A Secular Age: Marriage Plots* by (http://blogs.ssrc.org/tif/208/01/08/marriage-plots/).

50. See Manuel Vasquez, *More Than Belief: A Materialist Theory of Religion* (Oxford: Oxford University Press, 2010).

51. Guider, *Daughters of Rahab*, 90.

52. Guider, *Daughters of Rahab*, 161.

53. Guider, *Daughters of Rahab*, 156.

54. Ghider, *Daughters of Rahab*, 156. See also her related presentation of Gabriel Marcel's work.

55. See Karl Rahner, "Christian Living Formerly and Today," *Theological Investigations 7* (London, United Kingdom: Darton, Longman and Todd, 1971), 15. The source for this insight can be traced to Ignatius of Loyola and Ignatian spirituality more generally. See Harvey Egan, *Karl Rahner, Mystic of Everyday Life* (New York: Crossroad, 1998).

56. The first meeting of the Jesus Network, in fact, was simply prayer. In the words of leadership, the insight was to pray first, above all. See *The Jesus Network Report*, 8.

57. *Rahab Project Report*, 10.

58. Guider, *Daughters of Rahab*, 97.

59. Regarding the religious imagination, see discussions of a related concept, the social imaginary, in Charles Taylor, *Modern Social Imaginaries* (Durham: Duke University Press, 2003) and *A Secular Age* (Cambridge: Harvard University Press, 2008). See also Guider, *Daughters of Rahab*, 12.

60. This recalls the saying of Irenaeus: Christ and the Spirit as the two hands of God: "The Holy Spirit and the Christ being the hands of God the Father, reaching in from the infinite into the finite." Irenaeus, "Preface to Book IV", *Against Heresies* in Philip Schaff, *Ante-Nicene Fathers*, Volume I, (Grand Rapids: Eerdmans, 2001). See Ralph del Colle, *Christ and the Spirit: Spirit-Christology in Trinitarian Perspective* (Oxford: Oxford University Press, 1994). See also Catherine Mowry LaCugna, *God for Us: The Trinity and Christian Life* (San Francisco: HarperOne, 1993). Regarding the Trinity, it is sometimes most helpful to recall formulas used in prayer, such as:" God for us, we call You Father; God alongside us, we call You Jesus; God within us, we call You Holy Spirit." See http://archive.cacradicalgrace.org/conferences/post_sog/sog_prayers.html.

61. The use of a feminine pronoun derives from the grammatically feminine Hebrew biblical concept of Shekinah, meaning Divine Presence (as in the presence in the tabernacle). The use of the concept seems parallel to descriptions of the Holy Spirit in the New Testament, as in 1 Corinthians 3:16-17. There are also parallels with the Quranic Arabic notion of Sakina(h). See Karen Armstrong, *Muhammad: A Biography of the Prophet* (San Francisco: HarperOne, 1992), 224. A related biblical term, also grammatically feminine, is Sophia, for "wisdom" in the Septuagint translations of the wisdom books. In the Greek-speaking Christian world of the ancient Eastern Mediterranean, the term for the Holy Spirit, or Holy Wisdom of God, Hagia Sophia, as in the great church of Constantinople that was the patriarchal cathedral up to 1453.

62. Ormond Rush, "Sensus Fidei: Faith Making Sense of Revelation," *Theological Studies*, 62, 2001, 231-261. Guider, *Daughters of Rahab*, notes that prostitutes (and other marginal persons, particularly those marginalized in ecclesial praxis) ironically have power to upset ecclesial equilibria by the theological questions their very existence poses the church (77).

63. See Ormond Rush, "Sensus Fidei: Faith 'Making Sense' of Revelation," *Theological Studies* 62 (2001): 232.

64. Jeff Astley, *Ordinary Theology: Looking, Listening, and Learning in Theology* (Surrey: Ashgate, 2003).

65. See Manuel A. Vasquez, *More Than Belief: A Materialist Theory of Religion* (New York: Oxford University Press, 2011).

66. See Tom Bamat and Jean Paul Wiest, *Popular Catholicism in a World Church: Seven Case Studies Inculturation*, (Maryknoll: Orbis, 1999). Such a correlational approach almost implies some form of an analogical imagination. Note however, following Osmer and Wentzel van Huysteen, other related methods would be tranversal or transformational.

67. Jerome, "Letter 22," 38.6 in *The Letters of St. Jerome, Book 1: Letters 1-22*, translated by Charles C. Mierow (New York: Newman, 1963), 175 and "Homily 91: On the Exodus," 237. See also "Homily18: On Psalm 86 (87)" in *The Homilies of Saint Jerome, Volume 1: Homilies 1-59*, translated by Marie Liguori Ewald (Washington: Catholic University of America Press, 1964), 138. Cited in Guider, *Daughters of Rahab*, 31-32.

68. Clement sees the scarlet cloth that Rahab left as prefiguring the blood of Jesus on the cross, arguing further that she who saves her household prefigures the church. Clement of Rome, "Epistle to the Corinthians 12," in *Epistles of St. Clement of Rome and St. Ignatius of Antioch*, translated by James A. Kleist (Westminster, Maryland: Newman Bookshop, 1946). Cited in Guider, *Daughters of Rahab*, 31.

69. Augustine, "Psalm 87" in *Expositions on the Book of Psalms, Volume 4: Psalms 76-110* (London: Rivington, 1850), 219-220. Cited in Guider, *Daughters of Rahab*, 32.

70. As, for example, shown in Catherine Mowry LaCugna, *God for Us: The Trinity and Christian Life* (San Francisco: HarperOne, 1993).

71. Which as Heinrich Pesch, SJ, (1854-1926) and Oswald von Nell-Breuning SJ, (1890-1991) would have argued, include a theological anthropology that views solidarity as de facto human interdependence and an ethnics that sees solidarity as an imperative. See Gerald J. Beyer, *Recovering Solidarity: Lessons from Poland's Unfinished Revolution* (Notre Dame: University of Notre Dame Press, 2010).

72. Robert Michels, *Political Parties: A Sociological Study of the Oligarchical Tendencies of Modern Democracy* (London: Jarrod and Sons, 1915), http://etext.lib.virginia.edu/toc/modeng/public/MicPoli.html.

73. For that reason, Guider, writing on a similar topic in *Daughters of Rahab*, noted that the "Nature of this analysis is investigative and stems from a practical missiological interest in understanding the adaptive challenges that the so-called church of liberation faced in its efforts to minister among prostitutes" (75).

74. Guider, *Daughters of Rahab*, 72.

75. Guider, *Daughters of Rahab*, 97.

76. This phrase, sometimes attributed to Augustine or cited as a generic medieval aphorism, was used in one form or another by the leaders of the Reformation. The documents of the Second Vatican Council, such as *Lumen Gentium*, used similar language: "The [Catholic] Church, embracing sinners in her bosom, is at the same time holy and always in need of being purified, and incessantly pursues the path of penance and renewal" (8). Reform was a major issue among *ressourcement* theologians. See Yves Congar, OP, *True and False Reform in the Church*, translated by Paul Philibert, OP (Collegeville: Liturgical Press, 2011). The origin of this Latin phrase is. See Standing Conference of the Canonical Orthodox Bishops in the Americas, "Steps Towards a Reunited Church: A Sketch Of an Orthodox-Catholic Vision for the Future," October 2, 2010, available at http://www.scoba.us/articles/towards-a-unified-church.html.

77. In this sense, God is more a noun than a verb; the point is not what the church does but what God does. See Stephen Bevans, SVD, "The Mission has a Church: An Invitation to the Dance," *Australian eJournal of Theology*, 14,1 (2009). For a lengthier treatment of these topics, see Stephen Bevans and Roger P. Schroeder, *Constants in Context: A Theology of Mission for Today* (Maryknoll: Orbis, 2004).

78. *The Jesus Network Report*, 11-12.

79. Guider, *Daughters of Rahab*, 150.

80. Guider, *Daughters of Rahab*, 150-151.

81. In a way, this gets at Rodney Stark's argument for the success of early Christianity. Rodney Stark, *The Triumph of Christianity: How the Jesus Movement Became the World's Largest Religion* (New York: Harper Collins, 2011).

82. These are reflections, respectively, of Gabriel Marcel's notions of *inquietude, disponsibilite,* and *espirit*. See Gabiel Marcel, *Problematic Man* (New York: Herder and Herder, 1967), 67-71; Gabriel Marcel, *Being and Having* (Gloucester: Peter Smith, 1976), 72-73; Gabriel Marcel, *Reflection and Mystery* (Chicago: Henry Regnery, 1970), 64, 67-68. All cited and discussed in Guider, *Daughters of Rahab*, 157-158.

83. Guider, *Daughters of Rahab*, 156-160.

84. The Jesus Network Discussion, C-2 (author's notes). These were the words of Todd Johnson, but they reflected the sense that emerged within the entire theological reflection group on these cases.

85. This point is made very clearly in Guider, *Daughters of Rahab*, 136-137.

86. As noted by Guider, *Daughters of Rahab*, 142: "[E]cclesial institutions are constrained not only by the inevitable changes that accompany the natural course of human history. Despite the church's desire and commitment to redress and solve specific problem associated with oppression and injustice, it was, is, and most likely will always be unable to realize fully its aspirations and longs because of any number of causes and conditions outside of its control."

87. Guider, *Daughters of Rahab*, 143-6. In other words, Christians "assume that they know the form that liberation and salvation of others should take and thus can endeavor to bring it about. Imitation of Christ as a license for individuals and group to control and confirm the *missio Dei* in accord with their own claims to know God's will for others."

88. The Jesus Network Discussion, D-9 (author's notes).

89. This is a reference to Paul of Tarsus, Catherine of Siena, and Martin Luther King, Jr. Of course, it could be just as well a reference to Martin Luther. The great voices of Christian revitalization through the centuries are legion.

90. The theological concept "artisans of a new humanity" is developed further in Clemens Sedmak, *Doing Local Theology: A Guide for Artisans of a New Humanity* (Maryknoll: Orbis, 2002). In addition, the five volume book project of Juan Luis Segundo, SJ from the early 1970s bore the collective title of "Artisans of a New Humanity," and the concept was also reflected in *Evangelii Nuntiandi*, Paul VI's 1975 exhortation on Evangelization in the Modern World (31). The term originally came from *Gaudium et Spes* (30). The translation of the original passage below is the original one and thus does not reflect contemporary English use of gender inclusive forms.

Let everyone consider it his sacred obligation to esteem and observe social necessities as belonging to the primary duties of modern man. For the more unified the world becomes, the more plainly do the offices of men extend beyond particular groups and spread by degrees to the whole world. But this development cannot occur unless individual men and their associations cultivate in themselves the moral and social virtues, and promote them in society; thus, with the needed help of divine grace men who are truly new and artisans of a new humanity can be forthcoming.

91. I John 4:8. See also the encyclical of Benedict XVI, *Deus Caritas Est* ("God is love").

92. This material is taken from Guider, *Daughters of Rahab*, 147, and continues, noting that this "theological orientation for ministry merits the attention of practical theologians. ...The primary purpose of the Incarnation must be understood in broader theological terms than those identified with the utilitarian end of supplying for hu-

manity's need of redemption... [through] understand[ing] the Incarnation as rooted in the mystery of God's love.

93. Which is arguably analogous to the Covey principle of "beginning with the end in mind."

94. Or as noted in Guider, *Daughters of Rahab*, 171, and quoting the Franciscan Paulo Evaristo Arns (Archbishop of Sao Paulo from 1970 to 1998), "Do the churches have the courage to be the heart of God?"

95. *Rahab Project Report*, 10.

Chapter Four

Summary Chapter: Insights and Implications for Christian Revitalization in the Twenty-First Century:

J. STEVEN O'MALLEY
BEVERLY JOHNSON MILLER
AND MICHAEL PASQUARELLO

What We Were About

J. STEVEN O'MALLEY, PHD

We have now presented the cases that were prepared for Toronto, as well as the interpretations provided by the three tables of participants who reflected on their meaning and significance. Participants represented a diversity of academic disciplines, and faith traditions ranging from Catholic and Orthodox to mainline Protestant, evangelical, Pentecostal, and indigenous churches from the Global South and East. and seventeen nations on five continents.

This summary chapter offers perspective from the vantage point of faculty members of the planning team from Asbury Theological Seminary, who also participated in the first two consultations of this Luce project and write from the perspective of the contributions of Toronto to the project as a whole. They actually write from two perspectives. First, Beverly Johnson-Miller considers the viewpoint of the dynamics represented in the table discussions. Second, Michael Pasquarello, who served as grand synthesizer for the daily discussions of the consultation, offers a theological perspective to facilitate working with revitalization movements on the world stage -- particularly in the megacities of the Global South and East, which will be the focus of the second Luce project (2012-2016).

The Toronto consultation demonstrated the increasing influence of diaspora and transnationalism as driving issues in twenty-first century social demographics, impacting a wide range of Christian communities, both traditional and contemporary/indigenous. Amid this mix, Pasquarello formulates a cogent way forward for coming to terms with movements of revitalization. His recommendation stands contrary to the "conventional wisdom" of emphasizing the primacy of human agency in producing self-chosen outcomes for the ministry of revitalization and renewal. In a "non-utilitarian" way of thinking and acting, this approach seeks to track with how the Holy Spirit is present and active to "awaken the Church's desire for the reign of God in ways congruent with its calling to be a holy people in the world." The key to this proposal is to recast ministry as the virtue of prudence, or the practice of wisdom in cultivating a grassroots attention and receptivity to God's Word in Christ who indwells the life of the church, in all its authentic expressions in the world.

Relating to burgeoning revitalization movements in the Global South from this vantage point will help us engage the ways in which preaching, worship, catechesis, and social outreach are done in the megacities where that vitality is now occurring at levels unseen in the Global North. Lessons learned from the Global South will be instructive in pointing the way forward for the churches of North America, which are increasingly experiencing reverberations from the great expansion of world Christianity occurring in the Africa, Asia, and South America.

A. Revitalization in the Crucible of Discussion: The Mosaic of God in Motion

Beverly Johnson-Miller, PhD

Creating a mosaic involves assembling many disparate parts into a whole. Each part has a significant role in the larger design yet any single piece is insufficient apart from the whole. Any group of parts can potentially compose many different designs, and a Mosaic can be composed of multiple patterns or designs within a meta-design. Any part does not describe the whole, nor can the whole be grasped from any single part. The whole emerges from patterned assembling of the various parts.

Everything in the universe moves, including all aspects of life and creation. We have the motion of human life from birth to death, the motion of history in space and time, and the motion of personal growth, social development, and cultural change.

A mosaic in motion could be likened to the creative and colorful moving formations of a marching band halftime show. The design is dependent upon rhythmic movement of each and all participants, and vice versa. The design and the movement are interdependent.

To view Christian revitalization as a *mosaic* is to recognize the complexity, significance, and beauty of countless interlaced components and patterns. A complex web of numerous interdependent dimensions and components characterized each revitalization movement. The configuration of the intertwining elements varied from movement to movement, but every movement demonstrated some significant form of ecclesial renewal or reconstitution, testimony of divine encounter, and evidence of personal transformation. Each case study of revitalization illustrated a significant segment of God's redemptive work in the world.

Understanding revitalization as a mosaic *in motion* means acknowledging the dynamic, ever evolving and revolving kaleidoscopic patterns. Shifting patterns and practices occur in conjunction with an ever shifting society and dialectical interaction between the past, present, and future. In this regard, the Jesus Network illustrates a shifting perspective from hospitality as a means to conversion to embracing hospitality as a Christian virtue.

Each of the consultation case studies embodied intersecting theological, social-cultural, functional or practical, spiritual, and historical dimensions. Multiple elements comprise each dimension of revitalization.

Ecumenical engagement, incarnational models, recovery of the importance of the cross, theological anthropology, critical practices of forgiveness and social justice, proclamation wed with liberation, and ecclesial identity crisis were among the many theological elements at work in the various movements. Examples of social-cultural components included globalization, marginalization, ethnic cross-fertilization, immigrant networking, religious freedom via transnational immigration, violent persecution, and social crisis of poverty and human commodification.

Functional elements included activities or practices such as intentional diversity, holistic ministry focus, cultural accommodation in ministry form and style, incarnational ministry practice, renewed attention to ancient church tradition, emphasis on mission, openness to vulnerability, and solidarity with human need. Among other things, spiritual elements represented prayer, worship, compassionate service, sacrificial love, Bible study, and personal testimonies of divine encounter. Historical aspects were exhibited by recovery of ancient church practices as well as generational roles in revitalization.

The intersections among these various dimensions can be seen in the diasporic revival within the Toronto Coptic Orthodox Church in which praise and worship practices were adapted for the sake of cultural integration, and yet ancient church liturgical traditions and orthodox doctrines were simultaneously maintained. The practice of sharing personal stories of divine encounter and transformation illustrate the intersection of theological, spiritual, and functional elements. Intentional ministry within the Toronto diaspora churches to members from all ethnicities and nationalities illustrates the intersection of functional with social-cultural aspects of revitalization.

Each element or pattern consisting of multiple components contributes to the beauty, message, and function of the whole. However, unlike a typical mosaic where the elements or parts can stand apart from other elements or parts, the elements at work in revitalization are usually so deeply meshed or interlaced that they are inseparable and at times indistinguishable from the whole.

No given revitalization movement could be understood apart from the web of revitalization movements throughout history, and each movement of revitalization occurs or has occurred as a part of a larger picture. There was no such thing as a "solo" form or force of revitalization. No individual element, dimension, or dynamic stood alone, and the entire network of pieces and patterns are incapable of being described with completeness . Any particular aspect of revitalization that may be identified could not be contained within any single category. The pieces of the picture, and pictures within the meta-picture of God's redemptive work defy or defied autonomous and linear categorization.

The case studies examined in the research consultations along with the insights and expertise of scholars and established practitioners provided realistic illustrations of the nature and complexity of Christian revitalization in context. The concrete examples of revitalization revealed these feaures among others: an experiential recognition of divine activity; spiritual vitality grounded in the undisguised realities of life; a very pronounced pattern of tension and conflict; and, responsive participation in an ever-moving purpose driven process. These generative themes provide perspective on the nature and meaning of Christian revitalization. The insights and questions that emerge from these findings are identified in these cases with a view to inform and guide new expressions of Christian revitalization as they are manifested.

Dependent on Divine Activity

Revival cannot be organized, but we can set our sails to catch the wind from heaven when God chooses to blow upon His people once again. (G. Campbell Morgan)

The design and movement of revitalization is guided and empowered by the rhythmic work of the Holy Spirit. The consultation research makes clear that the work of the Holy Spirit cannot be measured, controlled, or contained by human effort, however, all of the case studies demonstrated divine activity via at least two types of evidence. One type of evidence was the testimony of personal, spiritual transformation, among groups of individuals such as the widespread change that took place in the African and Asian contexts.

A second type of evidence was the testimony of Christian spiritual transformation occurring in difficult, unusual, or unprecedented contexts or forms. This would include places or people groups closed to the gospel such as the Muslim contexts, and places of great darkness and evil such as the human trafficking industry.

The work of the Holy Spirit cannot be measured but also should not be underestimated. The birth of fresh vision in response to unusual contexts and needs, the inspired creation of new ministry forms, the unprecedented unity amidst unfathomable diversity, the unexpected accessibility to unreached people groups, the unpredictable church growth, and, the dynamic surge of mission vitality and opportunity confirm the presence of the Holy Spirit. This divine activity may be widespread and unmistakable, but it cannot be measured, predicted, or controlled.

Grounded in Reality

Christian revitalization does not occur in a cosmic vacuum. Each case study and every specific example within each case study revealed that God's redemptive work in the world is deeply intertwined with every dimension of human existence, including the conflicts and tensions of life. Every circumstance, issue, and event that connects with human life on this planet in any degree or form, both past and present, contributes to a dynamic web of reality that is intimately intertwined with the process and experience of revitalization.

The reality grounded nature of Christian revitalization can be seen in the response of Toronto diaspora churches to the various forms of human brokenness such as economic poverty and social alienation experienced by immigrants. Immigrant communities settled in very secularized context within Toronto, yet gospel transformation is thriving and multiplying. The Rahab ministry emerged in response to the dark social reality of human trafficking, and the social and economic realities that fuel and sustain this vile industry necessitated a holistic ministry approach. The political turmoil and related religious persecution ignited a unifying spiritual renewal in the Coptic churches of Egypt. The East African revival was a subversive response to political oppression and colonial authority.

Christian revitalization occurs at the intersection of the social forces of relationship, community, culture, and society. Social forces are at work in all forms and dimensions of revitalization. Individuals, or group of individuals, may experience some element of revitalization in a way that is particular to them, such as participants in the Jesus Network. No individual or group however experiences alterations in their spiritual life apart from the social context or their interactions within their social context. This was evident in every case study. Social realities of every kind, including many forms of conflict, contribute to the birth and spread of revitalization movements.

The Inescapable Role of Conflict

One table participant at the Toronto consultation commented, " [there is] no revitalization apart from crisis". Is it possible that tension and conflict, something we usually avoid and often consider *unchristian* is *a*, or perhaps even *the*, key propelling dynamic of revitalization? Tension and conflict in various forms, degrees, and roles were major themes in the analysis of every revitalization case study in the Toronto Consultation. Even the identification and discussion of the tensions and conflicts was at times a source of significant tension and conflict among consultation participants.

The case studies demonstrated that Christian revitalization in any context involves a significant relationship to some form of conflict. The type and degree of conflict varied from case to case. Some of the tensions and conflicts evident in the case studies may be identified. There were social conflicts such as political oppression of colonial authority in East Africa, religious persecution suffered by the Coptic Christians of Egypt, and the human exploitation addressed by the Rahab ministry. There was conflict regarding the nature of Christian community evident in the need for cultural accommodation by the Filipino and Coptic diaspora churches in Toronto. In addition, the limitations of the first generation immigrant church faced by second and third generation Korean-Canadians generated intergenerational conflict. Conflicts were also evident within individuals: the beginning of the East African revival Balokole movement can be traced to one man's conflict with the spiritual lethargy of the native Anglican Church in East Africa.

Engagement with one conflict often led to the emergence of other conflicts. The Balokole movement triggered by one man's conflict brought attention to the oppressive nature of the colonializing missionary movement. The Balokole challenged the self-perceptions of missionaries as well as African Christians by their hostility toward the hierarchical authority structures within the institutional church, as well as the hierarchical authority structures of colonial rule and traditional rulers.

The Balokole hostility toward the hierarchical authority structures became a subversive challenge to traditional family values. It encouraged non-traditional roles for women, valued advanced education, cleanliness but not fashion or luxury, character but not charisma, disregard for wealth and materialism but a high regard for healthy living, and intolerance of subterfuge. Another theological dimension of the Balokole hostility involved rejection of the missionary and African Christian cultural accommodations which the Balakole perceived as a contradiction of the personal, spiritual, and moral implications of the gospel message of the cross (truth telling/brutal honesty/ modesty/ transparency). Here was evident a passion for core values over expected social civility.

The conflicts and tensions identified in the case studies played significant roles in revitalization movements. These may be enumerated.

First, conflict contributed to the birth of revitalization. Persecution of the Coptic Christians prompted overnight and weekly extended prayer meetings throughout Egypt. Thousands of people attend a weekly two-hour Bible study led by the Coptic pope in the Cairo cathedral. The Rahab ministry confronts the evil of human commodification. Further, it was one man's deep dissatisfaction with the spiritual lethargy of the Native Anglican Church in Kampala, Uganda, that led to the development of a network of committed disciples that in turn ignited the revival in 1932.[1]

Diaspora tensions between faith and culture gave birth to new "multicultural" forms that bring new life to the immigrant communities as well as the nationals. Ancient Church traditions of Coptic immigrants give spiritual depth to the church in Canada, and Canadian culture also transformed the worship practices in Coptic immigrant communities. Tension between embracing cultural diversity and uniform assimilation to the dominant culture among Southeast Asian immigrants led to local church mission initiatives instead of mission societies/agencies or denominational missional programs. Through the intentional subversive efforts of Dr. Joe Church, the Balokole revival flourished through the leadership of African converts rather than through foreign missionaries.

Second, conflicts and tensions fueled revitalization by exposing the limitations of traditional missional efforts. For example, the Balokole commitment to a heart-felt Christian conversion experience challenged church members and missionaries alike to reassess their previous Christian experience. The deep division within the Ruanda Mission in response to the Balokole revival transformed over time into "an organ for revival values".

Young Nak's first generation immigrant Korean-speaking congregation gave shape to a second and third generation English speaking multicultural congregation enabling movement beyond the limitations of the first generation immigrant church. The challenges faced by Young Nak's first generation Korean immigrants also influenced the development of a major missional church planting initiative among South East Asian Buddhist immigrants. The missional initiative of Young Nak's first generation Korean immigrant congregation involved the development of ministry partnerships within Toronto with Vietnamese, Manmar, Laos, and Thai communities enabling new congregations to develop and even thrive in the face of the challenging immigration realities.

Third, conflicts fueled many fresh concrete opportunities for evangelism. The missional initiative of Young Nak's congregation made possible the development of a Thai ministry in the face of major challenges (e.g., the predominant faith in Buddhism with ties to Thai nationalism and culture, and no existing precedent of a Thai church in Canada).

Young Nak's Korean congregation of over 4000 members has through their missional initiative partnerships enabled the development of many ethnic congregations in the United States as well as Canada. Young Nak's congregation responds to the needs of immigrant communities with practical assistance, including providing without cost services such as funerals, weddings, and the use of facilities, means of transportation, clothes, food, pastoral care, and more.

The struggle of Southeast Asian immigrant congregations in Toronto with the heavy Buddhist influence has been transformed into a new friendship form of evangelism in which Asian immigrants build relationships around shared experiences as ethnic minorities. This emphasis includes interfacing the moral values of Buddhists and Christians as an opening for enhancing the opportunity for significant Christian education. The conflicts

Buddhists experience with oppressive elements within their religious tradition, such as the need to satisfy many gods, serve as opportunities for introducing the liberating message of one God who provides salvation by grace in Jesus Christ.

Eye-opening oppositional interactions occurred among some of the consultation participants. The passionate concerns expressed by an American participant regarding the unfounded fear and despicable acts of hatred toward Muslims in the post- 911 United States came face to face with the firsthand experiences of an Egyptian Coptic Bishop who was in the midst of transnational political advocacy in response to radical Islamist persecution of Egyptian Coptic Christians, including the recent murder of twenty-five of their number in Egypt, that preceded the consultation.

These contradictory viewpoints stemmed from perspectives deeply rooted in painful realities of their personal stories and contexts. This, and other similar conflicts at the Toronto consultation, brought to light a complex web of realities encountered in global revitalization efforts.

Pertinent issues illumined amid the conflict reflected in the table discussion may also be enumerated. First, international differences in the relationship between politics and religion (e.g., the pattern of separation of church and state in the United States, and the tendency toward a theocratic interface of religion and politics in Muslim societies). Second, there was a tendency to polarize conflicting perspectives rather than addressing realities in a dialogical manner (e.g. there was the bifurcation between viewing Islam as the adversary in contrast to denying altogether a problem of violence associated with Islam. Third, there were some untested assumptions with reference to international political and religious realities (e.g., the substantial differences between the interfaith respect in the United States and the interfaith conflict in Egypt). This observation indicates the ongoing presence of political engagement remaininf at play within revitalized forms of Christianity.

The question of *how to define Christian revitalization* emerged as a dominant theme in all three of the consultations. Some consultation participants found it difficult to see *new* or *unusual* movements as a *re*-vitalizing of Christianity. Some participants expressed a desire for concrete, closed-ended definition or defining criteria. Others assumed Anthony's Wallace's definition of revitalization movements as the standard or norm for understanding Christian revitalization movements, a definition that, though perhaps true for some forms of culture change, did not correspond with many examples and dimensions of revitalization illustrated in the consultation case studies.

In this reference, it may be noted that Paul Seungoh Chung's assumption that the work of Anthony Wallace provided "The conceptual framework through which the case-studies of revitalization movements in Christianity were examined" does not reflect the vantage point of those who were engaged in the core-planning group. As a member of the core-planning group for all three consultations, I am very aware that Wallace's model was never assumed or intentionally chosen as the defining conceptual framework of our Christian revitalization research. To the contrary, the qualitative research process was intentionally designed to allow the data to reveal fresh insight.

Participants were invited to listen to the case studies through the lens of their experience, scholarship, and/or expertise, and it was clear from the discussions that perspectives of several participants had been shaped or influenced by the work of Wallace. This contributed to substantial discussion of the possible relationship between his conceptual framework and the case study narratives. Rather than imposing the conceptual framework of Wallace on the case studies, however, the case study discussions illumined the limitations of Wallace's paradigm. This inductive approach, though uncomfortable for some, invited deeper and more empirically informed reflections on the nature and meaning of Christian revitalization.

Ever-Moving Phenomenon

The diaspora case studies of the Toronto consultation revealed emerging and evolving gospel-transforming movements. Each case study discussion illumined a variety of intersecting parts, and the combined insights from all the case study discussions offered hints, clues, and even glimpses of the magnificence and unfolding mystery of God's revitalizing meta-mosaic in motion.

The mosaic of God's redemptive work in the world cannot be separated from motion in all aspects of life and creation. Every revitalizing action contributes to the ever-changing design. The creative, colorful moving formations are dependent upon the rhythmic guidance and empowerment of the Holy Spirit. Every element and dimension is grounded in the realities of human existence including the inevitable ordinary and profound conflicts and tensions in life.

The many forms of conflict and tension play vital roles in the emergence and motion of kaleidoscopic patterns. Human brokenness in its many forms elicits the compassion of Christ. Transnational encounter and immigration inspire new ministry forms and multidimensional multicultural spirituality. Social, political, and religious oppression demand liberative action, both overt and covert, and, sometimes subversive.

When Christians encounter alternate forms of Christian expression, it changes their vision of what the church could and should be. The ongoing emergence and spread of transnational, multicultural diaspora ministry in a diasporic setting brings into existence unimaginable beauty within the ever-evolving Mosaic. At the beginning of the Toronto consultation, Todd Johnson raised the question,"*Is God bringing us to see the richness that is possible?*" Perhaps here is disclosed the purpose of God's mosaic of revitalization in motion.

B. Advancing Christian Revitalization by Following the Spirit: A Summary and Projection

MICHAEL PASQUARELLO, PHD

("The wind blows where it chooses, and you hear the sound of it, but you do not know where it comes from or where it goes. So it is with everyone who is born of the Spirit" – John 3:8, NRSV).

Advancing Christian Revitalization in the Twenty First Century, a consultation hosted by Tyndale Theological Seminary of Toronto, Canada, was held October 20 - 23, 2011. The consultation consisted of six case studies focusing on "diaspora" people living in the Toronto area. While this final consultation drew from the findings of the Center's previous consultations in 2009 and 2010, it was rather unique in testing our accumulative understandings by attending to the reality of diaspora in our time. We live in a time of unprecedented movements of peoples, both voluntary and involuntary, that are surprising signs bearing witness to the mission of God in reaching global peoples. This gathering of diaspora community leaders, missiologists, theologians, practitioners, and representatives of the global church was informative and encouraging. Participants were privileged to hear of surprising ways the Spirit is at work among communities of people on the move. As a participant in the consultation I would offer the following summaries of the case studies:

1) *Greenhills Christian Fellowship* (GCF) in Toronto. The GCF is the story of Filipinos in diaspora. Its origin is in Manila, the Philippines. GCF has been led by the Holy Spirit to follow a missional vision shaped by the Great Commission. This has resulted in the sending of families to Canada as new immigrants. A Canadian church planting vision has arisen out of this global movement of people: a Missional Church, A Metropolitan Community, and a Multicultural Country. We learned much in hearing about GCF as "sojourners in Canada on a new journey among diaspora people." We were grateful for the representatives of GCF, and especially their pastor, Dr. Narry Santos, who shared with us the desire to interpret our present time in order to be responsive to God's movement in the world.

2) *The Jesus Network* provided us with a challenging case study emphasizing an "incarnational" model of ministry. Members of the Jesus Network seek to make their homes in communities of immigrants, many of whom are Muslims, sharing in their joys and trials, learning first hand of the cross cultural challenges and opportunities presented by this way of life and witness. As we learned from the case study, the Jesus Movement is a fairly young ministry in the diasporic community of Toronto, and as such, its leaders find they must be reliant on the leadership of the Spirit in an ongoing process of discernment. In other words, this form of ministry cannot be planned in ad-

vance and then "applied" to a chosen situation. They take seriously the scriptural admonition that Christians walk by faith and not by sight. Perhaps the most encouraging characteristic of this ministry is the strong desire displayed by new disciples of Jesus who return and serve among the people of their own cultures. Much of the discussion revolved around the importance of hospitality, lasting relationships, the gift of children, and the importance of sharing hardships and difficulties within relationships of trust and love.

3) *Young Nak Korean Presbyterian Church* shared their story of ministry to other Southeast Asian communities. They have named this work, "Mosaic Cultural Ministry." The Young Nak Church, led by the Rev. John Cheng, sees its ministry as contributing to a great mosaic that comprises a beautiful whole through the work of the Holy Spirit. Their support of diaspora people in Toronto, specifically those from Southeast Asia, aims to assist their fellow ethnic minorities in forming and building up autonomous congregations that serve and participate in the Kingdom of God. We were pleased to hear about the deeper theological convictions that have shaped this strong commitment to servant leadership, a ministry that supports and encourages congregations from Thailand, Myanmar, Viet Nam, and Laos. As Pastor Chung pointed out in his presentation, this is not a cross cultural ministry but a ministry that seeks to nurture and strengthen particular ministries within a particular culture. The ministry, then, aims to serve people groups who are seen as a sign of God's providential work, rather than a sociological category to be studied, analyzed, and "reached."

4) *The Rahab Ministry* presented a very different kind of case study, a ministry with Asian women in the Toronto area who are caught in the sex trade. The model for the ministry has been the compassion extended by Jesus to sinners, outcasts, and prostitutes. In this manner, the witness of the gospel was the starting point for Rahab Ministry. Its members see their present work as a continuation of and participation in the mission of the Triune God who hears the cries of those in bondage and acts to deliver them from captivity to enjoy the blessings of the reign of Jesus Christ. What was most informative about this case study was the strong theological foundation on which it is based. Much study and prayer has gone into the process of arriving at an appropriate and substantive theological understanding of the sex trade and the women who are bound by its power. Moreover, this strong theology of the human person is joined with an equally strong theology of salvation and the church. Thus, Rahab Ministry provided keen insight into the humanness of diasporan women, who, created in the divine image, have been caught in the dehumanizing grip of abusive and destructive powers.

5) *St. Maurice & St. Verena Coptic Orthodox Church* in Toronto, led by Fr. Pishoy Salama, provided a study of a multicultural, missionary Coptic Orthodox Church in the diaspora. Fr. Pishoy described the way by which this congregation was established with the blessing and authorization of H.H. Pope Shenoude III of Cairo, Egypt. The ministry was seen as a potential means of revival for the Coptic Church in Toronto and North America. The identity of this ministry is deeply rooted in the Coptic Orthodox faith, its

doctrine, and its traditions. Yet, this ministry, which has also been affected by its diasporan location, reflects and celebrates the diverse, multicultural ethos of Toronto. St. Maurice & St. Verena presented a good test case for thinking about how diaspora communities remain true to the faith of their ecclesial traditions while moving their home and mission to a strange and distant culture. Fr. Pishoy stated that this is an ongoing challenge requiring constant self - examination and evaluation to discern how to best carry out its commitment to evangelism, social ministries, and leadership development. Hospitality, an openness to graciously receive seekers and strangers has been a key to the flourishing of this ministry.

6) *The East African Revival*, a movement of the Balokole (Luganda for the Saved People) in the Anglican Church of Uganda, offered much to the discussion of revitalization movements. The designation of "saved people" or Balokole, points to the core identity of the East African revival, a call to all, both those within and outside the church, to head the call of God to salvation and a life of wholesale commitment. We learned that this revival was not organizational or institutional in form, but rather was a fellowship of brothers and sisters which comprises a distinct type of evangelical Christianity, not unlike the evangelical revivals in the UK during the eighteenth century. One of the unique characteristics of the Balokole has been the strangeness of this call to both European/North American and African sensibilities. This is because the cross has been central to this form of life, devotion, and experience which is marked by the confession of God's cleansing power. The fruit of this confession has been a life of serious, ethical rigor, separation from the world and its values, and a willingness to sacrifice to remain faithful to the call of the gospel. Such gospel diligence may provide an example of faithfulness as a form of resistance to more culturally accommodated forms of revitalization and mission.

Practicing the Spirit's Gift of Wisdom

("I thank you, Father, Lord of heaven and earth, because you have hidden these things from the wise and intelligent and have revealed them to infants, yes, Father, for such was your gracious will" - Mt. 11:25 - 26, NRSV).

The question I would like to raise in reflecting on these case studies is as follows: how may we account for the diversity we have observed in the forms and shape of these ministries? And if we acknowledge the primary significance of the prompting and leading of the Holy Spirit in engendering and giving shape to such forms of ministry, how do we account for the particular human judgments, decisions, and actions that have been intimately involved in the giving visible expression to the work of God in particular times and places? I want to suggest in the remainder of this essay that the virtue of prudence, or practical wisdom, provides a way of understanding the exercise of judgment in ministry that illumines the discernment displayed in the cases I have described.

As a way of "knowing in action," practical wisdom, or prudence, is sustained by good character and habits that enable discernment of the good for the sake of doing good acts that are a source of joy. Joseph Dunne comments, ".... the good practitioner has been formed by a history of participation in the practice itself. His or her experience of serving the end or *telos* of the practice - and recurrently trying to discover what this concretely requires - has laid down certain dispositions of character which, through discipline and direction, enable and energize."[2] He continues,

> For this reason, a practically wise person will possess skills of deliberation, discernment, and decisiveness that make him or her capable of transforming knowledge of reality into virtuous speech and action: "Prudence not only includes making the right decision, but also demands we carry out the decision. In this way prudence links the intellectual and moral virtues (knowing and doing). Moreover, prudence shapes the other moral virtues insofar as it enables the just person to act justly, the courageous person to act bravely, and the temperate person to act with self - control."[3]

Dunne's discussion challenges an instrumentalist, "cause and effect" approach to practice which frames objectives in advance, anticipates plans, controls the moves one will make, and then evaluates both the activity and results on terms defined by "effectiveness."[4] He argues persuasively that practice is irreducible to external techniques or procedures but requires a nontechnical, personal and participatory way of knowing which cannot be framed in terms of detachment, universality, and utility.

Dunne defines this type of activity as a form of "making" which is specified by a maker who determines its end or goal in advance; a way of construing ministry that is pervasive in our time. In contrast to the activity of making or producing which proceeds by explanation, prediction, and control for acting externally upon the raw material of one's work, Dunne discusses the social activity of practice. A practice is conducted in public places in cooperation with others and with no ulterior purpose or goals external to sharing in the truth and goodness of the practice itself and with a view to no other end or outcome than the moral intentions, habits, and qualities exemplified by wise, experienced participants of the practice.

This definition of shared communal activity may be extended to our understanding of Christian practices, or means of grace, such as prayer and worship, the use of Scripture in preaching and teaching, evangelization, catechesis, training in discipleship, pastoral care, and works of mercy and justice. Activities of this nature are carried out in such a way to realize and demonstrate as their end those virtues, dispositions, and excellences that are valued by the church as a historical community and constitutive of its life through faith that works through the Spirit's empowerments of love. In this alternative picture, practical knowledge is seen as a fruit which grows only in the soul of a person's experience and character. One is at the same time a feeling, expressing, and acting person; and knowing is inseparable from one's life as such.[5]

Dunne's description of these two distinct modes of activity can illumine how ministry springs from and embodies the practical wisdom that we are to love God and our neighbor as ourselves. Seen from this perspective, good ministry will be characterized by a particular kind of history, experience, judgment, and influence which, while rooted in the wisdom of Scripture and guided by the Christian tradition, remains open to the gifts, dispositions, and habits appropriate to responding to the Word and Spirit in assessing and interpreting present circumstances and situations.

What we love plays a significant role in shaping our judgments. Love moves the intellect to engage in the process of practical reasoning and focuses the intellect's attention upon certain objects rather than others because of the intensity of its love.[6] Prudence is therefore akin to "love discerning well" with the power of the intellect working through practical judgment, counsel, and direction; an insightfulness which directs one's reason, desire, and actions to the end of love for all things in God.[7] Because prudence is "love choosing wisely," it is in the service of human excellence in the service of God - loving the truth and desiring the good - so that the person who knows, judges, speaks, and acts well is truly happy in God.[8]

There can be no wisdom or virtue without the Spirit's gift of love since the goal of moral discernment is dependent upon knowing God through faith that is energized and penetrated by love. Flowing from the will to the intellect, love transforms prudence for knowing the right end and choosing the right means in conformity to that end. The wisdom of Scripture as illumined by the Spirit is a key element of the Law of the Gospel which inspired the prophets and apostles and moved the saints to act. Moreover, in addition to the union of heart and mind with God through the theological virtues of faith, hope, and love, the virtue of practical wisdom requires intellectual and moral skills that enable assessment of specific situations and the transformation of knowledge into appropriate action: speaking or doing the right thing, for the right reason, in the right manner, for the right persons, and in the right circumstances.[9]

Prudence, then, is neither a procedural method nor technical skill. Rather, it is a capacity linking the intellectual and moral virtues for choosing good ends that are appropriate to particular activities by following the Spirit's leading in obedience to Christ in particular times, places, and circumstance. Seen from this perspective, the practice of ministry can be understood as the practice of wisdom which is cultivated and given shape through attentiveness and receptivity to God's Word revealed in the scriptural witness to the risen Christ who dwells within the Church and continues to extend his ministry to the whole creation. Contrary to the "conventional wisdom" of our time concerning the ministry of revitalization and renewal - that our agency is primary and that we are capable of predicting and producing outcomes we desire - this will be a non - utilitarian way of thinking, perceiving, and speaking through which the Spirit awakens the Church's desire for the reign of God in ways that are congruent with its calling to be a holy people in the world.

Notes

1. Simeoni Nsibambi, "regarded as pre-eminently the founding figure" of the East African Revival, Simeoni Nsibambi, a baptized confirmed member of the Native Anglican Church in Kampala, Uganda, who experienced conversion to Christ and became "critical of what he saw as the lethargy of the Native Anglican Church." Nsibambi's experience of spiritual conversion to Christ that transformed his lifestyle to embrace simplicity and native rather than western dress shaped a critical view of the "lethargy" of the Native Anglican Church. Nsibambi developed a network of people committed to these values, as cited in Kevin Ward, "The East Africa Revival and the Revitalization of Christianity," 13.

2. Joseph Dunne, *Back to the Rough Ground: Practical Judgment and the Lure of Technique (Notre Dame:* University of Notre Dame Press, 1993) 378.

3. Michael Dauphinias and Mattew Levering, *Knowing the Love of Christ: An Introduction to the Theology of St. Thomas Aquinas* (Notre Dame: University of Notre Dame Press, 2002) 57.

4. Dunne, *Back to the Rough Ground,* 235.

5. Ibid 358.

6. Sherwin, *By Knowledge & By Love: Charity and Morality in the Moral Theology of Thomas Aquinas* (Washington D.C: Catholic University of America, 2005) 102.

7. Ibid., *By Knowledge & By Love,* 106-118.

8. Ibid., *By Knowledge and By Love,* 120.

9. John Mahoney, S.J., *Seeking the Spirit: Essays in Moral and Pastoral Theology* (London/Denville, N.J.: Sheed & Ward and Dimension Books, 1982) 67-69.

www.ingramcontent.com/pod-product-compliance
Lightning Source LLC
Chambersburg PA
CBHW021843220426
43663CB00005B/379